The shadow and its shadow
Surrealist writings on the cinema

ONE WEEK LOAN

THIRD ... ...SED AND EXPANDED

... ..., ...troduced by

Paul Hammond

City Lights Books
San Francisco

10 9 8 7 6 5 4 3 2 1

Book design and typography: Small World Productions, San Francisco
Cover: Stefan Gutermuth
Cover photo: "Are you cold?" from *Le Surréalisme au service de la révolution* (Paris) 1 (July 1930). Photographer unknown, but probably Albert Duverger, cameraman on *Un chien andalou* and *L'Âge d'or*. The young woman is Suzanne Christy, who screen-tested for the Lya Lys role in *L'Âge d'or*. The bishop is Marval, production manager on both films, and one of the two tugged curés in *Un chien andalou*.

Library of Congress Cataloging-in-Publication Data

The shadow and its shadow: surrealist writings on the cinema / edited, translated and introduced by Paul Hammond.-- 3rd., rev. and expanded.
    p. cm.
    ISBN 0-87286-376-X (pbk.)
    1. Surrealism in motion pictures. 2. Motion pictures. I. Hammond, Paul.

PN1995.9.S85 S5 2000
791.43'61163--dc21   00-034639

CITY LIGHTS BOOKS are edited by Lawrence Ferlinghetti and Nancy J. Peters and published at City Lights Bookstore, 261 Columbus Avenue, San Francisco, CA 94133. Visit our web site at www.citylights.com.

For the shadow is his and the penumbra is his
and his the perplexity of the phenomenon.

—Christopher Smart, *Jubilate Agno,* line 313

Contents

Available light

Paul Hammond

Light sets up its festive tents in spaces unsuspected.
—Novalis

The Surrealist response to cinema was passionate, poetic, Romantic. André Breton once defined Surrealism as "the prehensile tail" of Romanticism. To the epigram above, coined by the German Romantic poet-philosopher Novalis, who died in 1801, you could append others of his so as to shade in an anticipatory program for the production and consumption of a Surrealist cinema:

> Dark memories hovering below the transparent screen of the
> present will project images of reality in sharp silhouette, to create
> the pleasurable effect of a double world.
> Plots without any coherence, and yet with associations, as in
> dreams.
> Directed through the twigs, a long ray entered his eyes, and through
> it he could see into a distant, strange and marvelous space,
> impossible to describe.

Splice to these another Novalis maxim:

> More heavenly than the distant stars that twinkle are those bright
> eyes of the infinite which night has opened within us.

This yearning for a lost plenitude, for setting the revelations of night alongside those of day, fueled the Surrealist desire to follow the exemplary "trajectory of the dream" as it revisioned daily life. Their inspiration was anthropocentric and, in the widest sense, materialist. Only by reforging links with what Jamake Highwater calls "the primal mind"—the mind at one with nature, expressing itself through the imaginary—could the real be fully comprehended and thus recast according to human need. An ex-

1

tremely Romantic project; an inspired salvage operation no doubt, both courtly and cavalier, bullish and fragile.

Octavio Paz has described the irruption of the night light of Romanticism as the libertarian Other of *le Siècle des lumières,* the Century of Enlightenment. For the Romantics, as for their heirs, the Surrealists, the overarching rationalism of the Enlightenment, and of its avatar, positivism, had led to an alienating diminution of the polysemic fulsomeness of the world that man inhabited and that inhabited him. Echoing Weber echoing Herder, those "dark chroniclers" Adorno and Horkheimer characterized this parsimonious socialized logic and the capitalist order it buttressed as dependent upon "the disenchantment of the world," and they saw one of its baleful long-term consequences in the cretinizing narrowness of the mass culture industry, a view the Surrealists didn't always share, as the texts in this book make clear. The too sharply focused light of Enlightenment reason "plunged all things around it into deep shadows," wrote August Wiedmann, "shadows it then deemed insignificant or non-existent." The Romantics, and the Surrealists, took umbrage (a word deriving from *umbra,* shadow) with the repressive clarity of diurnal rationalism, instead devoting themselves to the reenchantment of nature, and of man, through a mythopoeic, totalizing investigation of existence's shadow side.

However, in evoking nature we shouldn't forget that the Surrealists were city folk, acculturated beings. In her book on Walter Benjamin's *Passagen-Werk* Susan Buck-Morss yokes the Surrealist vision to Benjamin's own. Under conditions of capitalism, she argues, "industrialization had brought about a reenchantment of the social world . . . and through it, a 'reactivation of mythic powers.'" It was Benjamin's intention to sift the capitalist commodity world for signals of the forgotten or repressed utopian dimension of things. Inspired by Aragon's *Paris Peasant* and its auratic evocation of the explosive metaphysical power of the threatened arcade—the site of the first film showrooms, let it be remembered—Benjamin developed his theory of the dialectical image. His messianic Marxism, built on an insight into the revolutionary potential of the recently outmoded commodity as wish-image, looked back to Romanticism:

> In the early nineteenth century, German Romantics, in protest against Enlightenment rationality, had called for a rebirth of

mythology, and what Schelling termed a new, "universal symbolism," based on the things of "nature" which "both signify and are." By the twentieth century the "new nature" of industrial culture had generated all the mythic power for a "universal symbolism" that these Romantics might have desired.

It is indeed true that, with Benjamin, the Surrealists rewrote the book of commodity fetishism, finding subversive mythic traces in the objects created by capitalism—and here their attitude toward the film image is crucial—but I would argue that after the first flush of creative engagement with capitalist modernization—between the years 1924 and 1935, say— they intermittently turned back to the idea of nature as the imaginary ground of utopia. Symptomatically, when Breton was exiled in America during the war, he rejected the skyscrapers of Manhattan and went botanizing, à la Rousseau in his *Reveries of the Solitary Walker,* in the meadows of New England and on the shores of the St. Lawrence River. What had begun as an ironical disavowal of nature in favor of the enchantments of the urban life-world was reversed, in an historical era that saw the post-1918 Americanization of Europe, the Depression, the rise of totalitarianism in Russia and Germany, the Second World War, and the Cold War confrontation of Stalinist state capitalism and the democratic Society of the Spectacle, in favor of the Arcadian potential of the embattled natural world, with its elective sites in Mexico, the Antilles, Canada, and in rural France itself (the summer retreats to Breton's house in the Lot). The poetry of Breton, Paz, and Césaire, and the painting of Tanguy, Gorky, and Lam bear this out.

Where a prehensile Surrealism wags the tail of Romanticism is in its privileging of the poetic imagination as the keystone, the binding agent, of authentic understanding. Shelley said "Poetry is at once the center and circumference of knowledge." A century and a half later the Surrealist poet Benjamin Péret reaffirmed that "Poetry is the source and crown of all thought." The Surrealists were not against reason per se. They simply believed it had to be refashioned, supplemented, by other, metarational ways of knowing. And knowing entailed *being,* so that if poetic imagination (and its reasoned metonym, *irrational knowledge*) was to furnish man with "the key to the fields," he had to comprehend by "poetry" not the mere

3

writing of lyric poems—although such a rehearsal of "words making love" had its place—but the investigation, through language and action, of the force fields of instrumental desire, love, the dream, play, and revolt. Poetry—"ontological possession," as Cortázar phrased it—was immanent harmony symbolized: imaged holism. The light in the shadow.

From this general program to *cinema* as oneiric illumination is but a short somnambulist's step. The movie auditorium was, the Surrealists held, the festive tent of that quest after our tenebrous originary depths. Philosophizing in the boudoir of cinema became a passion with them. And yet "romanticism" and "cinema" are words rarely conjoined. (Lotte Eisner, Henri Agel, P. Adams Sitney, and the Surrealist Ado Kyrou stand apart here.) Doubtless there's a hint of perversity in my spotlighting the idealist aspect of the Surrealist project, since such special pleading omits mention of its post-Romantic genealogy: the philosophers, poets, artists—and filmmakers—whose impact was to sublate Novalis's "magic idealism" into Breton's "magic materialism." But to take your seat in such a stall may perhaps disorient expectations of an approach akin to most mainstream interpretations of cinema. (And, as we shall see, disorientation has a value all its own.) Both cinema and Surrealism are more spectral, more sublime than such reductionist hermeneutics will allow. Surrealist cinema—in production and as consumption—is a marginal, utopian enterprise, at once scandalous and prefigurative, ludic and lucid. Millenial, too, as Ado Kyrou declaimed in his 1951 essay, "Romanticism and Cinema": "We seek a shock cinema with lightning and thunder, murderous passions, a lust for revolt, a cinema that explores the unexplored, that assays the boiling blood of extraordinary tales. Eroticism, imagination, exaltation, infernal tension are the elements of a cinema that will have at last rejected the void to forever advance with giant strides toward 'something else.'"

It was circa 1912 that Guillaume Apollinaire and the poets and painters in his entourage latched on to cinema. One of the novelties of Apollinaire's review, *Les Soirées de Paris,* founded that year, was its "chronique cinématographique," compiled by the art critic Maurice Raynal. Reading his column today, you can witness the inception of the cult of cinema and of cinemagoing: a love of the new, brash, and amoral Hollywood melodrama, Western, and comedy; a canonization of the Stirnerite antihero Fantômas; an affection for marginal genres like animation; a predilection

4

for the chancy eroticism of the darkened auditorium. By 1916, and in the provincial town of Nantes, André Breton and Jacques Vaché, medical intern and patient, were wandering from cinema to cinema, charging their mental batteries with film images (cf. Breton, "As in a Wood," q.v.).

The First World War finally won cinema its pluralist audience in France. Unlike theater, film exhibition was simple and mobile, and the movies had propaganda value. The state, through the new Section Photographique et Cinématographique de l'Armée, covered the country with a team of three thousand trained projectionists. In this way, many civilians and off-duty soldiers really engaged with the medium for the first time. Some of these neophytes were intellectuals, and out of this mood of conversion emerged the first specialized film magazines, like Henri Diamant-Berger's *Le Film,* resuscitated in 1916 when the future champion of French avant-garde cinema, Louis Delluc, became its editor. Delluc, Colette, Léon Moussinac, and Marcel L'Herbier wrote for it, as did Louis Aragon (cf. "On Décor," q.v.). Like Raynal, the cinema they championed was as much imported American as homegrown French. By August 1914 the French cinema, until then world leader, was spiked on its own tripod of creative doubt, conservatism, and xenophobia. The war opened the door to the burgeoning American film industry which, without the dead weight of the European theatrical tradition, and displaced to the California sunshine and its raw landscape, rapidly consolidated a dynamic new film form. (This became known in the Old World as "American montage.") In contrast to the antediluvian comedies and chauvinistic melodramas that emanated from French studios, the novelty and élan of films by Griffith, Ince, De Mille, Sennett, and Chaplin converted French audiences to the American Way. The leaders of the home industry responded with alacrity. Léon Gaumont gave his arrière-garde auxiliary, the great Feuillade, free rein to make *Les Vampires,* in response to the U.S.-produced serial, *The Perils of Pauline.* With *Fantômas* and *Judex,* Feuillade's series kept the Gaumont flag flying. The differing strategy of Louis Nalpas, now head of the stodgy Film d'Art company, was to gamble on the talents of the young tyro Abel Gance, with *Mater Dolorosa* and *La Dixième Symphonie* (1917). A year later, Charles Pathé backed Gance to make the innovatory *J'accuse.* Caution, then, persisted alongside daring, Feuillade's penny-a-liners doing battle alongside Gance's prestige pyrotechnics in a rearguard action against American cultural domination.

Such was the protean setting for the first-generation Surrealists' response to film: the dawning of a French avant-garde cinema of montage (often anchored in pictorialist melodrama); cheek by jowl with it the more demotic, yet wildly inventive, imported Hollywood product; plus, of course, the seemingly passé work of Feuillade and his ilk, directors like Henri Fescourt; and, lastly, the reception of revolutionary cinema from Soviet Russia. In a period of modernist iconoclasm and partisanship the Surrealists were to excoriate the formalist film culture of Delluc, Gance, Marcel L'Herbier, Germaine Dulac, and Jean Epstein—now lumped together as "the Impressionists"—in favor of the lowbrow cinema of Chaplin, Sennett, Pearl White, *Fantômas,* Douglas Fairbanks, Stroheim (cf. Philippe Soupault, "Cinema U.S.A.," q.v.). (Having said this, the Surrealist filmmaker Jacques Brunius—assistant director on *L'Âge d'or*—conceded the importance of Delluc and Epstein; L'Herbier went on to direct the much admired *La Nuit fantastique;* and Gance was to be reconciled with Breton in the 1950s, thanks to Nelly Kaplan.) In a mood of messianic fervor and scandal-mongering, the Surrealists came to blows more than once with avant-garde cinephiles in the film clubs that mushroomed in the 1920s (cf. Brunius, "The Lights Go Up," q.v.).

There was, for sure, a functionalist strand of thought in this early Surrealist defense of Hollywood. Writing about Buster Keaton's *College* (1927)— and in defiance of what he saw as the mystificatory syntax of the Impressionists—Luis Buñuel thought the comedian's film as "beautiful as a bathroom." There was, he noted, such complete harmony between Keaton, the objects, and situations he bent to his will and the technique he used to describe these, that no one noticed that technique: "Just as when living in a house we remain unaware of the calculus of resistance of the materials that go to form it." ("Buster Keaton's *College,*" q.v.) This assumed zero degree of style was to become Buñuel's own antivirtuoso credo as a director.

To rewind the spool a little, we must go back to the first writings on cinema of those young poets, inspired by the ambiguous specter of Apollinaire, who were the French Dadaists and future Surrealists: Breton, Aragon, Soupault, Tzara, Ribemont-Dessaignes, Péret, Éluard, Rigaut. Their outpourings are lyrical, subjective: notations made mentally in the dark, of images that crystallize the poetic response, that in turn become poetic material. Aragon's "On Décor" (q.v.), his first published essay, which appeared in the

September 1918 issue of Delluc's *Le Film,* is a good example of this kind of writing, which has ramifications for all Surrealist film theory:

All our emotion exists for those dear old American adventure films that speak of daily life and manage to raise to a dramatic level a banknote on which our attention is riveted, a table with a revolver on it, a bottle that on occasion becomes a weapon, a handkerchief that reveals a crime, a typewriter that's the horizon of a desk, the terrible unreeling ticker tape with its magic ciphers that enrich or ruin bankers.

Aragon was in awe of the movie camera's power to instrumentalize the commonplace object by making it photogenic, to confer a dignity and poetic value on the things of everyday life, to turn them into what Freud called "thing-representations," indices of the unconscious. In isolating objects, magnifying them, and recombining them in new ways, things were revealed—and *reveiled,* as Breton demanded—in all their fulsome, hieratic mystery. Jacques Vaché, who had been sent Aragon's essay by Breton, emphasized this primal transubstantiation of the material world in his "War Letter" (q.v.), sent from the front line:

. . . what a film I'll play in!—With runaway cars, you know the kind, bridges that give way, and enormous hands crawling across the screen toward some document or other! . . . Useless and invaluable!—With such tragic conversations, in evening dress, behind an eavesdropping palm tree!—And then, of course, Charlie Chaplin, grinning, with staring eyes. The Policeman forgotten in the trunk!!!

Telephone, shirtsleeve, people rushing about, with those bizarre, jerky movements—William R.G. Eddie, who's sixteen, thousands of black servants, with such beautiful gray-white hair, and a tortoiseshell monocle. He'll get married.

Aragon first employed the term "synthetic criticism" in a review of Apollinaire's *Calligrammes.* It soon came to signify the tangential reading of film, the bringing to the surface of a film's second, secret life, its latent content. Instead of criticizing a film from a soi-disant objective position, the Surrealist viewer deconstructed it according to his or her lights. "We are too sympathetic," Aragon wrote, "to what, in a work or in an individual, is *left to be desired* to be very interested in perfection." A way to do this was to purloin images or sequences whose poetic charge, when liberated from the narrative that held them prisoner, was intensified. These detourned images were reedited into a parallel scenario in the critical text. Once detached from the metonymic chain, the elective fragment functions as metaphor, as symptom, as a condensation of human need. The spectator, as Robert Desnos argued in his essay "Eroticism" (q.v.), while caught up in the narrative presented to him, cannot help but mentally rewrite the script, "a more miraculous adventure," *his* cinema of facts and gestures.

These synthetic-critical texts appeared in a variety of forms, from the poem to the shooting script, the purely elaborative to the practicably realizable. Soupault's "cinematographic" poems, for example, are composed in the first person in a didactic prose. A prose poem like "Rage" (1925) is synthesized from recognizable filmic situations—the shady character in a bar, a car chase—and the circularity of its construction, with the last scene repeating the first, is undoubtedly cinematic; yet it has something about it that is neither poem nor shooting script. (However, Walter Ruttmann did film three of Soupault's poems in 1922.) It comes closest to the dream accounts Freud included in *The Interpretation of Dreams* and, indeed, we have Soupault's own testimony to substantiate this: "I wanted, thanks to the film, to give an impression, neither clear nor precise, but similar to a dream." Compare Soupault's

> I enter a café. Leaning on the bar, I see a customer sitting alone at a table. I survey his arm, then his hand, and finally his fingers, which are closed around a glass. The customer gets up and leaves. I follow and overtake him just as an automobile flashes by at top speed. I stop to button my jacket, then I take off after the car, into which I am able to leap. I seize the wheel after knocking the driver out. . . .

With Freud's own dream, recounted in his magnum opus:

> I am very incompletely dressed, and I go from a flat on the ground floor up a flight of stairs to an upper story. In doing this I jump up three stairs at a time, and I am glad to find that I can mount the

stairs so quickly. Suddenly I notice that a servant-maid is coming down the stairs—that is, towards me.

For Soupault and his confreres the synthetic-critical method was an iconoclastic attempt to register the latent content present in the "dream thoughts" that made up commercial cinema. The Surrealist notion of film language as an analog of oneiric thinking is as fruitful and ultimately as metaphorical a conceit as, say, Eisenstein's notion of dialectical montage. To be sure, this Surrealist critique was akin to psychoanalysis, but with one important difference. While Freud underlined the materialism of the dream—its origins in everyday life; the secret, parallel activity of unconscious thought during waking; the squirreling away of material for use when asleep—the Surrealists sought to extend the process the other way, to complete the circle. They wanted everyday life to be emphatically and consciously permeated by the dream, by its scabrous language, its transgressive remodeling of normative constraints. "Day for night," as they say on the back lot. Here was a project to be realized on every level: aesthetic, moral, social. Objectivized subjectivity could transfigure and redeem our perception and experience of reality by letting us into the affective clandestine life of the material world; it could reconnect us with the utopian promise our "night thoughts" have. (I'm filching the title of Edward Young's Romantic poem, much admired by Breton.) Breton's books *Les Vases communicants* (1932) and *L'Amour fou* (1937) chronicle this dialectic. The magic materialism of film, inherent in its power to suggest the spatial, temporal, and psychological dimensions of the real— by heightening these, by making reality uncanny—is taken as read. And this imagistic "surplus value" could be consolidated by the poetic imagination decanting the unconscious life from the precipitate image.

The fecund shuttle between synthetic-critical text and film is activated in Man Ray's movie, *L'Étoile de mer* (1928). The director's images reverberate with lines drawn from a poem by Robert Desnos. When, for instance, Desnos' intertitle tells us that "women's teeth are such charming objects," Man Ray's next shot shows us a woman's legs. Word and image contradict each other, as in certain Magritte paintings. A poetic space—"the space of a thought," to use the title of one of Magritte's own films—is opened up between signified and signifier. *L'Étoile de mer* decomposes itself in the ricocheting silence of its own synthetic-criticism.

Written by members of the Romanian Surrealist Group in 1947, "Malombra, Aura of Absolute Love" (q.v.) celebrates, in a synthetic-critical way, the "involuntarily Surrealist" *Malombra,* a metaphysical romance directed by Mario Soldati in 1942. This delirious exegesis on *Malombra* draws its power from the collision of discourses: poetic, philosophic, didactic, automatic. Such fragmentation is helped, no doubt, by the collaborative nature of its writing. The text may evoke the reverie of the cinematic experience through compulsive repetition:

> The convulsion of beauty, the feebleness of memory, the color of regret, the charm of life, the mediumism of motion, the rarity of love, the madness of the senses, the beauty of madness. . . .

The film has an ethical dimension, it touches on moral truths:

> Never has the difficulty of raising revolution to the heights of poetry so confounded us, seduced us so. Never has it been so obvious in our eyes that in the flashing beauty of the woman destined for love there resides the concentration of the universe's most restless dialectical moments.

Snippets of collaged dialogue bring home the hypnotic and enigmatic quality of the decontextualized word:

> "Do you recall that evening, Renato? The lake, the lanterns, the far-off sounds. . . . It's strange what happens to me, I don't belong to this world. You haven't understood me, you don't understand me because you don't know. Today I depart for an unknown destiny, unknown reader, goodbye."

A film image can be vandalized to become the starting point for a chain of automatic responses:

> So brief the eye was blinded by it, like an edgy scorpion for all that, the shadow passed through the gray diurnal light like a wound, a ruin, a sleepy waterfall.

Stripped of their causal relations in the film, a rapid-fire of reported images emphasizes their latent content, their capacity to signify bottomless sighs, occult rage, the horror of living, raucous cries, bloody hair, dresses cut by a razor, the suicide exhibition, the speed of crazy glances, arrogant imposture, murderous scandal, lost cries, voluptuous spasms. . . .

The voluptuous spasms of "Malombra" (the text) flay the celluloid to reveal the dark heart, the "baleful shadow" or *malombra*, of Soldati's film. Discursive subjectivity guts this "closed" work, opens up its reading, setting a vertiginous dialectic in motion. We are on the road to surreality, the visionary, fugitive point of the mind where hierarchies and antinomies are to be abolished, where obstinate difference collapses into the flux of exchange. Analogy is everything.

The arrogant imposture of interpretive delirium, *le délire d'interprétation*, as the French have it. In his magisterial work, *The Discovery of the Unconscious*—which, by the by, proposes that many of the categories crucial to psychoanalysis find an origin in German Romanticism—Henri Ellenberger fleetingly introduces us to the "reasoning madness" of Hersilie Rouy, a celebrated paranoiac who penned a brace of autobiographies wherein she described the delusions she lived of her "royal" genealogy. In the figure of convulsive beauties like Hersilie we find two abiding preoccupations of the Surrealists conjoined. First, an affirmative interest in the spontaneous pathological utterance, read not so much as a distress flare but as a fireworks display of linguistic inventiveness: no "Mayday," but the broadcasting of quintessentially human powers, communicated by the incarcerated from the Ship of Fools. (The "antipsychiatry" movement may be said to originate in the Surrealist defense of madness, and in their critique of the asylum.) Second, a male passion for the psychotic or criminal woman as *femme inspiratrice*, symbol of the transgressive Other, victim and therefore perturber of the repressive patriarchal order. The Surrealist transference of mental disorder into poetic illumination—social negative into ontological positive—finds expression in the reasoned irrationalism of Salvador Dalí's theory of paranoia-criticism, a wayward chip off the old synthetic-critical block; and in Breton and Éluard's simulations of delirium in *L'Immaculée Conception* (1930), a work itself triggered by the electrifying induction of the Spaniard into the Surrealist Group, following the Paris showing of *Un chien andalou* in June 1929.

Paranoia-criticism thrives on contrived delusion, on the assiduous ambi-

11

tion to get things wrong, to see something as something other. Dalí explored his baffling analogical methodology in any number of visionary paintings in which one or more set of signifiers can be read in two or more ways as differing signifieds. The eye scuttles from pillow to post. His elaborate, disorienting visual puns and double meanings are a sort of libertarian phenomenology, demonstrating the power the mind has to refute the one-to-one gestalt of the world dear to positivists. In *L'Amour fou* Breton wrote eloquently of this Dalínian panic of the logos: "Interpretive delirium begins only when man, ill-prepared, takes fright in this *forest of indices.*" The title of Breton's 1951 essay on cinema, "As in a Wood" (q.v.), suggests that it be read as a coda on this polysemic enchanted forest, the luxuriant tangle that is everyday life. And, in a madly loving meditation on Leonardo's famous wall at which you gaze until you see a battle scene delineated in the cracks, Breton conjured up the image of the *écran* (screen or grid) that functions as a brittle palimpsest for hallucinated yearning: "Everything man wants to know is written on this screen in phosphorescent letters, in letters of *desire.*" A short shuttle across the lobby carpet, a brief tussle with the muffled doors: once you're inside the artificial night of the auditorium, the projector beam becomes your phosphorescent precipitate, the screen your delusory palimpsest. You pays yer money and you takes yer chances. . . .

The most sustained literary example of Dalí's interpretive vision is contained in his barnstorming exegesis on a painting not obviously consonant with Surrealism. *Le Mythe tragique de L'Angélus de Millet: Interprétation "paranoïaque-critique"* was completed in the late 1930s, but the manuscript, lost during the Occupation, was only published in 1963. Calling on an analogical iconography—his own and others' paintings, popular postcards, cartoons, everyday objects—Dalí intensifies his haunting and haunted brainstorm to uncover the enigma at the center of Millet's famous picture: the oedipal triangle of father, mother, and, invisible to the eye, the object over which they pray, the corpse of their son. (Dalí had an X-ray photo taken of *The Angelus* and read a dark form Millet had painted out as a child's coffin.) The Spaniard prefaces his disinterment of the picture's latent content with a challenge: "Here you have the most bewildering 'secret' scenario for whomsoever will dare make the most ambitious film."

Before helping make *Un chien andalou* Dalí had written on both photography and film, but his most sustained essay on the movies is his 1932

"Abstract of a Critical History of the Cinema" (q.v.). The cranky monomania so often mined by Dalí finds full expression here. His perverse argument is that the more "cinematic" cinema is, the more it is to be deplored. All that are worth preserving are certain theatrical melodramas made in Italy around the First World War, with their obsessional femmes fatales and doomed heroes, and comedy films of the Sennett school (forgetting the lachrymosity of Chaplin), in which the gratuitous and imaginative use of objects and bodies enables man to explore the world's essential "concrete irrationality." "Idealizing" montage should step aside for "materialist" mise-en-scène. Thus Dalí welcomes sound's arrival since it puts paid to the formal preoccupations of silent avant-garde cinema. The nefarious inauthenticity of "pure cinema" is substituted by a redemptive filmed theater that had, of late, seen its apotheosis in the work of the Marx Brothers.

Salvador Dalí was, it appears, éminence grise behind Breton and Éluard's *L'Immaculée Conception*. Composing it in a fortnight during the autumn of 1930, the poets constructed their semiotic two-hander by using automatic writing and the tactics of detournment as practiced by Isidore Ducasse in his *Poésies* (1870). Their automatism, much subject to secondary elaboration, is a mimetic play on the words of psychotic discourse. Especially pertinent is the section of their book called "The Possessions" (as in "to be possessed"), a simulation of the more creative disorders defined at the century's turn by Emil Kraepelin: mental debility, acute mania, general paralysis, delirium of interpretation, dementia praecox. Breton and Éluard's stated aim was to demonstrate that the poetically trained mind could, at no particular expense to its own equilibrium, inventively replicate seemingly alienated, irrational modes of thought. By doing this the poets hoped to discredit the repressive antinomies of sane/insane, normal/abnormal, free/unfree.

Five years later Éluard and Breton set their caps toward cinema. Their scenario, "Essai de simulation du délire cinématographique," was composed one summer's day in 1935. The poets and their wives were, with Man Ray, guests at the country house of the writer Lise Deharme. Man Ray describes the episode in his *Self Portrait:* how he intended to put a souvenir of their stay on film (much as he had done for the Vicomte de Noailles in his short *Le Mystère du Chateau de Dés* (1929)). He shot sequences of the women wandering around Deharme's rambling manse and of a neighboring farmer's daughter riding bareback on a black horse. Eventually, Breton

13

grew bored with his acting role and blew his top. The film was finally abandoned, and all that remains is a page of seven stills and their captions in the review *Cahiers d'art* (no. 5–6, 1935): Nusch Éluard rests her chin on a spindly branch, her face shaded by black lace hanging in the boughs above, a curious pyramidal lump of stonework in the background. The caption reads, "You would always find me again, says the sphinx." In a star-spangled dress and pearls Lise Deharme gazes in Nusch's general direction, an odd twig-bisected skullcap on her head: "Nothing in the north well." Breton with a dragonfly on his forehead gazes through a window-pane at Lise: "And he sighed. . . ." Jacqueline Breton slumbers on the ground in deep shadow, surrounded by a holed and grooved wooden ball as big as her head and a turned wooden pole (elements of an obscure *bilboquet*-like game?): "Extinguish everything!" The same odd implements, plus a further bulbous rod stuck in the ground, in deep shadow: "Following a sinister vision, Don Juan." The girl on horseback and Lise Deharme, the arm of each around the shoulders of a man (the farmer?), their feet obscured by a pile of gravel: "The twilight man." Eight men and women, including the above, cluster on a hillside around the bole of a leafy tree: "They were meeting each other for the first time."

The enigmatic charge of these fragments of a fragment is heightened by the hiatus of meaning between them and by the further tangential nature of the captions. There are enough formal and metaphorical equivalencies to bind the images together, but not too tightly. Later in the same issue of *Cahiers* Breton elaborated on the way he and Éluard arrived at their scenario. Discussing "the automatism of the variant," he describes a game in which the participants whisper a given phrase one to the other in a chain. The game hinges on errors of transmission, on getting things subtly wrong. (It's an old parlor game, a favorite of Lewis Carroll's, called "Chinese Whispers." A well-known example is of Tommies in a trench. The first one whispers to his comrade, "Send reinforcements, we're going to advance." The last man in the long line hears, "Send three-and-four-pence, we're going to a dance.") After giving various examples, transmitted in part by an old woman, a five-year-old child and a person who didn't really know French, Breton continues:

> One cannot help . . . but convince oneself of the constancy here of a certain process of dramatization analogous to that of the dream,

which would be enough to reveal the circular functioning of censorship. I have been able to follow it by dint of a written shooting script reproducing the intermediary states of a sample phrase, in this instance the text of a telegram I had the intention of proposing as the pivot of the scenario Paul Éluard and I were then preparing for Man Ray:

> The fog thickens. Nothing in the north well.
> Unmake the sheets while thinking of your William.
> My ninth wedding in the rain is an embrace.

Clearly, from this sparse and somewhat obscure evidence it's impossible to know how Breton and Éluard defined "cinematic delirium"—the play of light and shade, indoor and outdoor, and the arrested, hieratic nature of the stills, suggest the uncanny rather than the delirious—but it is interesting that, by associating it with Kraepelin's nosology, they should have connoted *le délire cinématographique* as a psychotic dysfunction of language. And the film's origin in the whispering game, with its privileging of the lapsus as a source of linguistic pliability, of poetic invention, stands as a paradigm for the desired relation of spectator to film image: mutual misconstrued murmurings from deep within the psyche; the revenge of mind on mind—of mind on matter.

Another French word for you: *le dépaysement,* disorientation. We take our orientation from the four cardinal points, from their intersection at right angles; disorientation is when "the needle goes wild in the compass," as Jacques Prévert put it. Bakunin said something to the effect that if the cops give you a piece of lined paper to write your confession on, turn it through ninety degrees and write across the lines. The gut anarchism of the Surrealists led them to cross-examine cinema, to go at it like a bull at the projector gate. To disorient the ruled order of the screen was to add a fillip of frisson, to convulse both text and reader. The Surrealist interrogation of cinema's latent meanings drew inspiration from a game they played in 1928, "Question and Answer," in which an answer is formulated in ignorance of the question (or vice versa, it doesn't matter). "What is a cannibal?" Suzanne Muzard asked. "It's a fly in a bowl of milk," replied Max Morise. Of course, the non sequitur functions just as piquantly if "a cannibal" gives way to the word "cinema." *Cinema is a fly in a bowl of milk.*

15

The mind quickly grasps the emblematic symbolism of a flailing, doomed, black organism on the whiteness of a screen. (I can't help thinking of Larry Semon.)

Later, the Surrealists developed their question-and-answer game. Researches into "irrational knowledge" were undertaken in the sixth issue of *Le Surréalisme au service de la révolution* (May 1933) and involved elucidating the "possibilities" of an object (a crystal ball; a scrap of pink velvet), a painting (by De Chirico), an arbitrary date (409 AD), and a city (Paris). Apropos of Paris, the question posed was: "Should we preserve, shift, modify, transform, or knock down its landmarks?" The answers were spontaneous, if not automatic, and had Breton razing the Palace of Justice and covering the site with a huge graffito, Arthur Harfaux supplementing the statue of Henri IV with three diminishing replicas marching in Indian file behind it, and Maurice Henry replacing the Sacré-Coeur with a woman's enormous hand holding what seems to be a toilet roll. The results of this collaboration were sifted and analyzed. Two decades later the Surrealists assembled their "Data Toward the Irrational Enlargement of a Film" (q.v.) in much the same way. This time the "interpreted found object" was Josef von Sternberg's exotic melodrama, *The Shanghai Gesture* (1941). Questions were posed about its content, questions like:

How might the film be symbolized?

which was answered

By a salamander, the one Benvenuto Cellini saw
By a giant nettle in flower
By a steel blade protruding slightly from a window
By premature baldness
By a snail
By a town inhabited exclusively by hands

Such nonutilitarian, metarational discourse, in which spontaneity and surprise aerate understanding, uncannily exemplifies Habermas's "ideal speech situation" as defined by Peter Dews: "a situation of dialogue characterized by full reciprocity, and by an absence of external coercions and internal distortions."

Dews' "external coercions and internal distortions" provides us with as fine a definition of sublimation as you could wish for. If sublimation describes the mental process whereby instinctual, unconscious thought is rendered serviceable for both psyche and society in being rechanneled by "higher" forms of thinking—and for "higher thinking" read "the cinematic apparatus"—then the Surrealists wanted to desublimate cinema, not to bring it down to earth, but to go deeper, to crack open the volatile magma at its core, the brimstone beneath the treacle. For them, authentic knowledge grew out of willful ignorance. A transgressive, liberating dialogue could unfold in the ellipsis between discrete monologues, in the slippery sovereign space of amnesia:

> "Do you remember everything? Everything. I don't remember a thing. But I know that moment had to come, Cecilia. What a world you lived in. I'm suffocating. The lake can only be seen from the left wing of the chateau." ("Malombra, Aura of Absolute Love," q.v.)

The Surrealist lust for disorientation is a sumptuous "remake" of Rimbaud's programmatic *dérèglement de tous les sens:* "The Poet makes himself a *seer* by a long, prodigious, and reasoned *disordering* of *all the senses.*" *Les sens* also signifies "meanings." If the Surrealists merrily scrambled their senses, it was through disorienting the meanings offered them by cultural products, films included. In 1936, at a time when he was intimately involved with Surrealism, Joseph Cornell made his film *Rose Hobart* by "disordering" a found object. (It was an idea Dalí had had but never realized, and he was most miffed when he saw Cornell's film.) Cornell took George Melford's Hollywood melodrama *East of Borneo* (1931)—Melford was a poor man's Tod Browning—and recut it into a fifteen-minute movie, *his* cinema of facts and gestures.

In speaking generally of Surrealist attitudes toward cinema in his 1936 book *Surrealism,* Julien Levy—New York gallery owner and the first American champion of Surrealism, and of Cornell—accurately defined the specific charm of *Rose Hobart:*

> It is never the plot of such a film that should receive attention, but rather the wealth of innuendo which accompanies each action and which forms an emotional pattern far richer than that of the usual straight story to which our logical mind is accustomed.

17

In leaving three-fourths of *East of Borneo* on the cutting-room floor, Cornell eliminated any obligation to the linear time and causality, the straight story, of Melford's film. Instead, we have a dreamlike rereading of the original and a fetishistic homage—not the last proposed by Cornell, as his "'Enchanted Wanderer': Excerpt From a Journey Album for Hedy Lamarr" (q.v.) makes clear—to an idealized female performer. The new narrative describes the disorientation of a desirous, rather boyish young woman—the actress Rose Hobart—as she drifts skittishly in search of epistemological enlightenment through an exotic, chaotic, largely nocturnal landscape, constantly perplexed by her ambivalent and metamorphic paramour(s). *Rose Hobart* is a film built on pregnant hiatus, chill, often cruel emotion, confounded expectancy, sabotaged continuity; on accepted contradiction; on displacement, condensation, and overdetermination. Even though Cornell affirms many of the Hollywood cinematic codes—reaction shots, reverse angles, match cuts—he purposively gets things wrong. He subverts the seamless continuity that is the hallmark of mainstream cinema by rendering problematic, and thus poetizing, the relation of shot to shot and sequence to sequence. Sometimes he retains elements of Melford's montage, but for the most part shots are juxtaposed rather than spliced, so that the classical relations between them— cause and effect, gaze and object—jar rather than gel. This is a film that never gets going. It's an accretion of irrelevancies, of momentary excitations and subterfuges. Yet we are more than happy to live in its enigma, its deferred resolution.

"That kind of dilemma, the inexplicable impossibility of fulfilling a simple desire, often occurs in my movies," Buñuel told us with his last gasp. Cornell had comprehended that the substance of all the first wave of Surrealist films (1927–30) is the surfacing of desire, the self-imposed and socially imposed repressions that this unconscious impulse suffers, and its desublimated—or pseudosublimated—expression in an impassioned symbolic ritual of compensation. Just think of Gaston Modot's flaming spruce, plow, archbishop, and giraffe tossed from his lover's bedroom window in *L'Âge d'or;* Kiki's attack on the starfish, dagger in hand, in Man Ray's *L'Étoile de mer;* and the priest's oedipal reverie of watery grottoes, schooner, and glittery gothic castle in Dulac and Artaud's *The Seashell and the Clergyman.*

It's only in recent years that *Rose Hobart* has truly revealed herself, her image being lodged in archives in London, Paris, and New York. Cornell well understood the oneiric possibilities of the "Surrealist cut" as formulated by Buñuel and Dalí in *Un chien andalou.* (In all probability it was an idea they'd appropriated from Buster Keaton.) This strategy, later dear to Deren, Resnais, and Ruiz, works by perturbing the parallel continuum of time and space. An example: when we read the intertitle "Sixteen years before" in *Un chien andalou,* we assume the next shot will be different in content to the preceding one. Not so: Buñuel contradicts the temporal leap by maintaining an impossible spatial continuity (same décors, costumes, and physiognomies). And Cornell's use of sound—Melford's original dialogue and mood music being replaced by the incongruous use of samba rhythms—suggests that he'd absorbed the idea of what Karel Teige called the "sound defect." Striving to pursue the formal inventiveness of their 1920s cinema and to stave off the static, theatrical naturalism which threatened it with the advent of talkies, Eisenstein, Pudovkin, and Alexandrov theorized that "Only a contrapuntal use of sound in relation to the visual montage piece will afford a new potentiality of montage development" ("A Statement on the Sound-Film," 1928). With *L'Âge d'or* Buñuel made it clear he'd heeded the Russians' words. And in Georges Hugnet's Surrealist scenario for *La Perle* (1929), a film with clear echoes of Buñuel and Dalí, we read of the requirement that all sound accompaniment be "mistranslation," "countersound." For instance, Hugnet has a seduction accompanied by a banging door, a kiss by the rolling of a drum. (Jacques Brunius, and Goldfayn and Heisler were to pursue these sound/image researches.)

Probably without knowing Cornell's epoch-making opus, the Belgian Surrealist Marcel Mariën elaborated on the issues it raised in his essay "Another Kind of Cinema" (q.v.). Echoing Eisenstein, et al.—whose high hopes were soon dashed with the displacement of their 1920s NEPotism by Stalinist Filmmaking in One Country—Mariën argued for the superiority of silent montage cinema over the dialogue-bound sound film. (His credo is a far cry from Dalí's conclusion in his "Abstract of a Critical History of the Cinema," q.v.) Writing in 1955, Mariën maintained that sound cinema had reached an impasse and that the only way forward was to revert to the idea of montage as the determining factor. The economic problem could be overcome by taking existing films and reediting them: "It is a question of cutting the narrative thread, while retaining the emotional effects" (a succinct definition of *Rose Hobart!*). Perhaps Mariën had lent an ear to his young friends Debord and Wolman, the proto-Situationists who were currently propounding their theories of detournment in his magazine *Les Lèvres nues*. Anyhow, in his essay Mariën suggests ways of detourning found footage: (1) Take any film, strip it of its sound track, study its purely visual makeup. Invent a new script from this with new dialogue. (2) Start from the sound track and match it with new visual images from other films. (3) Destroy a character's identity by modifying his voice and dialogue from shot to shot. (4) Have the same voice coming from different mouths. (5) Edit together the performances of one actor. (6) Swap over the sex of the voices. (7) Compose a film of several versions of the same story, Joan of Arc's, say.

We have, Mariën stressed, to rediscover cinematic inventiveness and the power the mind has to poeticize. He attempted to do this with *L'Imitation du cinéma,* made in 1959. Mariën's film contains two films. Like many Surrealist works, it has elements of critical reflexivity. The first film tells the story of a man with a crucifixion complex and is a series of gags. But scandal is not restricted to the narrative. As Mariën says, it "is situated on the plane of the aesthetics of cinema; it results mainly from the exceptionally poor way [the film] is put together." The director sets out to perturb our usual expectations of continuity in raising error to a poetic principle. At the same time, he wants to rehabilitate montage. He does away, so to speak, with the continuity girl, "the real Cerberus whose task consists of examining the smallest details, to prevent life from interfering at all costs," and emphasizes discontinuity by having his characters' appearance chop and change from shot to shot: although the montage maintains the unity of time and place, a character may be wearing a striped tie in one shot and a spotted one in the next. The splice, then, becomes contradictory since it affirms continuity and subverts it at the same time. The Surrealist cut is the deepest.

In their attempts to disorient themselves through film, the Surrealists aestheticized the cinematic experience itself: "It has not been said often enough," wrote Albert Valentin, "that the cinema, like the automobile, owes a part of its interest to a taste of recent origin which it flatters and maintains in us: a scorn for timetables. One comes and one goes, one enters and exits when it suits." ("Introduction to Black-and-White Magic," q.v.) Breaking the narrative thread was easy if you simply drifted into the cinema after the film had begun and left as soon as you were bored or felt yourself slotting the fragments of plot back into place. Breton and Vaché first practiced this in 1916, as Breton tells us in "As in a Wood" (q.v.):

When I was at "the cinema age" (it should be recognized that this age exists in life —and that it passes) I never began by consulting the amusement pages to find out what film might chance to be the best, nor did I find out the time the film was to begin. I agreed wholeheartedly with Jacques Vaché in appreciating nothing so much as dropping into a cinema when whatever was playing was playing, at any point in the show, and leaving at the first hint of boredom—of surfeit—to rush off to another cinema where we behaved in the same way, and so on (obviously, this practice would be too much of a luxury today). I have never known anything more *magnetizing:* it goes without saying that more often than not we left our seats without even knowing the title of the film, which was in no way of importance to us, anyway. On a Sunday several hours sufficed to exhaust all that Nantes could offer us: the important thing is that one came out "charged" for a few days; as there had been nothing deliberate about our actions, qualitative judgments were forbidden.

The aleatory discovery of the marvelous nooks and crannies of the metropolis was inaugurated by Baudelaire, redeemed by Apollinaire, resuscitated by the Surrealists (and later the Situationists), and, in between times, elucidated by Walter Benjamin. Paul Éluard was to discover *Peter Ibbetson,* a seminal, "involuntarily Surrealist" Tinseltown melodrama, when he slipped into a cinema on the heels of a woman he'd been pursuing. Yet even as the authors of *Nadja* and *Paris Peasant* lyricized over the chance encounter, their City of Light was evolving. It's the late 1920s and Breton and Aragon are already lamenting Paris's waning potential for Surrealist discovery. That potential seems all the more fragile today: we have only to think of the pedestrian zoning of many a modern metropolis—rendering us refugees from the all-pervasive automobile—to realize that the unwonted is all but forbidden, or contrived to the point of virtual disappearance. And where "Surrealist" film is concerned, one vital element is missing now: the fleapit. The fleapit was the ideal setting for Surrealist seeing: "Above all, cinema auditoriums must be afflicted with the same decay as the films they show," said Robert

Desnos. It provided a rapid turnover of films; the staple diet was precisely the despised, wholly popular, almost anonymous trash the Surrealists found revelatory. The lumpen proletarian ambience of the largely empty venue—water dripping through the ceiling, rats running over the feet, dark stains on the screen, demented people wandering about—enhanced any Surrealist reading, since communal *skepticism* reigned there. But the fleapit has disappeared, and today different patterns of consumption, the concatenation of shoe-box-sized auditoriums in the mall multiplex, the greater critical coverage films receive, the specific cultural quest that takes you to the movies now, mean that these interestedly disinterested strategies have gone by the board. But in 1951 such dystopian decay could give way to utopian promise in Bernard Roger's "Plan for a Cinema at the Bottom of a Lake" (q.v.). One of the rare Surrealist architects—others being Frederick Kiesler, Yves Laloy, Guy-René Doumayrou, and the Italian "anarchitect" Fabio de Sanctis—Roger revisioned Rimbaud's "pure hallucination" of "a drawing room at the bottom of a lake" in his scheme for a sock-shaped glass movie theater that would float, to a depth of five fathoms, in a volcanic lake in the Auvergne. As visionary as anything in Ledoux—a favorite architect of the Surrealists—Bernard Roger's design for a submarine cinema was never built.

You'd think, perhaps, that TV is an ideal "Surrealist" medium, since drifting is accomplished at the push of a button. When I had a television I never found it so. The homeliness and incomplete darkness of the sitting room with its intrusive visual field; the petiteness and pettiness of the images with their round-the-clock formulaic content and conjunctions; the mobility and the familiarity to us of other spectators, if there are any: all these things militate against the oneiric and vitiate the exercise of reverie, instead encouraging the passive, half-hearted, guilty absorption of an enervating stream of facile detritus that consolidates the "voluntary house arrest" (Paul Virilio) most modern consumers cleave to. It may well be that, as James Monaco contends, TV's tendency is to be "diarrhetic and diuretic," to saturate us with images and dry us out at the same time. However that may be, these largely negative attributes exist in antithesis to the inherent uncanniness of cinema. (The uncanny is, in German, the *unheimlich,* the "unhomelike.") I mean, would you rather watch *The Piano, Institute Benjamenta, Lamerica,* or *Felicia's Journey* on the box or see them at the movies? Does anybody use the mercurial phrase "silver screen" apropos of the telly?

Attempting to define the "marvel" of cinema, the capacity it has for smoothing the way for an empathy with the unwonted, Breton said:

> From the instant he takes his seat to the moment he slips into a
> fiction evolving before his eyes, [the spectator] passes through a
> critical point as captivating and imperceptible as that uniting
> waking and sleeping (the book and even the play are incomparably
> slower in producing this release).

This hypnagogic marvel is founded on several things: the sumptuous concreteness and scale of the film illusion; the isolation from normal reality conferred by the darkness, the night of cinema; the curious contradiction of active, giant, hyperreal phantoms inducting prone, depersonalized beings of flesh and blood into their imaginary world. Which brings us to the dream/cinema equation so dear to the Surrealists.

During the five years that span the review *La Révolution surréaliste* (1924–29), the same five that separate the first and second manifestos, the Surrealists placed great emphasis on the dream and on automatism, on dream recitation and automatic writing. The first critical writings on Surrealism and cinema (by Artaud, Desnos, Soupault, Goudal) are bounded by this still rudimentary elaboration. What, people asked, was the relation between dream and cinema? Brunius argued that, up to 1920 or so, the film was incapable of realism, "in the sense of an illusion of reality." He implies that this was due to the inexperience of audiences and the clumsiness of film language. Since film was incapable of realism, it was incapable of representing a dream. "Voluntarily," he added. It was, however, capable of doing so *involuntarily.* How?

To begin with, entering the dark auditorium was like closing your eyes. Your isolation from the crowd, your body submitting to a feeling of depersonalization; the droning music obdurating the sense of hearing; the stiffness of the neck necessary for the gaze's orientation: all this was like going to sleep. Then there were the intertitles—we're watching a silent film—with their white letters on black suggesting hypnagogic visions. The very technique of film evoked the dream more than it did reality:

> The images *fade in* and *fade out,* dissolve into each other, vision
> begins and ends in an *iris,* secrets are revealed through a keyhole,

the mental image of a keyhole. The disposition of screen images *in time* is absolutely analogous with the *arrangement* thought or the dream can devise. Neither chronological order nor relative values of duration are real. Contrary to the theater, film, like thought, like the dream, chooses some gestures, defers or enlarges them, eliminates others, travels many hours, centuries, kilometers in a few seconds, speeds up, slows down, stops, goes backward. It is impossible to imagine a truer mirror of mental performance. (Jacques Brunius, "Crossing the Bridge," q.v.)

The monochrome sobriety of the film image, its pre-Technicolor dearth of mimesis, played a part. In "Surrealism and Cinema" (q.v.) Jean Goudal invoked Taine's notion of "the reductive mechanism of images." When we are awake, imagined images have a pallor made all the more dramatic by the vigor and relief of reality as perceived by the senses. When asleep our senses are idle, or seem to be so, and this contrast ceases to obtain as the imaginary images take over. We believe in their actual existence. The film, Goudal said, was "conscious hallucination," and the trance-like atmosphere in the cinema enhanced the feeling of immediate revelation.

Around 1920, Brunius went on to argue, the cinema became more capable of realism, because of the refining of syntax. But it still remained the least realistic of the arts, because of the tension between the "fidelity" of photography and the "infidelity" of montage. (This tension was the subject of Buster Keaton's much admired *Sherlock Junior* (1924).) It qualified cinema to portray the dream *voluntarily* since, to put it crudely, the dream is elemental waking reality (= photography) retraced, sectioned, jumbled (=montage). Sound added another dimension to the antithesis because it was capable of duplicity. Used naturalistically, it fortified photography's fidelity; used unnaturalistically, dissonantly, it strengthened montage's infidelity. This sonorous double-dealing excited the Surrealist filmmakers. From the start, the Surrealists were conscious of the analogical role film language played: it could *simulate* the dream, but that was all. René Clair was one of the first to fall into the trap of confusing thought with the tool used to transcribe it. Pondering the problem of unconscious thought being put on film in the way you could write it down spontaneously, using the automatic method, he came to the conclusion that the complications of film technique, the time and effort needed to bring any film project to fruition, precluded success. Brunius pointed out Clair's error by observing that the Surrealists had never disputed that the transcription of unconscious thought, including the dream, by word of mouth, pen, brush, camera or whatever, always involved a degree of secondary elaboration.

As the "intuitive period" of 1919 to 1929 drew to a close, Breton and his comrades grew uneasy about the stereotypical constrictions of the automatic text and the dream account. The idea of a "pure psychic automatism" was naive, they realized, since language itself always structures thought, rendering the notion of "unalloyed"—prelinguistic—access to the unconscious chimerical. Whatever form it takes, all thought is, in the last analysis, magical, an act of instrumental, if ambivalent, faith communicated linguistically through the trope. If, say, Breton's dreamlike praise song of a poem "Free Union" is about the idealizing heterosexual imagination, it is also about the trope of *effictio,* "the head-to-toe itemization of a heroine's charms," as Richard Lanham defined it. When we turn our attention to film we can read "the Surrealist cut" (see above) as tropic in nature. Something of a "triste tropique" because, craving the ineffability of irrational discourse, the incantatory oddness of language per se, the Surrealists were wary, even, of dogmatizing the work of secondary elaboration. (In that sense "Free Union" is not about tropes at all; nor is *L'Âge d'or* about "the Surrealist cut.") Instead, they craved the plenitude of immanence rather than the contingency of affirmation. Within the symbolic order there was a fissure formed by what Georges Bataille called the *informe,* formlessness, a space where meaning had gone out of shape: "What it designates has no rights in any sense and gets itself squashed everywhere, like a spider or an earthworm." (Taking a lead from Bataille, and during analysis of a clutch of Eisenstein stills, Roland Barthes dubbed this fugitive overspill "the obtuse meaning.") In *L'Âge d'or* the "amorous egoism" of Gaston Modot has him deliberately flattening a beetle underfoot, but before that—and speaking of *Un chien andalou*—Buñuel stressed that he, coming later to Surrealism and therefore unburdened by the discoveries of the "intuitive period," was not directly concerned with either the dream or automatism but with describing a playfulness of mind, an irrational humor akin to the dreamwork, but no more than that. Artaud's cavil is important here. His script for *The Seashell and the Clergyman* was, he emphasized, meant to demon-

25

strate how far a scenario could identify with the mechanics of the dream "without being a dream itself." He wanted to suggest the free play of thought, and not a dream, which has an axiomatic structure. Although he actively colluded with director Germaine Dulac on the film, the wayward Artaud subsequently protested her structuring of his deliberately incoherent scenario as a dream. ("Rêve d'Antonin Artaud" appears on the credits.)

Although there was some questioning of their original emphasis on the dream account in itself, the nocturnal nevertheless remained a touchstone for the Surrealists. Freud dubbed that core of our night thoughts ever resistant to analysis "the navel of the dream." This is the space of Bataille's *informe,* and the Surrealists were attached to it as by an umbilicus. The all-seeing blind spot: irreducible and exemplary.

All aesthetic objects have their blind spot. There's an edificatory Surrealism the Surrealists made, but there's also a latent Surrealism discernible in artifacts that owe nothing to it. The scopophiliac "wild eye" evoked by Breton in *Surrealism and Painting* is forever on the lookout for the gratificatory images it needs. In his prologue to *Un chien andalou* Buñuel spectacularly bisected the rational, Cartesian eye. Returned to its "savage state," the razored eyeball is obliged to look behind itself: so, following that famous violatory moment, the film describes the avaricious play of unconscious thought hurtling osmotically from within to without and back again. "Go to the Louvre," Félix Fénéon advised, "and discover the sexual spot in some famous canvas, the part the artist treated with love." For "Louvre" read "Essoldo," for "canvas" read "film." The Surrealists went prospecting for the latent meaning of movies, "the sexual spot" that heralded the return of the repressed. Epicureans of detritus, they uncovered treasures of poetry and subversion in the bargain basement of cinema. "The worst films I've ever seen, the ones that send me to sleep," Man Ray claimed, "contain ten or fifteen marvelous minutes. The best films I've ever seen contain only ten or fifteen valid ones." ("Cinemage," q.v.) Breton mentions a film he saw in the late 1920s that completely disoriented him, *How I Killed My Child,* made by a priest known as Peter the Hermit, "a film of unlimited insanity in which everything was used as a pretext to show the 'Lord's Table.'" ("As in a Wood," q.v.) And, speaking of a puerile screen version of the Aladdin tale, Gérard Legrand referred to the film's power to "*liberate* the intellect from its moorings by pushing vacuity and foolishness as far as they can go, to the point where they outstrip themselves" ("Turkey Broth and Unlabeled Love Potions," q.v.). Ado Kyrou was unequivocal in his advice: "I ask you, learn to go and see the 'worst' films; they are sometimes sublime." Only with the knowing—and ambiguous—cult of kitsch have these proscribed movies been rescued today from the dustbins of oblivion. This more or less wretched oeuvre takes in the horror and science fiction genres, teen movies, serials, peplum movies, pornography, ads. Often adored at a forlorn distance through secondary material like stills, posters, and press books, they find their audience via the anthological book and the specialist magazine or, if extant, in the form of the videotape, a kind of celluloid samizdat available to the discerning fanatic, the fetishist. "Each of us," counseled Kyrou at a time when this cultural slag was still a part of the day-to-day life of the masses, "must find his or her own sublime films, since in this domain objectivity is to all intents and purposes impossible":

> For my part I confess to a weakness for almost all of Couzinet's films, for certain religious melodramas made by Léo Joannon, and some biblical films like Richard Thorpe's delirious *The Prodigal* (1955), in which Astarte, the High Priestess of Love, makes a human sacrifice as half-naked damsels play the part of wooden carousel horses and a potbellied character bangs the gong. But I'd prefer to forget those Nordic potboilers, with their midnight bathing, noble fathers, and metaphysical anguish (have you seen *The Hour of Desire*, by Egil Holmsen (1958)?), and the Italian travesties from which the superb *Beneath the Bridge of Sighs* (1954) alone stands out, wherein we can admire a striptease at sword-point (two heroines engaged in a duel of cutting the other's nightdress to ribbons), together with the incredible *Ship of Lost Women* (1953), made by Raffaele Matarazzo, in which sadism, revolt, eroticism, religion, and melodrama conspire to form a series of problematically linked scenes dependent on the commonplace, raised by its rigor to the level of pure involuntary poetry. ("The Marvelous Is Popular," q.v.)

In her book *Fantasy: The Literature of Subversion* Rosemary Jackson intimates how nominally realist, "bourgeois" texts often contain a fantastic subtext which "reveals itself at those moments of tension when the work threatens to collapse under the weight of its own repression." This aperçu could be applied to the conventions dear to Hollywood cinema, in which the very closures of generic and formal codification and the weight of the star system more or less guaranteed breaches of intentionality on the part of the director. Sometimes a sequence stood proud, came adrift from its setting in the narrative. These wayward segments could disorient the spectator, acquiring a force of meaning because they were both unforeseen and shocking. Nora Mitrani cites a scene from Hugo Fregonese's *One Way Street* (1950) in which a sleeping James Mason is courted by a pretty girl wafting a *fish* under his nose ("Intention and Surprise," q.v.). A better director, she argues, would have rejected this sequence "because it smacks of incoherence or vagabondage of the imagination." Being overwhelmed by the erotic import of the scene—the blunt olfactory equation that is made—we are invited to think of the characters in a different way. We put them on another, poetic plane: "It pleases us that from time to time characters live according to *their* will, obeying *their* imagination more than the director's intelligence. A sticky problem, perhaps, for the latter to reckon with the imagination of his own characters." This happens because the director is imaginative on occasion, or because he is not completely conscious of the situation and his logical intelligence fails him. Lapses like this are not uncommon and take their place among the psychopathological gaffs Freud analyzed in his book on everyday life. This is how Jacques Brunius put it:

Precisely because of the richness of its means the cinema makes total control of images, gestures, and words by one man alone very difficult. Often enough a film leaves the head of its creator and the hands of his colleagues like a ship in a storm, as best it may, the bearer not only of what they meant to say but also of some things no one wished to say. But is not the participation of chance in this clash of wills a fascinating thing? (*En marge du cinéma français* (Paris: Arcanes, 1954),189)

I remember seeing William Wyler's *The Heiress*, a 1949 melodrama enlivened by the definitely sexual ritual both the wealthy heiress's stern father (Ralph Richardson) and her conniving suitor (Montgomery Clift) performed when removing the paper bands from their cigars. Olivia de Havilland caught the bug, too, when she lovingly caressed the starched thumb of the white gloves Clift had "accidentally" left on the hall table. Whether or not the mise-en-scène was consciously contrived, so as to describe preconscious motivation—which is quite possible—it remains a fact that these overdetermined fragments, shifting as they do from the metonymic to the metaphoric register, eclipse the rest of the film for me. In my imagination they stand erect, so to speak, while the rest of Wyler's images remain flaccid, detumescent, forgettable.

Don't get me wrong: I'm as in awe of narrative grain as the next man at the Clapham Odeon, but I *do* respond to the splinter. We each of us chip our own shards from the communicating vessel of film. Film is, after all, an unstable emulsion of pullulating emblems, emblems we live directly, in a preconscious way. We're all dialecticians when we go to the movies, converting quantity into quality. The awesome satisfaction we might get from the fragment, against which the film as a whole may pale, is by definition fetishistic. "Nobody sees the same film," says Gérard Legrand in "Female x Film = Fetish" (q.v.), a point demonstrated by the way the most sympathetic of friends could argue fiercely about the meaning of a movie. The desire to make *the* definitive assessment in a debate in which such judgment is chimerical is likened by Legrand to the public revelation of one's most secret sexual preferences. Fetishism, the o'erweening predilection for a part of the body or article of dress, to the exclusion of the whole sexual object, is the very mechanism that binds us to the film fragment. Given the male Surrealist view of woman as erotico-sacred redemptrix, Legrand tends to cleave to the female film presence: "all fetishism results in the 'cutting out' of the woman and her attributes along a preferred dotted line of oneiric iridescence, barely justifiable in the eyes of someone else." Here we have an embryonic aside on the star system, wherein everything is rendered secondary to the fetishized tics and traces of the known but always defamiliar body. (The cult of Louise Brooks really cranks up, for instance, with the lyrical eulogies of Legrand's confrère, Kyrou.) However, as Legrand intimates elsewhere in his essay, erotic allure does not necessarily have to find its subject in a woman's body. For my own part, I have been dumbstruck by other "compensatory rituals," ones that describe human, often manual, gestures, actual or implied: the footprint in the mud that fills up with water (*Giant*, George Stevens (1956)); the rushing waterfall that forms a backdrop to an inverted guitar that emerges in a man's hand

29

from behind a ridge (*Trader Horn*, W.S. Van Dyke (1931)); Gregory Peck's fingers groping for and grasping a rock in the milky water to brain Robert Mitchum with (*Cape Fear*, J. Lee Thompson (1961)); the love letter left on a doorstep that slowly dissolves in a downpour of rain (*They're a Weird Mob*, Michael Powell (1966)). To be sure, the symptomatic clairvoyance of examples like these—which are specific to me; you'll have a different set, right?—takes us back full circle to the imaginative manipulations of Modot in *L'Âge d'or*, Kiki in *L'Étoile de mer*, and Alex Allin, the priest in *The Seashell and the Clergyman*. Like Barthes, we've been pricked by the *punctum*, in that fulgurating moment when we egoistically recuperate the "off-center detail" and thus scupper the cultural contract encoded in the *studium*, the polite, half-interested reciprocation of creator and consumer. There's something both winning and winsome, feisty and forlorn, about such perverse special pleading. It's hard not to laugh at Karl Kraus's observation that "There is no more unfortunate creature under the sun than a fetishist who yearns for a woman's shoe and has to settle for the whole woman."

The subtitle of Edward Young's *Night Thoughts* is "The Complaint and the Consolation." The consoling excitement felt by the first Surrealists for the films of Chaplin, Pearl White, and Douglas Fairbanks had floundered and flopped into complaint by the late 1920s. Soupault's valedictory understanding that "the cinema was not a perfected toy but the terrible and magnificent flag of life" ("Cinema U.S.A.," q.v.) quickly gave way to René Crevel's sarcasm—"once the light's back on, after having put up with the banalities on the screen you count all those gold moldings on the ceiling" ("Battlegrounds and Commonplaces," q.v.)—and then to Benjamin Péret's bilious accusation that "the cinema, a cultural form without precedent, has developed into an industry governed by sordid market forces incapable of distinguishing a work of the mind from a sack of flour" ("Against Commercial Cinema," q.v.). The pessimism that gradually overtook the Surrealists was not wholly extramural: some of them were working in film and saw it from within the prison walls. For Desnos, writing in 1927, this new pessimism was due to the intervention of technical interests, to the petrifaction of cinematic codes, and to the consolidation of big business. The arrival of sound prompted further gloomy prediction.

Things had indeed changed dramatically in a few years. The cinema that originally thrilled Breton, Soupault, Aragon, and friends was, in 1918, truly in the melting pot, fermenting in its own "intuitive period." Mack Sennett's *A Film Johnnie* (1914) demonstrates this well. It's set in a studio where a film is being made. Sennett—of whom Breton said "Mack Sennett is Surrealist in movement"—appears as the director. We see camera setups, rudimentary sets, etc. Charlie Chaplin inevitably contrives to get under everybody's feet, of course, but where the film is interesting is in its allusion to the spontaneous—a Surrealist might say "automatic"—way films were being made at that time. We cut from the mayhem in the studio to an employee in the street who telephones Sennett with news of a fire: "Just what we need to finish the picture!" Straightaway the cast and crew drive to the burning location and complete the now revised film. The violent, libidinous character Chaplin plays stands in marked contrast to the dreary, inadequate waif he has become by 1925 and *The Gold Rush*. The one disturbing image in that film is of Chaplin disemboweling a feather pillow after a visit from the girl he loves. The onanistic symbolism would be reprised by Modot in *L'Âge d'or*.

(This is perhaps the moment to open a parenthesis on Chaplin and "Chaplinism." Like many radical intellectuals of the interwar period, the Surrealists eulogized Chaplin—"Charlot"—as both creator and man. A typical pen portrait was inscribed by Paul Guitard in *La Révolution surréaliste*'s sister review *Clarté* in 1925:

> Always, and at every moment, Charlot strives to escape reality, because reality is ugly, demeaning, a dead end. But he always knows how to be TRUTHFUL within fantasy, real within the unreal. He is the first among our Surrealists. . . . A poor blighter, instinctual, too, close to nature, to authentic life; done down by the law and by social conventions. . . . Charlot appears as an irreducible enemy of the law. He is, logically so, in permanent revolt against this law's representative, the policeman. He is, as we've said, the poor blighter society oppresses and exploits.

In the *Second Manifesto* Breton placed Chaplin alongside Hegel, Feuerbach, Marx, Lautréamont, Rimbaud, Jarry, Freud, and Trotsky as an authentic *révolté*, one of the privileged witnesses "of a century of truly lacerating philosophy and poetry." When Chaplin was hauled over the coals for his "depraved" morals in 1927, the Surrealists leapt to his defense in their manifesto ("Hands Off Love," q.v.). However, Chaplin's waxing sentimentality, and the displacement of Surrealist interest toward other more cerebral screen comedians—Keaton, Langdon, Fields, and the Marx Brothers—ensured that by 1952, and Jean-Louis Bédouin's polemical "Chaplin, the Copper's Nark" (q.v.), the worm had well and truly turned.)

With the hardening of political attitudes after Breton, Aragon, Péret, Éluard, and Unik joined, albeit briefly, the French Communist Party in 1927, a more reflective, less delirious, attitude toward cinema developed: to what extent did the content of any given film support the Surrealist revolution? Here the Surrealists were echoing, and broadening, contemporary leftist debates about *Tendenzkunst*. Cretinizing as it was by definition, being an eddy in the gulf stream of merchandise that traversed the Atlantic—cf. the first paragraph of "Hands Off Love"—the Surrealists maintained that Hollywood cinema was still capable of producing the odd film, "Surrealist" in inverted commas, that expressed libertarian ideas sympathetic to theirs. W.S. Van Dyke's *White Shadows of the South Seas* (1928) was one such. The film's tendentious Rousseauism, its motif of *amour fou*, and its unremitting pessimism about Western civilization and its god were congruent with their point of view. Necessity dictated this turning toward mainstream cinema for comfort. The first wave of Surrealist films, beginning with *The Seashell and The Clergyman* in 1927, taking in *L'Étoile de mer* (1928), *Un chien andalou* (1929), Georges Hugnet's *La Perle* (1929), and peaking with *L'Âge d'or* in 1930, had come and gone. The ideological realignments in the group following the battles of 1929 muddied the waters. Then the introduction of sound helped put the means of production beyond the reach of most independent filmmakers. Equally crucial was police chief Chiappe's banning of *L'Âge d'or*: after that, where was there to go?

To be sure, from a revolutionary standpoint the impact Hollywood had on the masses couldn't be ignored. Although there was little chance that they could appropriate the means of production for themselves, the Surrealists continued to believe that in extremis Hollywood could argue their case for them. The overwhelming evidence of films like *Seventh Heaven*, *Berkeley Square*, and *Peter Ibbetson* suggested that this was so. The "Surrealist" content of *Peter Ibbetson* still staggers today. In *L'Amour fou* Breton placed Hathaway's "prodigious" film alongside *L'Âge d'or* as "a triumph of Surrealist thought." It addresses the same problems Breton does in his book: the transcendent materialism of desire, the dialectic linking reality and the dream. In *Peter Ibbetson* Peter and Mary, childhood sweethearts, are parted after the death of the boy's mother. Twenty years later, practicing as an architect, Peter is employed by the Duchess of Towers. The pair, who do not yet recognize one another, gradually feel a mysterious rapport evidenced in shared dreams. When Peter blurts out his love to Mary's suspicious husband, their childhood relationship is revealed. In the ensuing fight he kills the duke. Jailed for life, his back broken by a vicious jailer, Peter is given only hours to live. That night he dreams he is visited by Mary in his cell. Though he can miraculously walk again, he cannot summon up enough belief to walk through the bars as she has done. Mary promises to prove the power of dream by visiting the prison next day and giving him a ring. Peter lives; Mary brings the ring. As a warder gives him the ring Peter says: "It looks like a ring but it isn't. It's the wall of a world. Inside it is desire. Inside she lives. It's a world, with every road, every path, and the eighth sea." Peter now believes; he walks through the bars. And in their nightly dream Peter and Mary are united in a paradisal landscape.

The symbiosis of mental and material life is asserted from the start of the film. Childhood obsessions and symbolic actions are shown to determine adult life (the maquettes Peter builds as an architect are adult toys). The prison bars through which Peter passes every night are prefigured by the railings he squeezed through as a boy to get into Mary's next-door garden. Peter's adult fixations, his longing for Mary's love, hinge on two incidents from childhood which predicted his mother's death: a quarrel in which he accidentally broke a doll's face, a wagon he couldn't complete because he lacked the wheels. In the dream both are reconstituted.

Sad to say, *Peter Ibbetson*'s happy ending tends to undermine the film's main thrust. Mary dies; Peter is alone in their dream. Her voice comes down from heaven: he can join her there for eternity. Such Christian closure runs through many of the Hollywood *amour fou* films canonized by the Surrealists, and seems at odds with their own atheism and anticlericalism. In these movies Eros gives way to agape, or so it seems (but observe the erotic underpinning of Peter's obsessions, as discussed above). When love and metaphysics are in the frame, Christianity comes to the rescue. (We should also bear in mind that between 1934 and 1948 all Hollywood movies were vetted by the Roman Catholic–dominated production code.) But beggars can't be choosers. . . . And indeed this very straining after conventionality can have contradictory results, as in *Seventh Heaven,* when Chico, the atheist street-cleaner, ultimately finds God "within himself," but only because he is blinded/castrated: an unwitting (?) indictment of the Christian idea.

The diaspora wrought by the Second World War only interrupted the elaboration of Surrealist cinema, it didn't end it. The situation in 1945 bears comparison with 1918. Occupied Europe had been starved of films, of a nonfascist variety, anyway. René Clair estimated that between 1940 and 1944 French audiences were denied a thousand Hollywood features. (Actually, the figure was twice that.) Serge Guilbaut tells us in *How New York Stole the Idea of Modern Art* that, as a sneaky codicil to the May 1946 Blum-Byrnes Accord on U.S. economic aid, the Americans pushed through a revised quota for Hollywood films, upping the old figure of six out of thirteen weeks exhibition for their product on French screens to nine out of thirteen. As well as hampering the revival of the French film industry, the measure opened the floodgates to a huge backlog of American movies. In response to this inundation, various factions within a renascent French film culture began to tackle the ideological and aesthetic problems of popular Hollywood film. In 1918 Hollywood was a balmy hot bath; in 1945, and on the eve of the Cold War, a fetid cold douche. Yet, however watertight the nascent Cold Warriors wanted things, there was still the odd bit of soap to slip on. A previously uncharted, worm-in-the-bud genre could declare itself, a genre like film noir, admirable in its amoral pessimism, its violence and perversity, its corrosive critique of corrupted power. (It was during this period that a young Surrealist sympathizer called Raymond Borde, who was to make a film with Breton in 1964 about the artist Pierre Molinier, began the researches that culminated in his ground-breaking book, co-authored with Étienne Chaumeton, *Panorama du film noir américain, 1941–1953.*) Their euphoric beaching on the sandbars of popular film stood the Surrealists in good stead. Pessimism about Hollywood cinema remained a constant, however, punctuated only by the odd "Surrealist" *trouvaille* like *Dark Passage* or *Gun Crazy,* or the occasional flash of poetry in some celluloid sliver or other. Neither the Marshall nor the Molotov Plan! Given their hatred of Stalinism and their postwar suspicion of Marxism *tout court,* the Surrealists rejected the Manichean cleft stick: East privileged over West,

Russian over American imperialism. In this they plowed a lonely furrow. Such outsider status had its stresses, but its epiphanies, too. The production of a clutch of short films, plus the founding of a review devoted solely to cinema, demonstrated the importance of the medium for the Paris group around Breton. In 1951 Georges Goldfayn and Jindrich Heisler completed their collage film *Revue surréaliste*. A year later Michel Zimbacca and Jean-Louis Bédouin made *L'Invention du monde,* with commentary by Péret. The review *L'Âge du cinéma,* invoking the "cinema age" Breton alluded to in "As in a Wood" (q.v.), ran to five wonderful issues through 1951. The publisher was Adonis (Ado) Kyrou; Robert Benayoun was editor-in-chief; the editorial board comprised Ion Daïfis, Maxime Ducasse, Georges Goldfayn, Georges Kaplan, J.C. Lambert, and Gérard Legrand. The editorial in issue 1 reads:

> For cinematic oneirism, contra drab realism, *L'Âge du cinéma* intends to illuminate every manifestation of the Avant-Garde. Cinema is not a static art and the Avant-Garde of 1951 does not consist, as some people think, in the clumsy plagiarizing of 1920s filmmaking; far from being a well-tried formula, it is a state of mind. It is reflected more in the personal visions of certain unusual individuals; it is discovered by chance in serials, comedies, musicals, adventure films, and productions for kids rather than in the "difficult" masterpieces of the kind of men considered as geniuses. Richness of inspiration, the prerogative of many low-budget films, seems to us more important than the retrograde tours de force of certain aesthetes.

In a statement that sits uneasily with most definitions of the avant-garde, the *L'Âge du cinéma* editors disavowed the customary benchmark of formal invention and antinarrative intent, invoking instead a viable oddness of vision on the vitiated periphery of mainstream cinema. Number 4–5 of the review is a bumper Surrealist issue. In many ways the crowning achievement of their thought on film and, indeed, one of the most important of all Surrealist collective statements, this number is a powerhouse of past and future obsessions. (Many of the translations in *The Shadow and Its Shadow* have come from it.)

After a brief hiatus, the Surrealists began collaborating on the film magazine *Positif,* founded in May 1952. Ado Kyrou and Raymond Borde black-ened its pages after issue 10. Issue 12, November-December 1954, had Robert Benayoun in it. He became an editor in May 1962 and celebrated by publishing his Surrealist colleagues, José Pierre, Legrand, and Goldfayn. *Positif,* though, was not a Surrealist journal. Various currents of the French left were to be found in it: Marxists, Surrealists, liberals. A 1974 policy statement outlined its original platform, well informed by Surrealism:

1. To restore films to their political and social context, thus mistrusting a purely formal and apparently "objective" approach which served as a criterion to conservative criticism. Needless to say, this work aims at the ideological content of the film itself, but also at the conditions of production, distribution, and reception (the relationship to the spectator).

2. To approach films without any political, aesthetic, or moral puritanism. Standing against Stalinist criticism, which refused all entertainment movies as "the opium of the people," and against bourgeois criticism which came to the same conclusions in the name of our national cultural values and the corruption of a "noble" art, *Positif* was to undertake an argumentative defense of popular genres.

Still going strong, *Positif* for many years defined itself in opposition to its almost exact contemporary, *Cahiers du cinéma.* In a 1962 polemic ("The Emperor Is Naked") against the New Wave of Truffaut, Chabrol, and Godard (who remained his bête noire), Benayoun described *Positif*'s line this way:

We shall not indulge in the unbelievable glibness of talking about the cinema solely in technical terms, we shall refuse to set any limit on our imagination, and we shall subject films to all kinds of analogy. We shall base our appreciation of cinema on the identification of the intellectual content with its external envelope, and we shall make a sharp distinction between personal style and the mannerisms of the day. We shall go back to the fundamental idea of a "personal universe" that was established by the review *L'Âge du cinéma.* We shall answer any attempts to confuse by applying unruffled analysis which, while completely impervious to notions of fashion, will not exclude the wildest interpretations.

The collective endeavor of *L'Âge du cinéma* and *Positif* spawned the crucial theorizing you get in books by Kyrou, Benayoun, Legrand, and Král. It's a body of work that, bar the enthusiasm of a Ray Durgnat, is more or less occluded from Anglo-Saxon scholarship. In *Le Surréalisme au cinéma* (1953; revised editions 1963 and 1985) Ado Kyrou gives us *his* reading of film history and an extended essay on Buñuel. As well as manifestly Surrealist films he glosses the latent kind. In this, his book even now provides a sure, if dated, guide to the use-value of a vast number of movies drawn from every genre. Some of his gleanings may need winnowing today, but that's because the book is a manic, even naive polemic intended to overwhelm and not convince the opposition. (For instance, in the preface to the 1985 edition, published only months before the author's death, Kyrou claimed Raul Ruiz for Surrealism.) *Amour-érotisme et cinéma* (1957; revised edition 1967) is a lavishly illustrated, lyrical, and iconoclastic tome with chapters on love/eroticism in horror movies, comedies, musicals, thrillers, Westerns, and melodramas; on screen divas like Clara Bow, Mae West, Louise Brooks, and Marlene Dietrich; on directors like Borzage, Von Sternberg, Murnau, Buñuel, and Resnais. *Manuel du petit parfait spectateur* (1959) is Kyrou's waggish guide to in-house liberty taking, along the lines of Breton and Vaché's disorienting wining and dining in the front stalls. Kyrou also penned a partisan study of Buñuel (1962; English translation 1963). After 1957 he made short films, the scenario of one, *An Honest Man,* being published in English in 1964. His second feature, drawn from a scenario by Buñuel and Jean-Claude Carrière, was *The Monk* (1972); it is, alas, of little merit. Robert Benayoun is perhaps best known today for his sumptuous volume *The Look of Buster Keaton* (1984; French edition 1982) and his study of Woody Allen (1986). Along with *Le Dessin animé après Walt Disney* (1961), his studies of his alter ego Jerry Lewis (1972), John Huston (1966), Alain Resnais (1980), and Tex Avery (1988) are of note. Benayoun directed two rarely seen feature films, plus a bio-documentary about the late Surrealist leader, *Passage Breton* (1970). Gérard Legrand always made a distinction between his Surrealist work—which included co-writing, with Breton, *L'Art magique* (1957)—and his film criticism. Nevertheless, it is worth signaling his *Cinémanie* (1979), which draws on Panofsky to present an iconological theory of mise-en-scène, focusing particularly on the work of Fritz Lang.

Readers of V.F. Perkins and Andrew Sarris will feel at home here. Legrand has also published a study of the Taviani brothers (1990). Petr Král, too, no longer foregrounds his Surrealist past—he was part of the Czech group that also included Jan Svankmajer; he left for Paris after the Prague Spring— but his magnificent two-part study of silent comedy, *Le Burlesque ou Morale de la tarte à la crème* (1984) and *Les Burlesques ou Parade des somnambules* (1986), is redolent with it. I have translated and published Král's *Private Screening* (1985), a meandering collation of personalized clips, involuntary films-within-the-film, together with reflections on the unique experience of filmgoing (cf. "The Ideal Summa," q.v.).

As to *this* book, there is much herein of a historiographical nature, especially material on that Hollywood "Surrealism" discussed above. The field is enormous, even if we look no further than Kyrou's books and the pages of *Positif.* I have had to be selective in choosing the texts and have kept to the Surrealist celebration of the marvelous, humor, and love.

The marvelous—our experience of the perturbing flux between the imaginary and the real—is the crucible of Surrealism. There is, though, a distinction to be made between the marvelous and its stunted relative, the fantastic. In "The Fantastic – the Marvelous" (q.v.) Kyrou associates the former with any religious or spiritualist interpretation of the awesome uncanniness of phenomena: sons of god, angels, life after death, and the like. Such a masochistic evasion of the law of desire is set against the absolute materialism of the marvelous, a sacred category, euphoric and tumultuous in nature, out of which man is driven to explore a nonalienated, holistic being-in-the-world. Thus, given its frame of reference—the world of reason cataclysmically dislocated by monstrous forces—the horror film often bears an oneiric, iconoclastic charge (cf. Jean Ferry's "Concerning *King Kong,*" q.v.).

Like Artaud in his 1932 essay on the Marx Brothers, Petr Král links humor with tragedy and eroticism in "Larry Semon's Message" (q.v.). Building on the ideas in Dalí's "Abstract of a Critical History of the Cinema" (q.v.), Král argues that the "materialist" gag—the kind found in silent comedy—is a supreme form of "concrete irrationality," in which a *quantitative* squandering, a kind of potlatch, is linked to the singular *quality* of certain objects—false beards, Model T Fords, hose pipes—to form an irrational system. What the Surrealists saw in silent screen comedy was the elevation of new mythic symbols on a par with the ones called for in the *L'Âge d'or* manifesto (q.v.). Semon actualizes the same unwholesome forces of the imagination, opposed to the hygienic, bourgeois world, as does Gaston Modot in Buñuel's film. The comedians the Surrealists adored are Sennett, Chaplin, Langdon, Keaton, the Marx Brothers, Fields, and Jerry Lewis, together with animators like Max Fleischer, Chuck Jones, and Tex Avery.

Mainstream cinema comes ethically closest to Surrealism in the expression of love. Breton claimed that

> What is most specific of all the means of the camera is obviously the power to make concrete the forces of love which, despite everything, remain deficient in books, simply because nothing in them can render the seduction or distress of a glance or certain feelings of priceless giddiness. The radical powerlessness of the plastic arts in this domain goes without saying (one imagines that it has not been given to the painter to show us the radiant image of a kiss). The cinema is alone in extending its empire there, and this alone would be enough for its consecration. ("As in a Wood," q.v.)

The phenomenon of the couple, the man and woman whose transgressive love unites them against a repressive society conspiring to contain their passion, characterizes mad love. Or at least this is one sociological version of a perennially potent myth, because we're speaking here of a kind of Surrealist *Tendenzkunst*, a content-based, propagandist appraisal of aesthetic objects. Kyrou's knowledge of cinema was of the widest and he reaffirmed and enlarged the canon of mad-love movies, but in so doing he blunted the dialectical finesse, the antireductionist lyricism, of Breton's own exposition of *amour fou* in his 1937 book, to the extent of substituting the latter's vision with his own more reified conception. (Perhaps this is unfair to Kyrou, since integration of the extra-Surrealist artifact is as old as the movement itself, Breton himself being always ahead of the game.) The Ur-expression of mad love remains, of course, *L'Âge d'or*. However, the commercial cinema has given us such amorous lights as *Seventh Heaven* (Frank Borzage, 1927), *White Shadows of the South Seas* (W.S. Van Dyke, 1928), *One Way Passage* (Tay Garnett, 1932), *Berkeley Square* (Frank Lloyd, 1933), *Peter Ibbetson* (Henry Hathaway, 1935), *Dark Passage* (Delmer Daves, 1947), *Gun Crazy* (Joseph H. Lewis, 1949), *Portrait of Jennie* (William Dieterle, 1949), *Manon* (Georges Clouzot, 1950),

Pandora and the Flying Dutchman (Albert Lewin, 1951), *Clara de Montargis* (Henri Decoin, 1952), and *I Died a Thousand Times* (Stuart Heisler, 1955). Since Kyrou's demise in the mid-1980s, the genre shows no sign of abating: I would argue for the inclusion of *No End* (Krzystof Kieslowski, 1984), *Made in Heaven* (Alan Rudolph, 1987), *Les Amants du Pont-Neuf* (Léo Carax, 1991), and *The Lovers of the Arctic Circle* (Julio Medem, 1998). (This theme can easily disintegrate into *amour flou:* I'd place Patrice Leconte's *La Fille sur le pont* in this category.) The fusion of love and eroticism, Kyrou argued, is consonant with mad love. He saw evidence of their separation everywhere, love without eroticism, eroticism without love: should a film fall into either category it ceased to be of interest ("Eroticism = Love," q.v.). (For all that, Robert Lebel's "Pornographers & Co." (q.v.), flies in the face of Kyrou's dyad.) In 1964 Nelly Kaplan, the director of *Dirty Mary,* called for a female seer, armed with a camera, to lambaste the monopoly men have had in the representation of eroticism ("Au Repas des Guerrières," q.v.). Closer to tantra, say, than to occidental ideas of sexuality—or, if occidental, refracted through the optic of Freud and of Sade (cf. Robert Benayoun, "Zaroff; or, The Prosperities of Vice," q.v.)—the Surrealist cult of Eros encouraged the valorization of the Eternal Feminine as a "naturalized," redemptive lever capable of overturning, for the good of humanity, bankrupt, repressive "male" ontologies. (Breton's *Arcane 17* of 1947 set the agenda here.) Ergo, in the cinema the auratic female star became the subject of this wistful libertarian male gaze (cf. Jacques Rigaut's "Mae Murray," q.v., and Joseph Cornell's "'Enchanted Wanderer,'" q.v.). Heroines of celluloid, heroines of paper: the Surrealists also idealized fictional redemptrixes like M.G. Lewis's Matilda, Wilhelm Jensen's Gradiva, Emily Brontë's Catherine. And paper into celluloid: Buñuel's rip-roaring version of *Wuthering Heights—Abismos de Pasión* (1953)—in which Yorkshire farmhouse gives way to Mexican hacienda, is a truly Sadean critique of elective love, underpinned by delirious cruelty and excess. A real gila monster. After 1924 and the eulogization of Germaine Berton, anarchist assassin, the Surrealists repeatedly lauded the female criminal as exterminating angel of the hated bourgeoisie. And so a film about the murderous Papin sisters was homaged by Alain Joubert in his essay on *Les Abysses,* "Iron in the Wound" (q.v.). A real coco-de-mer, Papatakis's movie.

André Breton died in 1966. Three years later diverse members of the Paris Surrealist Group, taking the oft-debated issue of the movement's occultation to a conclusion, opted for terminating collective activity. Doubtless the dashing of the hopes of May '68, the ethos of which the Surrealists had done much to prepare, played a part, but the truth of the matter is that as an organized international movement Surrealism could not survive the loss of its sheet anchor. The autodissolutionists, led by Jean Schuster, executor of Breton's legacy, were opposed in 1969 by figures like Vincent Bounoure, who, before lapsing a decade later into silence, continued a militant but embattled activity. Bounoure's faction broadened contact with the Czech Surrealists, forced underground after the Prague Spring by totalitarian repression, as they had been in 1939 and 1948. (Vratislav Effenberger, leader of the Czech Group, was fired from his post as a philosophy teacher and given work as a night watchman: a poetical circumstance given the Surrealist privileging of "night," and a droll echo of that other great revolutionary lantern man, Diogenes.) While other groups—in Chicago, London, Madrid, Paris, and elsewhere—have, during the 1970s, '80s, and '90s defended an epigonic "Surrealism in aspic," it was the Prague Surrealists who under extremely hostile conditions produced exciting and progressive work. Their playful and blackly humorous take on the contemporary world is well known in the West—largely thanks to the efforts of Atelier Koninck; the Quay Brothers, and Keith Griffiths, that is—through the films of Jan Svankmajer. Since the collapse of the Soviet bloc, the Czech Surrealists have reemerged from clandestinity as a visible collective force.

In the elective site of Paris, a certain historicizing activity centered, between 1986 and 1992, around ACTUAL, an assembly of ex-Surrealists whose ambition was to create an "ideal palace" housing the collected archives of forty-five years of activity. (Among the founding sponsors were Blanchot, Césaire, Paz.) Largely animated by Schuster, José Pierre, and Édouard Jaguer, this project was founded on the distinction between a historical Surrealism, which began in 1924 and ended in 1969, and an eternal one, a basic component of the human mind: a confidence in desire, a faith in revolt, a belief in the poetic voice.

Often, as the tarry pellicle uncoiled from the capstan of the projector our oceanic imaginations unpicked the braid of images that tarried on the screen's white sail, teasing out the occulted wisp, cinema's essential red thread. But the conspicuous consumption of a superabundance of filmic emblems is today under threat, if not already in abeyance. The dynamic, heterogeneric Hollywood Kyrou adored no longer exists. TV is too thin a gruel in too small a bowl to satisfy. The video samizdat is a poor second and encourages the further privatization of experience. In the year of his centenary Buñuel has achieved sainthood. The European art cinema that could throw up an oeuvre nourished on Surrealism—take Resnais'—has come and gone. Yet the vibration still resonates in the work of João Botelho, Arturo Ripstein, Julio Medem, and Raul Ruiz. Thanks be, then, for a film like Ruiz's *City of Pirates* (1983). Using automatic writing to elaborate his script, the Chilean ex-pat has given us a purely Surrealist heroine in Isidore, part Ophelia, Salomé, Berenice, prone to trances, somnambulism, contact with "the other side." Her calm violence links her to the real life murderesses exalted by Breton's circle, and by Jacques Lacan. Just as Lacan's confrontational psychoanalysis, in which the analyst assiduously stays off the analysand's wavelength, is inspired by the idea of "Surrealist dialogue," so Ruiz's scatty scenario draws on this exuberant mode of cross-purposeful discourse to depict the oneiric tale of a deluded woman wandering a phantom city by a briny bereft of buccaneers.

And you and I? Let us aspire to be that kind of stalwart analyst, frame our own cross-purposeful riposte to the spectacular image bank of neoliberal capitalism. Virtuality has nothing in common with immanence. We sense that real life is elsewhere, and with a vengeance. Would ours be, then, a countersimulacrum? Maybe, but who's to say that we cannot claim the freedom to act as if the swashbuckling project of realizing love, liberty, and poetry were not yet complete? *Could* ever be complete? As if the quest for wholeness were a fata morgana? However barnacled the cinematic apparatus, however lovelorn our cinephilia, cinema remains a treasure island entombing the doubloons of the cathartic image. Three pieces of eight make twenty-four; twenty-four, as in twenty-four frames per second. The screen's our Jolly Roger, the phosphorescent skull and crossbones a symbol of our deadly quest to relive the lustful, *dangerous* moment of looking, our shameless, originary scopophilia. From this all things proceed. Pandora dismasts the Flying Dutchman in the endless sleep of Davy Jones's locker. Wasn't one of the most moving and unfathomable objects recovered from the *Titanic* that rusted, squelchy tin of movie film? Some may see the incandescent ontological idea of Surrealism as the kind of lifeline that'll yank you down to the bottom. No, I take it to be Buster Keaton's floating anchor.

Gérard de Nerval's message in a bottle, his suicide note, read: "Don't wait up for me this evening, because the night will be black and white." Come hell or high water, we're shipping out for the Straits of Messina. Our manifest is the latent. We sail on . . . in the dark.

SELECT BIBLIOGRAPHY

Adorno, Theodor, and Max Horkheimer. *Dialectic of Enlightenment.* London: Verso, 1979 (1944).

Aragon, Louis. *Paris Peasant.* London: Jonathan Cape, 1971 (1926).

Barthes, Roland. *Camera Lucida.* London: Jonathan Cape, 1982 (1980).

Bataille, Georges. "Formless." In *Visions of Excess: Selected Writings 1927– 1939.* Manchester: Manchester Univ. Press, 1985.

Borde, Raymond, and Étienne Chaumeton. *Panorama du film noir américain.* Paris: Éditions de Minuit, 1979 (1955).

Breton, André. *Arcanum 17.* Los Angeles: Sun & Moon Press, 1994 (1947).

———. *Mad Love.* Lincoln & London: Univ. of Nebraska Press, 1987 (1937).

———. *Manifestoes of Surrealism.* Ann Arbor: Univ. of Michigan Press, 1969 (1924–53).

———. *Nadja.* New York: Grove Press, 1960 (1928).

———. *Surrealism and Painting.* New York: Harper & Row, 1972 (1928–66).

———. *Communicating Vessels.* Lincoln & London: Univ. of Nebraska Press, 1990 (1932).

———, and Paul Éluard. *The Immaculate Conception.* London: Atlas Press, 1990 (1930).

Buck-Morss, Susan. *The Dialectics of Seeing: Walter Benjamin and the Arcades Project.* Cambridge, Mass. & London: MIT Press, 1989.

Buñuel, Luis. *My Last Breath.* London: Jonathan Cape, 1984 (1982).

Cortázar, Julio. *Around the Day in Eighty Worlds.* San Francisco: North Point Press, 1986 (1980).

Dalí, Salvador. *Le Mythe tragique de L'Angélus de Millet: Interprétation "paranoïaque-critique."* Paris: J.-J. Pauvert, 1978 (1963).

Eisenstein, S.M., V.I. Pudovkin, and G.V. Alexandrov. "A Statement on the Sound-Film" (1928). In *Film Form: Essays in Film Theory,* by Sergei Eisenstein. New York: Harcourt, Brace & World, 1949.

Ellenberger, Henri F. *The Discovery of the Unconscious.* New York: Basic Books, 1970.

Guilbaut, Serge. *How New York Stole the Idea of Modern Art.* Chicago & London: Univ. of Chicago Press, 1983.

Habermas, Jurgen. *Autonomy & Solidarity: Interviews.* Edited by Peter Dews. London: Verso, 1986 (1977–85).

Highwater, Jamake. *The Primal Mind*. New York: Harper & Row, 1981.

Jackson, Rosemary. *Fantasy: The Literature of Subversion*. London & New York: Methuen, 1981.

Kraus, Karl. *Half-Truths and One-and-a-Half Truths*. Montreal: Engendra Press, 1976.

Lanham, Richard A. *A Handlist of Rhetorical Terms*. Berkeley & Los Angeles: Univ. of California Press, 1969.

Levy, Julien. *Surrealism*. New York: The Black Sun Press, 1936.

Man Ray. *Self Portrait*. London: Andre Deutsch, 1963.

Monaco, James. "The TV Plexus." *Sight & Sound* (London) (winter 1978–79).

Novalis. "Aphorisms on the Cinema." Edited and translated by Roger Cardinal. *The Moment* (Paris) 3 (1979).

Paz, Octavio. *Children of the Mire: Modern Poetry from Romanticism to the Avant-Garde*. Cambridge, Mass. & London: Harvard Univ. Press, 1974.

Wiedmann, August. *Romantic Art Theories*. Henley-on-Thames: Gresham Books, 1986.

ACKNOWLEDGMENTS

Aside from the copyright holders credited at the end of each text, I would like to thank the following people: Alastair Brotchie, Ania Chevallier, Victoria Combalía, Bertrand Fillandeau, A.K. El Janabi, Mireille Kyrou, José Pierre, Dominique Rabourdin, Michael Richardson, Jean Schuster, Mark Stokes, and Sasha Vlad. A special thanks goes to my editor at City Lights, James Brook.

Some surrealist advice

The Surrealist Group

See	*Don't See*
Méliès	Lumière
Cohl	Disney
Feuillade	Delluc
Mack Sennett	Capra
Chaplin	
Stroheim	Gance
Langdon	
Christensen	Dreyer
Wiene	Dupont
Murnau	Griffith
Paul Leni	Leni Riefenstahl
Kuleshov	Nicolai Ekk
Pudovkin	Dovzhenko
Eisenstein	Dziga Vertov
Richter	Deslaw
Fritz Lang	Lubitsch
Pabst (died 1932)	Steinhoff
Renoir	
Cavalcanti	Grierson
Dickinson	Carol Reed
Man Ray	Kirsanov
Buñuel	
Vigo	L'Herbier
Tod Browning	Duvivier
De Santis	Rouquier
Van Dyke	Wyler
Storck	Machaty
Clouzot	Cocteau
Sternberg	

Lewin	Pagnol
Cooper-Schoedsack	Bresson
Sjöberg	Sjöström
King Vidor	David Lean
Pierre Prévert	P. Sturges
James Whale	Feyder
John Huston	René Clément
Visconti	Genina
Lewis	Leenhardt
Hamer	Rossellini

See, besides, the following films, exceptions to the rest of their director's work:

Le Brasier ardent	Volkov
One Way Passage	Garnett
Viva Villa!	Conway
Peter Ibbetson	Hathaway
I Am a Fugitive From a Chain Gang	LeRoy
Laura	Preminger
Dark Passage	D. Daves
Hellzapoppin	H.C. Potter
Senza Pietà	Lattuada
Malombra	Soldati

One cannot fail to notice the possibly important omissions in this list. These omissions are deliberate, the favorable elements counterbalancing the unfavorable elements.

From *L'Âge du cinéma* (Paris) 4–5 (August-November 1951): 2. According to this list, the directors sans peer are Chaplin, Langdon, Renoir, Buñuel, and Von Sternberg.

War letter

Jacques Vaché

14.11.18

Dearest friend,

How depressed your letter found me!—I'm devoid of ideas, and not all that clever, doubtless more than ever an unconscious registering device of many things, all jumbled up—What crystallization? . . . I'll end the war slightly senile, perhaps OK, like one of those splendid village idiots (and I hope I do) . . . or else . . . or else . . . what a film I'll play in!—With runaway cars, you know the kind, bridges that give way, and enormous hands crawling across the screen toward some document or other! . . . Useless and invaluable!—With such tragic conversations, in evening dress, behind an eavesdropping palm tree!—And then, of course, Charlie Chaplin, grinning, with staring eyes. The Policeman forgotten in the trunk!!!

Telephone, shirtsleeve, people rushing about, with those bizarre, jerky movements—William R.G. Eddie, who's sixteen, thousands of black servants, with such beautiful gray-white hair, and a tortoiseshell monocle. He'll get married.

And I'll be a trapper or thief or explorer or hunter or miner or driller— The Arizona Bar (Whiskey—Gin and mixed?), and beautiful, workable forests, and you know those beautiful riding breeches with automatic pistols, and the clean-shaven look, and such beautiful hands at solitaire. It'll end in a fire, I tell you, or in a saloon, our fortunes made—Well.

What am I going to do, my poor friend, to endure these last months in uniform?—(I've been told the war's over)—I am at the end of my tether . . . and then THEY are mistrustful . . . THEY are suspicious of something . . . As long as THEY don't bash my brains out while THEY have me in their power.

I've read L.A.'s article on the cinema (in *Film*) with as much enjoyment as I can muster at present. There are very amusing things to be done, when

I'm given my freedom
so
LOOK OUT!
Can you write me?

Your good friend.

Harry James.

First published by Breton in 1919 as a memorial to the recent suicide of Vaché.
Reprinted in Jacques Vaché, *Lettres de guerre* (Paris: Eric Losfeld, 1970), 66–67.

On décor

Louis Aragon

On the screen the great demon with white teeth, bare arms, speaks an extraordinary language, the language of love. People of all nations hear it and are more moved by the drama enacted before a wall decorated poetically with posters than by the tragedy we bid the subtlest actor perform before the showiest set. Here trompe-l'oeil fails: naked sentiment triumphs, and the setting must equal it in poetic power to touch our hearts.

A barroom door that swings and on the window the capital letters of unreadable and marvelous words, or the vertiginous, thousand-eyed façade of the thirty-story house, or this rapturous display of tinned goods (what great painter has composed this?), or this counter with the row of bottles that makes you drunk just to look at it: resources so new that despite being repeated a hundred times they create a novel poetry for minds able to respond to it, and for which the ten or twelve stories told man since the discovery of fire and love will henceforth unfold without ever tiring the sensibilities of this time which twilights, gothic castles, and tales of peasant life have worn out.

For a long time we have followed our elder brothers on the corpses of other civilizations. Here is the time of life to come. No more do we go to Bayreuth or Ravenna with Barrès to be moved. The names of Toronto and Minneapolis seem more beautiful to us. Someone mentioned modern magic. How better to explain the superhuman, despotic power such elements exercise even on those who recognized them, elements till now decried by people of taste, and which are the most powerful on souls least sensitive to the enchantment of filmgoing?

Before the appearance of the cinematograph hardly any artist dared use the false harmony of machines and the obsessive beauty of commercial inscriptions, posters, evocative lettering, really common objects, everything that celebrates *our* life, not some artificial convention that excludes corned beef and tins of polish. Today these courageous precursors, painters or poets, witness their own triumph, they who knew how to be moved by a newspaper or a packet of cigarettes, when the public thrills and communes with them before the kind of décor whose beauty they had predicted. They knew the fascination of hieroglyphs on walls which an angel scribbled at the end of a feast, or that ironic obsession imposed by destiny on the unfortunate hero's travels. Those letters advertising a brand of soap are the equivalent of characters on an obelisk or the inscription in a book of spells: they describe the fate of an era. We had already seen them as elements in the art of Picasso, Georges Braque, and Juan Gris. Before them, Baudelaire knew the import you could draw from a sign. Alfred Jarry, the immortal author of *Ubu roi*, had used scraps of this modern poetry. But only the cinema which directly addresses the people could impose these new sources of human splendor on a rebellious humanity searching for its soul.

We must open our eyes in front of the screen, we must analyze the feeling that transports us, reason it out to discover the cause of that sublimation of ourselves. What new attraction do we, surfeited with theater, find in this black-and-white symphony, the poorest of means, deprived of verbal giddiness and the stage's perspective? It isn't the sight of eternally similar passions, nor—as one would have liked to believe—the faithful reproduction of a nature the Thomas Cook Agency puts within our reach, but the magnification of the kinds of objects that, without artifice, our feeble minds can raise up to the superior life of poetry. The proof of this lies in the pitiful boredom of films that draw the elements of their lyricism from the shabby arsenal of old poetic ideas, already known and patented: historical films, films in which lovers die of moonlight, mountain, and ocean, exotic films, films born of all the old conventions. All our emotion exists for those dear old American adventure films that speak of daily life and manage to raise to a dramatic level a banknote on which our attention is riveted, a table with a revolver on it, a bottle that on occasion becomes a weapon, a handkerchief that reveals a crime, a typewriter that's the horizon of a desk, the terrible unreeling ticker tape with its magic ciphers that enrich or ruin bankers. Oh! that grid of a wall in *The Wolves* which the shirtsleeved stockbroker wrote the latest prices on! And that contraption Charlie Chaplin struggled with in *The Fireman!*

Poets without being artists, children sometimes fix their attention on an object to the point where their concentration makes it grow larger, grow so much it completely occupies their visual field, assumes a mysterious aspect, and loses all relation to its purpose. Or they repeat a word endlessly, so often it divests itself of meaning and becomes a poignant and pointless sound that makes them cry. Likewise, on the screen, objects that were a few moments ago sticks of furniture or books of cloakroom tickets are transformed to the point where they take on menacing or enigmatic meanings. The theater is powerless where such emotive concentration is concerned.

To endow with a poetic value that which does not yet possess it, to willfully restrict the field of vision so as to intensify expression: these are two properties that help make cinematic décor the perfect setting for modern beauty.

If today the cinema does not always show itself to be the powerful evocator it might be, even in the best of those American films that enable a screen poetry to be redeemed from the farrago of theatrical adaptations, it is because the *metteurs en scène,* though sometimes possessed of a keen sense of its beauty, do not recognize its philosophical qualities. I would hope a filmmaker were a poet and a philosopher, and a spectator who judges his own work as well. Fully to appreciate, say, Chaplin's *The Vagabond,* I think it indispensable to know and love Pablo Picasso's "Blue Period" paintings, in which slim-hipped Harlequins watch over-upright women comb their hair, to have read Kant and Nietzsche, and to believe one's soul is loftier than other people's. You're wasting your time watching *Mon gentilhomme batailleur* if you haven't first read Edgar Allan Poe's "The Philosophy of Furniture," and if you don't know *The Adventures of Arthur Gordon Pym,* what pleasure can you take in the *Naufrage de l'Alden-Bess?* Watch a thousand imperfect films with this aesthetic in mind, then, and only then, seek to extract beauty from them, those synthetic elements for a better mise-en-scène. Films are the only film school, remember that. It's there you'll encounter useful material, providing you can discern it. This innovation isn't so presumptuous: Charlie Chaplin fulfills the conditions I'd like to see insisted on. If you need a model, look to him. He alone has sought the intimate sense of cinema and, endlessly persevering in his endeavors, he has drawn comedy toward both the absurd and the tragic with equal inspiration. The elements of the décor which surround Charlie's persona participate intimately in the action: nothing is useless there and nothing indispensable. The décor *is* Charlie's very vision of the world which, together with the discovery of mechanics and its laws, haunts the hero to such an extent that by an inversion of values each inanimate object becomes a living thing for him, each human person a dummy whose starting handle must be found. Drama or comedy, depending on the spectator, the action is restricted to the struggle between the external world and humanity. The latter seeks to go beyond appearances, or let itself be duped by them in turn, and by this fact unleashes a thousand social cataclysms, the outcome of some changes or other of décor. I insist you study the composition of the décor in a Chaplin film.

Let the cinema take care: it is fine to be deprived of everything verbal, but art must take the place of speech, and that entails something more than the exact representation of life. It is its transposition following a superior sensibility. Cinema, master of all its distortions, has already timidly tried this method, which seduced all our great painters after Ingres. An independent spirit has become its defender in audacious projects, as yet unrealizable. But the cinema tends to remain a succession of photographs. The "cinegraphic" ideal is not the beautiful shot: hence I would violently condemn those Italian films which have had their day and whose poetic nonvalue and exultant nullity is obvious to us now. To seek out filmmakers possessed of an aesthetic and a sense of beauty is not enough: this would get us nowhere, we would soon be left out in the cold. We need a new, audacious aesthetic, a sense of modern beauty. On this understanding the cinema will rid itself of all the incongruous, impure, and harmful base metal that links it to a theater whose indomitable enemy it is.

It is vital for cinema to assume a place in the preoccupations of the artistic avant-gardes. These have designers, painters, sculptors. Appeal must be made to them if one wants to bring some purity to the art of movement and light. One wants to leave it to academicians, to johnny-come-lately actors, and that's madness, an anachronism. This art is too deeply of *this* time to leave its future to the people of yesterday. Look ahead for support. And don't be afraid to offend the public who have indulged you up to now. I know those to whom this task falls must expect incomprehension, scorn, hatred. But that should not put them off. What a beautiful thing a film barracked by the crowd is! I have only ever heard the public *laugh* at the cinema. It's time someone slapped the public's face to see if there's any blood beneath its skin. The consecration of catcalls that will gain cinema the respect of people of feeling is still missing. Get it, and the purity that attracts spittle emerges at last! When, before the naked screen lit by the projector's solitary beam, will we have that sense of formidable virginity,

The white concern of our sail?

O purity, purity!

First published in September 1918 in Louis Delluc's *Le Film*. Reprinted in Alain and Odette Virmaux, *Les Surréalistes et le cinéma* (Paris: Seghers, 1976), 107–111. This is the Aragon essay Breton sent to Vaché at the front (Vaché, "War Letter," q.v.). The penultimate phrase quotes Mallarmé; the ultimate, Rimbaud.

Cinema U.S.A.

Philippe Soupault

Just when all French eyes were tired of seeing the same eternal "slices of life" over and over again on the theater stage, when the music halls alone could still move our poor hearts seared by poetry for at least a moment, the cinema was born.

But soon the disappointment was greater than one might have expected.

Films were lamentable, insignificant, boring. They weren't even idiotic; scriptwriters wanted to reach the people at any price, the people which supposedly thrived on melodrama and sentimental comedy. So to make their tears flow the bright filmmakers scattered plenty of pretty blue flowers on the celluloid.

The result wasn't long emerging. Audiences did begin to cry, but from laughter. You saw a little girl stolen by rascally gypsies, then discovered by accident by her parents; a poor mother and her twelve kids beaten by a brutal, drunken husband, ultimately avenged by drink and delirium tremens. As the old song goes: "It was beautiful, yet it was sad, the fire brigade chief was weeping into his helmet."

Nothing was possible any more.

The boredom of evenings that drift like cigarette smoke and make you yawn till sleep descends blossomed in the ardent lives of some young people, my friends.

We used to walk the cold, deserted streets in search of an accident, an encounter, life. To distract ourselves we had to hitch our imaginations to sensational dreams. Still more colorful than maps of the world, the newspapers used to distract us for a moment or two. For a few cents you could travel the world and witness the marvelous and bloody dramas that momentarily illuminated some dot on the globe. We were thirsty, terribly thirsty for that strange and powerful life, that life we drank like milk.

One of us, the strongest among us, Jacques Vaché, declared: "I'll be a trapper or thief or explorer or hunter or miner or driller."

One day you saw huge posters, as long as snakes, stretching out along the walls.

At each street corner a man, his face covered with a red handkerchief, was pointing a revolver at the unconcerned passersby.

You thought you heard galloping, a motor kicking over, screams of death.

We descended on the cinemas and understood that everything had changed.

Pearl White's smile appeared on the screen; this almost ferocious smile announced the upheavals of the new world.

We finally understood that the cinema was not a perfected toy but the terrible and magnificent flag of life.

The small, dark cinemas we sat in became the theater of our outbursts of laughter, rage, our great feelings of pride.

Wide-eyed, we read of crimes, departures, wonders, nothing less than the poetry of our age.

We did not understand what was happening. We lived at speed, with passion. It was a beautiful time. Doubtless many other things contributed to its beauty, but American cinema was one of its finest ornaments. . . .

From *Films* (Paris) 15 (15 January 1924). Reprinted in Alain and Odette Virmaux, *Les Surréalistes et le cinéma* (Paris: Seghers, 1976), 115–117. Courtesy Philippe Soupault.

Battlegrounds and commonplaces

René Crevel

Cinema, a commonplace. And a common place, what's more, in the literal as well as the metaphorical sense, since, once the light's back on, after having put up with the banalities on the screen, you can count all those gold moldings on the ceiling which, in private drawing rooms and suburban "Palais de Danse," seduce the shopkeepers on the day of their marriage, be this right- or left-handed.

Cinema, a common place. Yet we perennially seek to believe that this will be a place of refuge from our boredom, just as in the Middle Ages churches were a place of sanctuary from crime. But why do these walls and their pretentious frescoes, this screen we were hoping for miracles from, afford us such poor protection? In spite of all the gazes met with, the street had already proved a disappointment. In the absence of all those glances that might have done something for us, our indolence has expected a lot of those black-and-white creatures with whom most adult males would like to fall in love, as, once upon a time, adolescents did with the blond and rosy Gaby Deslys. At pavement level you used to tell yourself the marvelous bliss could never end, since the marquee announced *nonstop entertainment.* In her lair the cashier with her more than perfect curves and her smile pinned on in just the right place seemed like a benevolent goddess. A Circe in negative, who'd never turn men into pigs, but rather make of each bank employee a Don Juan.

Why should we have believed her? Many a postcard Melisandre had already tormented us with mad whims. A whole theory of femmes fatales, of big lumps of women got up as soi-disant empresses, should have been enough to disabuse us. Yet a single minute's lyricism, the detail of a face, the surprise of a gesture, have always been, and will always be, capable of making us forget all sorts of wretched stories. You think of Caligari's madman, of Lon Chaney's metamorphoses, of the silvery reflection of an African river, and you don't leave your seat when bits of "The Marseillaise" and the rumblings of national anthems announce a film about heroism. And then, you read, Slavonia and Gergovia (laugh not) are at war. Gergovia, Slavonia. From the Balkan hinterland anything's possible. Slavonians and Gergovians have a lot of national feeling, but the sad thing is there's only one country for the two peoples. A Corneille-like situation. And even more alarming since there's no braver man than a Gergovian, unless it be a Slavonian, something which doesn't, however, prevent there being no braver man than a Slavonian, unless it be a Gergovian. All this is genuinely tragic and the misery of those times even requires Pola Negri to become a waitress in an inn. To console her, the cheap joint she cleans the stairs of has been baptized "Hotel Imperial," pending the time when an enemy general will buy her dresses of gold lamé, with which she sweeps the steps she'd toiled at scrubbing with iron shavings.

So Slavonians and Gergovians who are fighting over a fatherland, a hotel, and Pola Negri raise a terrible amount of dust on the open plains and indoors, too. Whence such an heroic atmosphere. In the orchestra pit the brass section gives it their best shot. O Père Ubu, you, a great expert on Slav issues, who proclaim so judiciously "Long live Poland, because without Poland there'd be no Poles," if you, Père Ubu, could be present at this Gergovian-Slavonian hotchpotch, how joyously you'd intone "The Debraining Song."

Alas, there's a whole mass of spectators taking these inanities seriously.

Battlegrounds and commonplaces. Why flatter public fatigue and stupidity in this way? Can the inanity that's killed the theater suffice, then, to keep the cinema alive?

From *Close Up* (Paris & London) 5 (November 1927): 14–16.

Against commercial cinema

Benjamin Péret

Never has any means of expression engendered such hopes as the cinema. With cinema not only is anything possible, but the marvelous itself is placed within reach. And yet never have we seen such a disproportion between the immensity of its possibilities and the mediocrity of its results. In acting so directly on the spectator the cinema is capable of overwhelming, disquieting, and enthralling him or her like no other medium. Yet as well as awakening, it is also capable of brutalizing and it is this, alas, that we have witnessed as the cinema, a cultural form without precedent, has developed into an industry governed by sordid market forces incapable of distinguishing a work of the mind from a sack of flour. Nothing counts for a producer more than the return he may get on the millions he has shelled out on some idiot's legs, some cretin's voice. The net result of such an attitude can only be an interminable series of films devoid of the slightest interest—when they are not, frankly, odious and stupid—films that skillfully and purposefully set out to anaesthetize the public. What does it matter if three or four films in a hundred are exceptions to this rule and show themselves to be works of value! All that counts is the general tendency; the exceptions remain what they are, exceptions powerless to change the rule. The actual production of any film is vitiated at the outset by money, by capital, the goal of which is alien, antithetical even, to any disinterested undertaking. Take any medium and you'll observe that a worthwhile end product results only where mercantile considerations cease. Besides, those artists who have chosen to express themselves through cinema—I mean by that the scriptwriter and director, not the actor, whose role is secondary—always come up against capital, which basically asks them, "Just what return will I get on my money?" As long as this situation is unchanged the cinema will be condemned to stupidity, to inanity exacerbated by an anachronistic censorship, its prejudices hidebound by the foul stench of Christianity.

Nonetheless, the hope youth has invested in cinema from its inception is a sure sign that its almost unlimited, unexplored, and intrinsic possibilities still exist, despite the frustration this hope is perennially victim to. Already it seems that some young people have attempted individually to escape the emasculating hold of capital. However isolated and fragmentary the results, they are extremely promising and permit us to imagine an imminent renaissance in cinema, since these youngsters have understood that creativity and money are permanent enemies. They will associate freely to produce the cinema we have craved for since our youth, this cinema whose earliest manifestations—oases in a desert of asphyxiating dust—go by the name of *Nosferatu*, the first Chaplins, *Peter Ibbetson*, *L'Âge d'or*, etc.

From *L'Âge du cinéma* (Paris) 1 (March 1951): 7–8. Courtesy Association des amis de Benjamin Péret and Librairie José Corti.

Buster Keaton's *College*

Luis Buñuel

H ere's Buster Keaton in his wonderful new movie, *College*. Asepsia. Dis-
infection. Freed from tradition, our eyes have been rejuvenated in
the youthful and restrained world of Buster, a great specialist against sentimental infection of all kinds. The film was as beautiful as a bathroom; with
a Hispano's vitality. Buster will never seek to make us cry, because he knows
facile tears are old hat. He's not, though, the kind of clown who'll make us
howl with laughter. We never stop smiling for an instant, not at him, but
at ourselves, with the smile of well-being and Olympian strength.

We will always prefer, in cinema, the monotonous mien of a Keaton to
the infinitesimal one of a Jannings. Filmmakers abuse the latter, multiplying the slightest contraction of his facial muscles to the nth degree. Grief
in Jannings is a prism with a hundred faces. This is why he's capable of
acting on a surface fifty meters wide and, if asked for "a bit more," will
contrive to show us that you could base a whole film on nothing other
than his face, a film to be called *Jannings' Expression; or, The Permutations of*
M *Wrinkles Raised to the Power* n^2.

In Buster Keaton's case his expression is as unpretentious as a bottle's,
for instance; albeit that his aseptic soul pirouettes around the circular and
unambiguous track of his pupils. But the bottle and Buster's face have infinite points of view.

They are wheels that must accomplish their mission in the rhythmic and
architectonic gearing of the film. Montage—film's golden key—is what com-
bines, comments on, and unifies all these elements. Is greater cinegraphic
virtue attainable? The inferiority of the "antivirtuoso" Buster, when compared
to Chaplin, has been argued for, turning this to the disadvantage of the former,
something akin to a stigma, while the rest of us deem it a virtue that Keaton
creates comedy through a direct harmony with the implements, situations,
and other resources of filmmaking. Keaton is full of humanity, but streets
ahead of a recent and increate humanity, of a humanity à la mode, if you like.

Much is made of the technique of films like *Metropolis* and *Napoléon*. That of films like *College* is never referred to, and that's because the latter is so indissolubly mixed with the other elements that it isn't even noticed, just as when living in a house we remain unaware of the calculus of resistance of the materials that go to form it. Superfilms must serve to give lessons to technicians: those of Keaton to give lessons to reality itself, with or without the technique of reality.

The Jannings School: European school: sentimentalism, a bias toward art and literature, tradition, etc.: John Barrymore, Veidt, Mosjoukine, etc. . . .

The Keaton School: American school: vitality, photogenia, a lack of noxious culture and tradition: Monte Blue, Laura la Plante, Bebe Daniels, Tom Moore, Menjou, Harry Langdon, etc. . . .

From *Cahiers d'Art* (Paris) 10 (1927). (Keaton's film dates from the same year.) Copyright © Herederos Luis Buñuel. Courtesy Juan Luis Buñuel. Although written almost two years before Buñuel joined the Surrealists, and suffused with a particularly Spanish brand of avant-gardisme, this text is most heavily influenced by Desnos and Brunius.

Abstract of a critical history of the cinema

Salvador Dalí

Contrary to current opinion, the cinema is infinitely poorer and more limited when it comes to expressing the real functioning of thought than writing, painting, sculpture, and architecture. Just behind it comes music, whose spiritual value is, as everybody knows, almost nil. By its very nature cinema is consubstantially linked to the sensory, base, anecdotal face of phenomena, to abstraction, to rhythmic impression—in a word, to harmony. And harmony, the refined product of abstraction, is by definition diametrically opposed to the concrete [*le concret*] and, consequently, to poetry.

The rapid and continuous succession of film images, whose implicit neologism is directly proportional to a specifically generalizing visual culture, hinders any attempt at reduction to the concrete and more often than not annuls—given the factor of memory—the intentional, subjective, lyrical character of the latter. The mechanism of memory, on which these images always work in an exceptionally acute way, already tends of itself toward the disorganization of the concrete, toward idealization.

Within waking life latent intent and the violence of the concrete are almost always immersed in amnesia but frequently surface in dreams. In order to attain authentic lyrical existence the poetry of cinema demands, more than any other, a traumatic and violent disequilibrium veering toward concrete irrationality.

The experimental beginnings of cinema, up to and including Méliès, constitute (as much in the contemplative, quizzical exhibition of things and phenomena as in the presence of an action proffered as a simulacrum) its metaphysical stage. After the various gray periods during which technique is perfected, cinema, which has timidly broached an ephemeral pseudonaturalism, suddenly attains its authentic Golden Age in giving birth to the first materialist films of the Italian school (in the prewar period and just after). I am speaking here of the grandiose epoch of hysterical cinema, with Francesca Bertini, Gustavo Serena, Tulio Carminati, Pina Menichelli, etc.; of this cinema so marvelously, so properly close to theater, which not only has the immense merit of offering us real, concrete documents of psychic disturbances of all sorts, of the veracious course of childhood neuroses, of the actualization within life of the most impure aspirations and fantasies embodied before it by those admirable art nouveau buildings, but also the merit of having attained complete possession over its essential technical means. From this moment on cinema rapidly enters its decadent phase.

The actors were really living these films, in a sustained and immodest way boastful contemporary humor would no longer put up with. There, in all its glory, an arrogant female exhibitionism. I recall those women with their uncertain, convulsive walk, their castaway hands of love groping along walls, along corridors, clinging to each curtain, each bush, those women whose décolleté perpetually slipped from the nakedest shoulders on screen, in an unending night of cypresses and marble stairs. During that fleeting and turbulent era of eroticism, palm trees and magnolias were materially bitten into, torn apart by the teeth of women whose fragile, pretubercular complexions did not outshine bodies audaciously modeled by a premature, febrile youthfulness.

In one of these films, called *The Flame,* it was possible to see Pina Menichelli completely naked in a costume of feathers depicting an owl, and this for the sole reason of justifying, once dusk had fallen, an uncultured and lamentable symbolic comparison made between the owl she personified and a flame—the flame of love—she had just lit with her fateful hands before the eyes in ruins, eyes incommensurably ringed by certified onanism, that belonged to Gustavo Serena, who henceforth made no other movement than the indispensable, automatic, depressive ones necessary for a gradual, nervy descent into the waters of a lake, until the habitual concentric circles that reestablish calm on the water abated after this suicide, the moral lesson of the film. Automatic, depressive gestures comparable only to the aged William Tell's, a William Tell dazzled by the coppery light of the setting sun, ready for death, with bloody knees, eyes drenched in tears, still walking, a pair of eggs on a plate (without the plate) perched negligently on his shoulders.

After Italian cinema and the extraordinary *Perils of Pauline,* the dynamism, sportiness, and much other mythological dreariness brought us by nascent, standardized American cinema never cease establishing, in an imponderable way, constant osmoses which have their own avant-gardist, artistico-literary applications, to the delight of Europe's modern, catholic intelligentsia. The cinema deliberately takes the absurd and stupid path of abstraction. It creates a boring language based on a cumbersome visual rhetoric of an almost exclusively musical nature culminating in the rhythmic utilization of close-ups, tracking shots, dissolves, superimpositions, of découpage's monstrous divisionism, of montage's allusive and sentimental spirituality, and of a thousand other turpitudes which, running through the lamentable pre-talkie films of every country in the world, and aiming at an increasingly *cinematic* cinema (avant-garde, usually "Belgian" films[1]), would have arrived, without the sudden intervention of talking pictures, at an authentic "pure cinema," that is to say, at a more comfortable, more complete shamefulness, if this is possible, than that of pure painting—properly and correctly so-called.

Sound cinema brings with it a marvelous impurity and an estimable confusion that permits us to hear dialogue in a single shot slightly longer than the shots in silent cinema. It also brings to bear, before literature and art intervene (an imminent and already distinguishable intervention), the reestablishment of certain notions of the concrete, capable momentarily at least of suggesting anxieties and complexities, given the persistence within memory of words over images, to the magnificent detriment of the latter.

Throughout the history of cinema, and especially contemporary cinema, a single tendency, *concrete irrationality,* that delirious, pessimistic aspiration toward gratuitousness, manifests itself again and again in an increasingly sterilized, increasingly conscious manner in those films wrongly

---

1 I exclude *Entr'acte* here, by reason of the historical interest it presents. Despite René Clair, this film in fact brings together some of the ideas of Marcel Duchamp, Man Ray, and Francis Picabia, ideas representative of an isolated tendency running parallel to the products of American comedy film, but which because of the poetic, negativistic, and nonconformist preoccupations of the makers of *Entr'acte* display on a philosophic level a sort of semiconscious agnosticism, if one considers the scorn they have for phenomena and any attempt at a total reductivism of the latter, as well as the particular idea they have of the ungraspable, of the theoretical absence of knowing anything beyond the ruinous, aphrodisiac vertigo of accidents.

called "comedy films," for the simple and inadequate reason that they generally provoke laughter, an infinitely peculiar laughter, without this laughter implying the famous tears it is supposed to be hiding, an abominable and counterfeit invention of littérateurs, corroborated by pigs like Bergson, who thus aid and abet all the *laughing Punchinellos,* an inexhaustible and almost always abundant source of literature and art and which, in cinema, becomes the subject par excellence, the single subject, obligatory, solemn, omniscient, majestic, imperial, necessary, of consubstantial necessity, of apotheosiac rigor, of rigor mortis.

Analysis of the history of the so-called comedy film tends precisely to show the progressive elimination of the *laugh, Punchinello*[2] ilk, implying as it does, and in a very Latinate, swinishly picturesque way, all the seemingly transcendental seeds of abstraction in the domain of life.

For us to entertain contemporary cinema, that psychological, artistic, literary, sentimental, humanitarian, musical, intellectual, spiritual, colonial, departmental, Portuguese crap, for us to entertain, I repeat, the absolute crap of *laughing Punchinellos,* indistinctly cultivated and with the same affection by the Von Sternbergs, Von Stroheims, Chaplins, Pabsts, etc., etc., we needs must affirm that only comedy films of an irrational tendency mark the authentic route of poetry. Take those uncanny Mack Sennett movies, minor comedies with almost unknown actors of no especial talent as well as the ones due to somebody's genius, a Harry Langdon or a William Powell, as comic or as little comic as Langdon. Of late, *Animal Crackers,* with the Marx Brothers, is to be found at the pinnacle of the comedy film's development. There culminates, in this admirable film, a desire for systematic and concrete irrationality latent in all comedy films, a desire that gradually divests itself of all justification, pretext, subjective humor, etc., attenuating circumstances that hinder awareness of the violent moral category via which these films become *films à thèse. Animal Crackers* attains those kinds of grave, persistent and brutalizing, cold and transparent predispositions and contagions so rarely arrived at, and then only after having gone beyond the all too physiological stage of humor, the stage of frivolous solutions, not to say amusing schizophrenias, as soon as the ter-

---

2 [*Ris donc Paillasse.* Paillasse is Pagliaccio is Punchinello. "Laugh, clown, laugh" might be another way of putting this. Dalí may be echoing here the Surrealist Group's manifesto of the same year (1932), "Paillasse! (Fin de l'Affaire Aragon)." —*Trans.*]

rain of concession to instantaneous mental hypotheses is crossed, to attain the authentic and palpable lyrical consternation various passages in Raymond Roussel readily excite in me. It is equally possible for me to get close to this state of consternation via certain derivative notions of love, which might represent themselves to me in the form of a sudden and furious downpour of six or seven common-or-garden Anna Kareninas costumed in Portuguese cups, their handles covered partially or not at all in curdled milk, nunned-bollock.

The face of the Marx brother with the frizzy hair, a face of persuasive and triumphant madness, at the end of the film as well as during the all too brief moment when he interminably plucks the harp, contrives to disappear behind the horizon of psychological, pseudotranscendental, literary initiations, the infinitely prosaic gaze of Charlie Chaplin at the end of *City Lights,* the gaze of a gentle *arrivisme* which has no other equivalent save that implied by odious blind men or the phenomenal and stinking, pickled and vernal legless cripple.

In 1929 Buñuel and I wrote the scenario of *Un chien andalou;* in 1930 the scenario of *L'Âge d'or.* These are the first two Surrealist films.

Apart from revolutionary Communist propaganda films, which are justified by their value as propaganda, what one can expect of Surrealism and what might be expected of a certain "comedy" cinema are all that merit being considered.

From Salvador Dalí, *Babaouo: Scénario inédit; précédé d'un Abrégé d'une histoire critique du cinéma; et suivi de Guillaume Tell: ballet portugais* (Paris: Éditions des Cahiers Libres, 1932), 2–21. Courtesy Robert Descharnes. Perversely and tactically, Dalí flies in the face of his own pronouncements on cinema, published between 1927 and 1929. Was he hoping to settle scores with Buñuel after their internecine strife during and after the making of *L'Âge d'or?* Buñuel is being attacked in the paragraph beginning, "After Italian cinema and the extraordinary *Perils of Pauline.* . . . "

The marvelous is popular

Ado Kyrou

I loathe aristocrats and aristocracies (of class or otherwise). They can keep their Bressons and their Cocteaus. The cinematic, modern marvelous is popular, and the best and most exciting films are, beginning with Méliès and Fantômas, the films shown in local fleapits, films which seem to have no place in the history of cinema.

Those privileged in the marvelous exist no more: an elite no longer holds a monopoly of imagination, the cinema breaks open caches of arms, the double-edged swords of Arnim, to be distributed to all, and offers the example of Houdini, the man who cannot stay chained.

The great visionaries always addressed a very large public, but the diffusion of their works remains limited: society appropriates them. Today cinemas cover the globe, and if ever cinematic expression were not gagged the world could live in a climate from which the impossible was not outlawed. The ideal climate for Surrealist awareness.

But we don't deceive ourselves: psychological blabberings, dull realism do not become great cinematic successes, but those films the "aesthetes" disdain and the church reproves do. The popular films: serials with extraordinary heroes which the "quality" theaters refuse; the best *Tarzans* and old Westerns in which the lead wasn't a simple-minded sheriff but a man with the head of an eagle or a body of tin; Fairbanks's films, with their tree-men and giant spiders (*The Thief of Bagdad*, etc.), the films of the superb Houdini (*Terror Island, The Master Mystery*); those films forgotten by the historians where for ten episodes a gang snatched away the bride at the instant she was going to say that fateful "I do"; in which to get through a closed door the hero flattened himself like a sheet of paper, slipped underneath and gathered himself together on the other side; in which a hand, a single hand, ripped out the hearts of traitors who died like flies, in which each avenger let the world know about his joy at being free. Those despised masterpieces, like *The Raven* (directed by Louis Friedlander, alias

Lew Landers, with Karloff), *The Black Cat, The Mysteries of Dr. Fu Manchu,* and the admirable films drawn from the most cinematic of modern authors, Gaston Leroux: *Balaoo, The New Dawn, The Phantom of the Opera* (the first version, Rupert Julian's, made in 1925, with Lon Chaney), *The Perfume of the Lady in Black, Mister Flow,* etc. (How long must we wait for screen versions of *The Double Life of Theophrastus Longuet, The Haunted Chair, The Bleeding Doll, The Mohicans of Babel,* and *An Appalling Story?*)

A freedom of thought is often present in these "popular" productions, films that don't address themselves to pretentious pseudo-intellectuals. Impossible voyages (I'm thinking of certain films freely drawn from Jules Verne's and Conan Doyle's novels), exotic adventures (think of the delirious *Adventures of Hajji Baba* made by Don Weiss), certain peplum movies deliberately and sublimely idiotic, like Richard Thorpe's *The Prodigal,* more demented than biblical, are often the involuntary equivalents of Surrealist collages. The anecdote disappears, all that remains are some unexpected images as dazzling at times as Péret's prose or Trouille's paintings. All these films are *accepted* by the public, always ready to give itself over to mental exercises of liberating complexity, though this complexity disappears since basically everything is simple because everything is possible.

. . . .

You don't have to look for long to find films in your local cinema that are more often than not involuntarily sublime, films scorned by the critics, charged with cretinism or infantilism by the old defenders of rationalism. I say "more often than not" because sometimes fully conscious, extremely cultivated directors immerse themselves in a beauty to the power of two to give us sublime melodramas in which the most unbridled sense of the baroque remains senseless for those unable to read between the images. Here are some examples: *Pete Kelly's Blues* (J. Webb, 1955), certain of Douglas Sirk's melodramas (*Written on the Wind,* 1956; *Imitation of Life,* 1959), Minnelli's admirable *Some Came Running* (1959), the unique *Jeanne Eagels* (1957) from the underrated George Sidney, etc.

And as often as not there are involuntarily Dadaist or Surrealist films: disconcerting and surprising melodramas, from historical exploits to unintentional gags, films that break their chains and live their own full, free life. Each of us must find his or her own sublime films, since in this domain objectivity is to all intents and purposes impossible. For my part I confess to a weakness for almost all of Couzinet's films, for certain religious melodramas made by Léo Joannon, and some biblical films like Richard Thorpe's delirious *The Prodigal* (1955), in which Astarte, the High Priestess of Love, makes a human sacrifice as half-naked damsels play the part of wooden carousel horses and a potbellied character bangs the gong. But I'd prefer to forget those Nordic potboilers, with their midnight bathing, noble fathers, and metaphysical anguish (have you seen *The Hour of Desire,* by Egil Holmsen (1958)?), and the Italian travesties from which the superb *Beneath the Bridge of Sighs* (1954) alone stands out, wherein we can admire a striptease at sword-point (two heroines engaged in a duel of cutting the other's nightdress to ribbons), together with the incredible *Ship of Lost Women* (1953), made by Raffaele Matarazzo, in which sadism, revolt, eroticism, religion, and melodrama conspire to form a series of problematically linked scenes dependent on the commonplace, raised by its rigor to the level of pure involuntary poetry.

Even more unexpected are films belonging to a new category, "erotic terror." We may take as an example one of the peaks of the genre, *Ein töter hing in Netz* (by Fritz Bottger, 1960). The fantastic and soft-core pornography are wed in the complete absence of scenario, construction, mise-en-scène, to bring us some unforgettable images: the spider-man, the shipwreck, the Tahitian festival, the monster attacking the woman it loves, completely gratuitous disrobings, etc.

Let's have the guts to proclaim that some of the semipornographic shorts we used to see before the war in slot machines (the more recent ones are clearly in decline) were masterpieces. What could be more mysterious and unusual than those ladies in fur coats getting out of their bourgeois cars to plunge with dancer's steps into the forest where they revealed themselves to us in some strange rite or other? Much more than simple and base stimulants for old men, these short films constituted the sincerest, purest expression of cinematic magic. Automatism, objective chance, revolt, and love have met the most poetic of rendezvous in an immense commercial machine which they can transform from top to bottom. Obviously, these flashes of the spirit are scuttled (and for a long time yet) by mercantile and reactionary propaganda, but *I see them,* I see only them. From the screen to me perceptible links of great importance form, flames that only a few poems have been able to ignite up to now.

I ask you, learn to go and see the "worst" films; they are sometimes sublime.

From Ado Kyrou, *Le Surréalisme au cinéma,* 2d ed. (Paris: Le Terrain Vague, 1963), 90–91, 275–276. Courtesy Joëlle Losfeld and Le Terrain Vague.

As in a wood

André Breton

For my part it would be to gainsay myself, to disavow what conditions me in my own eyes, what appears to affect me beyond measure, to disown, as is customary, the disappointments wrought by the cinema, that form of expression one has been able to believe in to a degree greater than any other called upon to promote "real life."

In an era of *inhumanism,* when most writers consider it an honor to be "engagé," that is to say, in contempt of all that could qualify them spiritually (in the true sense of the word), when they opt for one of two contrary camps, each of which muses on the extermination of the other; when painters who have made a constant profession of atheism herald their work on religious edifices;[1] when for a whole hour on 28 September, under the title "The Variety Cup of France," French radio can inflict upon its listeners a concert given by "artistes" from the Prefecture of Police, complete with an Inspector's monologue, an air from *Pagliacci,* a bit of piano playing by a handcuffed man, a Prévert poem recited "from the heart," and a choir of "tiny singers from the pointed tower" (*sic*), in an era like this I don't think the cinema is a genre about which there are grounds for particular outcry.

I have never deplored the incontestable baseness of cinematographic production except on an altogether secondary, subordinate level. When I

---

1 Is there any scandal worse than Matisse declaring, or letting it be said, that the decoration of a chapel in Vence is his "life's work"? Similarly, what is more repugnant than the contortions of this emporium bully who, not content in having successfully imposed himself as the master of the abstract, the inexpressive, and the bestial—after a spectacular evolution from Pétainism to Stalinism via Gaullism—finds the wherewithal to "girdle" the walls of a new church with stained-glass windows and at the same time hang from the pegs of the Maison de la Pensée Française, under the title *The Builders,* a few workers' caps crowning the radical absence of thought and life! I pass over this with the intention of returning to it. . . . According to the latest reports, Miró himself—doubtless with the beautiful pansexual graffiti that made his name—would seem to be about to decorate the Baptistry at Audincourt!

was at "the cinema age" (it should be recognized that this age exists in life—and that it passes) I never began by consulting the amusement pages to find out what film might chance to be the best, nor did I find out the time the film was to begin. I agreed wholeheartedly with Jacques Vaché in appreciating nothing so much as dropping into the cinema when whatever was playing was playing, at any point in the show, and leaving at the first hint of boredom—of surfeit—to rush off to another cinema where we behaved in the same way, and so on (obviously, this practice would be too much of a luxury today). I have never known anything more *magnetizing*: it goes without saying that more often than not we left our seats without even knowing the title of the film, which was of no importance to us, anyway. On a Sunday several hours sufficed to exhaust all that Nantes could offer us: the important thing is that one came out "charged" for a few days; as there had been nothing deliberate about our actions, qualitative judgments were forbidden.

Nevertheless, it happened that certain "comic" films claimed our attention: they were, of course, by Mack Sennett, the first Chaplins, certain Al St. Johns. At this period I recall putting on an unrivaled footing a *Diana la charmeuse* in which a beautiful actress in the title role moved bewitchingly through a landscape of innumerable towers (it is useless to dwell on this: at this remove I only see a wasteland between the towers—magnificent). All we could grant of fidelity used to go to those serials previously so decried (*The Exploits of Elaine, The Laughing Mask, Les Vampires*): "Beginning on Saturday, on this screen, episode XIX: 'The Creeping Glove'—You can count on us."

We saw in the cinema then, such as it was, a lyrical substance simply begging to be hauled in en masse, with the aid of chance. I think that what we valued most in it, to the point of taking no interest in anything else, was its *power to disorient.*

This disorientation works on many levels, I mean to say, it admits of different degrees. The *marvel*, besides which the merits of a given film count for little, resides in the devolved faculty of the first-comer to abstract himself from his own life when he feels like it, at least in the cities, as soon as he passes through one of the muffled doors that give on to the blackness. From the instant he takes his seat to the moment he slips into the fiction evolving before his eyes, he passes through a critical point as captivating and imperceptible as that uniting waking and sleeping (the book and even the play are incomparably slower in producing this release). How come that the solitary spectator I have in mind, lost in the middle of these faceless strangers, at once takes up with them that adventure which is not his and is not theirs? What radiation, what waves, perhaps not resisting attempts to map them out, permit this unison? One dreams of what might be undertaken by means of this constellation, so that it lasts. . . . It is a way of going to the cinema the way others go to church, and I think that, from a certain angle, quite independently of what is playing, it is there that the only *absolutely modern* mystery is celebrated.

As to this mystery there is no doubt that the principal contributions made to it are love and desire. "Every week, for 150 million human beings," writes René Clair,[2] "the screen speaks of love. . . . And we may wonder if these representations of love are not one of the essential charms of the cinema, one of the secrets of the enchantment it exerts on the masses. . . . " One is surprised that he is not more sure of the fact. What is most specific of all the means of the camera is obviously the power to make concrete the forces of love which, despite everything, remain deficient in books, simply because nothing in them can render the seduction or distress of a glance or certain feelings of priceless giddiness. The radical powerlessness of the plastic arts in this domain goes without saying (one imagines that it has not been given to the painter to show us the radiant image of a kiss). The cinema is alone in extending its empire there, and this alone would be enough for its consecration. What incomparable, ever scintillating traces have films like *Ah! le beau voyage* or *Peter Ibbetson* left behind in the memory, and how are life's supreme moments filtered through their beam! But even if elsewhere the tension is much less sustained, nothing can alter the fact that on the fringe of the least dedicated as well as the emptiest lives the curve of a beautiful arm will reveal long shores of light.

The temptation is so great to make this disorientation last and to increase it to an impossible degree that it has been able to tempt my friends and me along the path to paradoxical attitudes. To be precise, it is a question of *going beyond* the bounds of what is "allowed," which, in the cinema as nowhere else, prepares me to invite in the "forbidden." And what if one

2 *Réflexion faite* (Paris: Gallimard, 1951).

chose to remain forever in this arbitrary but changing world which—just as it is—is worth so much more than the other. . . ? It is somewhat within this perspective that it came to me to evoke the time when "with Jacques Vaché we would settle down to dinner in the orchestra of the former Théâtre des Folies-Dramatiques, opening cans, slicing bread, uncorking bottles, and talking in ordinary tones, as if around a table, to the great amazement of the spectators, who dared not say a word."[3]

(The moment I cited this passage I thought of a *Declaration* printed by Malcolm de Chazal, dated Curepipe, Mauritius, 25 September 1951, of which this forms the conclusion: "The *Sense of Night* revealed is what gives the Key to the Opening. There is no other key, there cannot be one. Because the Secret of Success consists solely in breaking up antinomies. And only the Night has this power." The cinema is the first great open bridge which links the "day" to this Night.)

Always on the track of increasing disorientation, there was a time when I sought delectation in the most miserable cinematic productions. I used to find myself most at home with French films: "I have always been greatly attracted," I noted one day, "to the treasure of imbecility and vulgar eccentricity which, thanks to them, manages to sparkle weekly on the screens of Paris. For my part I swear by the French screenplay and French acting. With them one is assured of at least being able to amuse oneself resoundingly (as long as it is not, of course, a 'comic' film, then human emotion in its need for extreme exteriorization may be found there)."[4] A *superdisorientation* is to be expected here, not from the transference of a normal act from everyday life to a place consecrated to *another* life, which it profanes, but between the "lesson" the film teaches and the manner in which the person receiving it disposes of it. I speak in *Nadja* of a naked woman totally preoccupied with herself in the sidestalls of the Electric Palace (quite undressed, seen from the central stalls): she would have seemed to me to be of a less phosphorescent whiteness if she had not appeared during the projection of a film of unlimited insanity in which everything was used as a pretext to show the "Lord's Table." This was the work of a priest who signed himself Peter the Hermit, and I think the film was called *How I Killed My Child*.

---

3 *Nadja.*
4 *Les Vases communicants.*

One sees that as far as the cinema is concerned I remain comfortably "on this side," so that praise or complaint accorded such and such a film has little relevance. Nevertheless, that does not prevent me from pronouncing myself "for" or "against" and from defending such judgments with passion if need be. A hand is taken, then, in the necessary game of feelings and ideas, a game which can only be nourished and maintained by what is offered it. At this point it is fitting to make the best of a bad job. Once again social, ethic, and aesthetic criteria hungrily dispute their quarry.

Here as elsewhere one cannot refrain from a certain nostalgia for the idea of what the cinema might have become, and to allow that the sordidness of the epoch, together with certain conditions—worse than the others—of its "exploitation," were enough to clip its wings as soon as it flew the nest. I see Charles Fourier as a revolutionary only to the degree that he maintained and made sensible the idea that the whole cultural development of humanity has been effected in a sense which does not respond to any internal necessity, but only from pressures which might as well have been others, and differently exerted. Furthermore, such a conviction does not involve anything that revokes human success at any level, but accuses its strictly contingent and thereby *larval* character. And it is within our compass to perceive the original means of the cinema and to judge the more than parsimonious use to which they have been put. Twenty-five years have rolled by since Monsieur J. Goudal, in the *Revue hebdomadaire,* brought to light the perfect adequacy of these means for the Surrealist expression of life *second by second.* Nowhere else but in the cinema could we be fitted to receive that Key to the Opening which Chazal speaks of, which can make the mechanism of *correspondences* operate as far as the eye can see. But, of course, to keep to a theatrical type of action has been preferred. You can judge the result from these words, which I borrow from a professional: "I confess that today I rarely go to the cinema. Most films bore me, and I have the greatest difficulty in understanding what is going on. It's invariably necessary to explain the plot to me afterward."[5]

"We know now," I have had occasion to say, "that poetry must *lead somewhere.*" The cinema had everything it needed to subscribe to that view, but taken together—let us be specific: where its controlled activity is con-

---

5 René Clair, op. cit.

cerned—the least one can say is that it has not taken a single step in that direction.

From *L'Âge du cinéma* (Paris) 4–5 (August-November 1951): 26–30. Courtesy Mme. Élisa Breton. The cinema as an enchanted wood resonates with Baudelaire's idea of the universe as a dense "forest of symbols" which only humanity's capacity for analogical thinking can penetrate.

Picture palaces

Robert Desnos

There are cinemas where it's irritating to watch even the most beautiful film, others where the atmosphere is seductive enough to make the silliest story bearable.

Vainly have architects, modern and otherwise, desired to place their skill in the service of the cinema, which has no need of them.

All the velvet, gilt, and linear artifice adds up to nothing. The most beautiful cinema is perhaps the one on the Boulevard de Clichy, near the Place Pigalle, or the one on the Boulevard de Strasbourg; the first because it possesses the atmosphere of a great quay for those departing who knows where, the other because the women seen there are stunning.

Above all, cinema auditoriums must be afflicted with the same decay as the films they show: no luxurious seats and convoluted cornices as at the Opéra, no concrete verticals as in modernist theaters.

As for the orchestras, they do their utmost to irritate the nerves from the most idiotic *clairs de lune* to ridiculous adaptations of art music. How I miss the cinemas of days gone by, when an out-of-tune piano did its utmost to translate into sound the galloping of cowboys, the funeral march of the latest deceased celebrity, or the state of mind of two lovers beneath a setting sun reflected in a lake! The most touching romantic tunes from *Les Temps des cérises* to *The Blue Danube* followed each other without offending our ears. It was mere noise, that's all, but that was enough.

For there is nothing more ominous, after the cinema orchestras with their pretentious airs, than a film projected in silence. Noise is necessary, yet every attempt at imitative orchestration has been pitiful.

We cherish the memory of bass drum cannonades accompanying papier-mâché warfare. The art, ever the bungled art of those moving domains.

We are nauseated by artistic films, artistic orchestras, artistic cinemas.

And once again this applies as much to modern art as to its brother, academic art.

We are tired of these demonstrations of Western perversity.

We demand a cinema of beautiful heroines, action that does not pale into insignificance, an orchestra you don't notice, comfortable, unpretentious auditoriums. We also demand pleasant company. Too many cinemas are the setting for chauvinistic demonstrations; too many cinemas the meeting-place of the lowest company. As it happens, the last-named get the films they deserve, and it is they perhaps who are responsible for the insanities proliferating daily on our screens.

But where are the crowds of yesteryear?

First published in *Le Soir,* 28 May 1927. Reprinted in Robert Desnos, *Cinéma* (Paris: Gallimard, 1966), 183–184. Copyright © 1966 Éditions Gallimard.

Plan for a cinema
at the bottom of a lake

Bernard Roger

The instant when, into a sky disencumbered of any divine carbuncle, the conflagration of the last church disburses its ultimate wisps of smoke, we will recommence building the world. Not a stillborn world like the one we'll just have destroyed; ours will be a newborn world renewed again and again through its own vital impulse.

Among other things, we will build a cinema at the bottom of Lake Pavin. (Remember that Lake Pavin is an ancient crater in which water now assumes the place of fire.)

To build at the very bottom of the lake would only aggravate the technical difficulties without adding greater interest. Especially as this "bottom," adjudged to be ninety meters down, is actually but one stage in the lake's declivity.

Our cinema will float thirty meters or so below the lake surface. We will call on the expertise of nautical engineering to build it, assisted by the construction of submarines.

The entrance, the only part above the waterline, is in the middle of the lake. You reach it by boat, and from there descend to the auditorium via two lifts and intertwined helical stairways, the whole housed in a tower of glass. In its center is a ventilation duct for the auditorium.

Down below, the walls are in the form of a broad curve, without angles. The ceiling is an extended vault of glass (a double thickness of reinforced glass), through which you can see the lake above. In daytime the cinema is illuminated by the light of the lake. The seats are removable, permitting a variety of use. In the mornings it can function for the poetic and sexual initiation of children over seven.

Film projection takes place at night. Behind the screen is a glass panel. During the intermissions the screen disappears and you gaze on the nocturnal life of the lake.

From *L' Âge du cinéma* (Paris) 4–5 (August-November 1951): 48–49. Courtesy Bernard Roger.

The lights go up

Jacques Brunius

I t would be unfair not to mention the clubs here, different as they are from the cine clubs and film societies of today. The Club des Amis du Septième Art, the Ciné-Club de France, then the Tribune Libre du Cinéma not only permitted new ideas to be spread to a large audience, but illustrated these ideas by showing films.

The showings were sometimes tumultuous:

Potemkin was presented at the Ciné-Club de France sometime in 1925 or 1926. At the moment the sailors throw into the sea the officers who tried to make them eat rotten meat, applause breaks out. The lights go up. The guilty ones are denounced by their neighbors: it's the Surrealist Group. They are thrown out by the police. Nobody dares openly complain that they had applauded, since cheering can hardly pass for disturbing public order, or even that they had applauded a sequence for any but aesthetic reasons, but some are indignant that they had, it is claimed, got in without invitations.

At the Tribune Libre du Cinéma in 1926, one of Stroheim's first films, *Blind Husbands,* is shown and then debated. Edmond Gréville admires the fact that Stroheim had ended his film in having his hero, a Prussian officer, die, since this is the end that befits an officer. A gentleman gets up, declares himself to be an officer in the French army and that Gréville has just insulted the army. Other gentlemen reveal themselves as officers and, no less dedicated to defending the honor of the French and Prussian armies, as well as the right of all regular soldiers to die in their beds, surround the "insulter." A brawl ensues in which I hasten to defend Gréville and am felled by a courageous officer of the French army with a blow of the cane delivered from behind.

Another screening at the same club: Clarence Brown's admirable film, *Smoldering Fires,* with Pauline Frederick. A corpulent gentleman, the celebrated couturier Paul Poiret, declares, "this film is American, therefore idiotic." I demand the floor, await my turn, get to my feet, and in a modest tone that becomes my seventeen years pronounce that "one does not converse with imbeciles." Even though I am staring straight at him as I speak these words, Monsieur Poiret does not seem aware that they refer to him.

From Jacques B. Brunius, *En marge du cinema français* (Paris: Arcanes, 1954), 63–65. Courtesy Anne Cottance Brunius. Brunius's critical memoir of the "First Wave" of French avant-garde cinema formed part of the "Ombres blanches" series edited for Eric Losfeld by Ado Kyrou. Losfeld's going bust soon after meant that the book never had the impact it should have. Gréville went on to direct twenty-odd features, and his pulp inventiveness has been compared to that of Mexican-period Buñuel.

Surrealism and cinema

Jean Goudal

A new technique is born: immediately the philosophers come running,
armed with false problems. Is it an art?—Is it not an art?—Is it even
worthy of interest?

"In short," some of them say, "the cinema is only a perfected form of
photography." And they refuse to credit the new invention.

The indispensable extremists assume the other position. They tell us,
"Not only is the cinema an art, it will, moreover, gradually absorb all the
other arts" (Monsieur Marcel L'Herbier, in a lecture at the Collège de
France, repeated in Geneva during October 1924 at the showing in that
town of *L'Inhumaine,* previously published in *La Revue hebdomadaire* in
1923). The proof: the cinema takes the place of architecture (30 meters
devoted to the palaces in *The Thief of Bagdad*), music (a Negro jazz band
goes through the motions for 20 meters), dance (25 meters on a tango by
Valentino). Were they to draw the obvious conclusions from their ludi-
crous logic, they would have us believe that in future our meals will be
replaced by the image of Charlie Chaplin and the Kid tucking into a
plate of pancakes.

"Given its basic technical strictures, how do we see the future of the
cinema?" Now that's a more realistic question. To establish the correctness
of it, to begin to answer it, we need briefly to consider the evolution of the
other arts.

We see each of them in their turn follow the same general pattern.

First, they escape *literary* contamination (the renunciation of figurative
painting, of thematic music); next, they renounce the constraint of *logic*
considered as an intellectual element restricting sensory freedom, in favor
of inquiring after their guiding principles in terms of their *technique* (cub-
ism, musical impressionism).

(You can already foresee the third stage: thirsting for total liberty, artists
will thrust aside the last support of technique and claim the right to bring

into play, without any modification, the very *material* forming the basis of their art.)

We do not want to conceal the excessive simplification of these views or the dangers inherent in them, but nobody can contest this conclusion: in the evolution of every art there comes a moment, which may or may not be deplored, when the artist ignores every command of intellectual or logical origin in order to question the *technical* possibilities of his art. To us this moment appears to have arrived for the cinema.

Let us open a short parenthesis here on a literary movement whose origins are not recent but which manifests itself at present in a very noisy way.

We know the essential character of the Surrealist theses (we find an authentic expression of them in André Breton's *Manifesto of Surrealism*): that the unconscious activity of the mind, on which general attention has been focused through the work of thinkers like Freud and Babinski, or the novels of authors like Marcel Proust, has become the keystone of mental life. The artist's principal target is henceforth to search for a reality in the dream superior to that which the logical, therefore arbitrary, exercise of thought suggests to us. On the one hand, Surrealism presents itself as a critique of existing forms of literature; on the other hand, it presents itself as a complete renewal of the field and of artistic method and even, perhaps, as the renovation of the most general rules of human activity: in short, the absolute overthrow of all values.

You might think that objections to Surrealism (about which, however, you cannot deny the relative fruitfulness) are not lacking. Monsieur André Breton, even, shows himself to be ecstatic about the obstacles which already present themselves: "To its conquest [surreality] I go, certain of not getting there, but too heedless of my death not to calculate a little the joys of such possession."

The potential difficulties seem to us capable of being subsumed under two principal headings.

First, an objection as to method. It is not easy to determine if the Surrealists situate a superior reality in the dream itself, or in a sort of union or adjustment, difficult to imagine, of the two states, dream and reality. In both cases the same objection arises. If you admit that dream constitutes a superior reality, there will be insurmountable practical problems in attaining and fixing this dream. As soon as consciousness succeeds in rummaging through the unconscious you can no longer speak of the unconscious. On the other hand, if you accord a superior reality to a mystical fusion of the real and the dream, one cannot see by what means one can make two areas, by definition incommunicable, communicate with each other. (Our intention of progressing quickly here may lend too schematic an allure to our arguments. Furthermore, our real objective is not a critique of Surrealism.)

The second order of objection touches more profoundly on the antilogical ambitions of Surrealism. People have had the habit for so long now of using a language to communicate with each other that one asks if they can ever renounce this kind of usage. In short, what we call *reason* is the part of our mind common to all men: if it is to disappear, will we not lapse into an individual, incommunicable mode of expression? "I believe more and more," writes Monsieur A. Breton (*Manifesto of Surrealism*), "in the infallibility of my thought in relation to myself." Monsieur A. Breton is right; but why then have this "spiritual and mental mechanism" of Monsieur A. Breton's, once fixed in its absolute ingenuity valid only for Monsieur A. Breton himself, printed and published? Is it not so that we can make a comparison between his mind and our mind, and is this comparison even possible without some essential reference that only reason and logic can supply?

One fact seems remarkable to us. The objections we have just sketched out lose their value as soon as one applies the Surrealist theories to the domain of cinema. (That the theorists of Surrealism have wanted to apply their ideas to literature, that is to say, just where they are most contestable, should not be too surprising since the same pen suits the theorist and the poet.) Applied to the technique of cinema, the correctness and fecundity of the Surrealist thesis is all the more striking.

The objection toward *method* (the difficulty of uniting the conscious and the unconscious on the same plane) does not hold for cinema, in which the thing seen corresponds exactly to a *conscious hallucination*.

Let's go into a cinema where the perforated celluloid is purring in the darkness. On entering, our gaze is guided by the luminous ray to the screen where for two hours it will remain fixed. Life in the street outside no longer exists. Our problems evaporate, our neighbors disappear. Our body itself submits to a sort of temporary depersonalization which takes away the feeling of its own existence. We are nothing but two eyes riveted to ten square meters of white sheet.

But we must beware of vague analogies. It is better here to go into details.

Monsieur A. Breton, wanting to establish the superiority of the dream, writes: "The mind of the man who dreams is fully satisfied by whatever happens to it. The agonizing question of possibility arises no more." And, he asks, "what reason, what reason better than another confers this natural allure on the dream, makes me welcome unreservedly a host of episodes the strangeness of which strikes me as I write?"

The answer to this question lies in what Taine used to call the "reductive mechanism of images." When we are awake the images surging into our imagination have an anemic, pale color which by contrast makes the vigor and relief of real images stand out, the ones, that is to say, we get through our senses; and this difference of value is enough to make us distinguish the real from the imagined. When we sleep our senses are idle, or rather their solicitations do not cross the threshold of consciousness and, the reducing contrast no longer existing, the imaginary succession of images monopolizes the foreground; as nothing contradicts them we believe in their actual existence.

Awake, we imagine the real and the possible all at once, while in the dream we only imagine the possible. The Surrealists see an advantage in what, they say, one is used to seeing as inferior. Without going into the legitimacy of this paradox, let us return to the cinema. There we see a whole host of material conditions conspire to destroy this "reductive mechanism of images." The darkness of the auditorium destroys the rivalry of real images that would contradict the ones on the screen. It is equally important to ward off the impressions that can come to us through our other senses: who has never noticed the special nature of music in the cinema? Above all else it serves to abolish a silence that would let us perceive or imagine auditory phenomena of a realistic order, which would damage the necessary uniqueness of vision. And what spectator has not been embarrassed at times during the showing of a film at the attention he was giving, despite himself, to the music? In reality, the only music that would suit the cinema would be a sort of continuous, harmonious, monotonous noise (like the humming of an electric fan), the effect of which would be to obdurate the sense of hearing in some way for the duration of the show.

Someone might object that these are conditions common to all forms of spectacle and that even in the theater the darkness is there to facilitate the audience's concentration on the stage. But let us observe that the individuals performing on a theater stage have a physical presence that strengthens the trompe l'oeil of their setting; they have three-dimensionality, they live amid the noises of normal life; we accept them as our brothers, as our peers, while the camera aspires to give the illusion of reality by means of a simulacrum of a uniquely visual kind. An actual hallucination is needed here which the other conditions of cinema tend to reinforce, just as, in the dream, moving images *lacking three-dimensionality* follow each other on a single plane artificially delimited by a rectangle which is like a geometrical opening giving on to the psychic kingdom. The absence of color, too, the *black and white,* represents an arbitrary simplification analogous to those one meets in dreams. Once again let us note that the actual succession of images in the cinema has something *artificial* about it that distances us from reality. The persistence of images on the retina, which is the physiological basis of cinema, claims to present movement to us with the actual continuity of the real; but in fact we know very well that it's an illusion, a sensory device which does not completely fool us. Ultimately, the rhythm of the individuals we see moving on the silent screen possesses something jerky about it that makes them the relatives of the people who haunt our dreams.

We must add one last analogy. In the cinema, as in the dream, the *fact is* complete master. Abstraction has no rights. No explanation is needed to justify the heroes' actions. One event follows another, seeking justification in itself alone. They follow each other with such rapidity that we barely have time to call to mind the logical commentary that would explain them or at least connect them.

(Summary considerations, no doubt, but ones that allow us to make short work of certain illusions about the advisability of adding "improvements" like color, relief, or some kind of sound synchronization. The cinema has found its true technique in black-and-white film—forget three-dimensionality and sound. To try to "perfect" it, in the sense of bringing it closer to reality, would only run counter to and slow down its genuine development.)

The cinema, then, constitutes a conscious hallucination, and utilizes this fusion of dream and consciousness which Surrealism would like to see realized in the literary domain. These moving images delude us, by leaving us with a confused awareness of our own personality and by allowing us to evoke, if necessary, the resources of our memory. (In general, however, the cinema demands from us only memory enough to link the images.)

The cinema avoids the second order of difficulty raised by Surrealism just as happily.

Though the complete repudiation of logic is forbidden to language, which is born of this logic, the cinema can indulge itself in such repudiation without contravening any ineluctable internal necessity.

"The strongest image is the one that has the greatest degree of arbitrariness," declares Monsieur A. Breton, who cites, among other examples, this image from Philippe Soupault: "A church stood dazzling as a bell."

The word *church,* encompassed, by virtue of language, within a system of logical relations, just as the word *bell* is, makes the very fact of pronouncing these two words, of comparing them, evoke these two systems, makes us make them coincide. And, as they are not juxtaposable, the reader bridles at accepting the comparison.

On the other hand, when the cinema shows us a dazzling church and then, without transition, a dazzling bell, our eye can accept this sequence; it is witnessing two facts here, two facts which justify themselves. And if the two images succeed each other with the necessary rapidity, the logical mechanism which tries to link the two objects in some way or other will not have time to be set in motion. All one will experience is the almost simultaneous sight of two objects, exactly the cerebral process, that is to say, that suggested this comparison to the author.

In language the foremost factor is always the logical thread. The image is born according to this thread and contributes to its embellishment, its illumination. In cinema the foremost factor is the image which, on occasion, though not necessarily so, drags the tatters of reason behind it. The two processes, you see, are exactly inverse.

The above tends to demonstrate that not only does the application of Surrealist ideas to the cinema avoid the objection with which you can charge literary Surrealism, but that surreality represents a domain actually indicated to cinema by its very technique.

Just leaf through the dreamed poems Monsieur A. Breton has collected together at the end of his *Manifesto,* under the title of *Soluble Fish,* and you will see, perhaps, that the surest way of making the public accept them would be to treat them like film scenarios.

The adventures of the crate penetrated by human arms, sliding down hillsides, bashing against "trees that cast bright blue sunlight on it," then running aground on the first floor of a run-down hotel, and which is found to contain only starch, and the mysterious voyage of the barque which is the poet's tomb following the closing of the cemetery, and the tribulations of the lamppost, and the chase after the woman who has left her veil with her lover, a source of miracles and inexplicable bliss, so many marvelous tales with enough anacoluthon inevitably to shock the reader, but which, brought to the screen, would perhaps be accepted with delight by the spectator. The latter would see in its teeming lapses of logic no more than thousands of details, comic and strange, all ingenious.

It is time cineastes saw clearly what profits they may gain in opening up their art to the unexplored regions of the dream. Up till now this has only been done intermittently, as if by default. They should lose no time in imbuing their productions with the three essential characteristics of the dream: the *visual,* the *illogical,* the *pervasive.*

The visual

The cinema is already so by force of circumstance.

It will remain so exclusively.

(There is nothing for it to fear, we repeat, from the paltry attempts at phonographic synchronization.)

The illogical

Everything that is foolish about cinema is the fault of an old-fashioned respect for logic.

Sentimentality is the respect for logic within the framework of feeling. (All elegance, all un-self-consciousness results from the severing of one or more links in the traditional chain of feelings.)

The feuilleton is the respect for logic within the framework of episodes. (I term "feuilleton" any sequence of events whose unfolding, using basic characters and situations, can be understood by the average concierge.)

Slowness is the respect for logic within the framework of situations and gestures.

Etc.

The pervasive

But if you are to bring to the screen only various illogical series of images, assembled according to the most capricious associations of ideas, don't you risk alienating the public?

First, we reply that we are suggesting only one possible direction for the cinema here. *Other ways remain open besides this one.* Bit by bit the education of the public will occur.

Next, we feel we must not lose our footing through complete incoherence. Man is only interested in what is close to him. I am interested in my dreams, despite their incoherence, because they come from within me, because I find a particular quality in them belonging no doubt to what I can recognize in them of elements of *my* past life, though arbitrarily assembled. These memories are my own; but I have difficulty in identifying them. For want of a better word this is what I mean by the expression: the dream is *pervasive.*

This property of the dream is strictly personal, one can see that. How can a film, which must address itself to thousands of spectators, manage to be *pervasive?*

This is the place to reintroduce the human dimension.

One of Surrealism's points of departure is the observation that everything that emerges from the mind, even without logical form, inevitably reveals the singularity of that mind. Man retains his personality (all the more so perhaps) in his most spontaneous productions.

A film, then, will have a sufficiently pervasive and human character because it will have come from the brain of one of my peers.

We now come up against a serious problem. In the actual process of cinema, a film does not have one creator, it has two, three, ten, fifty. One person supplies the scenario, which usually consists of an extremely brief outline. This scenario is taken up by the director, who develops it, fills it out with detail; in short, brings it to the level of practical realization. It remains to note the contribution of each artist, the suggestions of the costume and prop departments, the requirements of the lighting technicians.

During the course of such a many-sided collaboration, doesn't the work risk losing the singular quality it owed to the individuality of the author, the singularity of its first conception?

This difficulty is, we believe, only temporary and soon tends to disappear. It is due to the exceptional conditions created by the too-rapid growth of the cinema. The cinema has met with such success since its beginnings (it is barely thirty years old, remember) that it has had to cope with demands disproportionate to its means. The public expects new films every week. To create them is the work of many. You employ whomever you can. Let us give the division of labor and the necessary specialization the time to find their way. Then, beginning with the original cell, the source idea born in his mind, the cineaste will be able to supervise it, thanks to a technique he must be master of, until it is seen on the screen without the idea being bungled by a commercial organization concerned only to exploit it. On that day the cinema will have its artists, and the question whether or not "the cinema is an art" will thereby get an affirmative response difficult to contest.

The cineastes are beginning to see the light.

It isn't too hard to see indications in their most recent productions that would confirm our previsions, yet with what awkwardness is this *Marvelous* in which the cinema finds its real voice still spoken of. Will results come from the comedy film side? We have memories of certain American films, almost without intertitles, in which girls, irresponsible individuals, and animals let their whims, of the most diverting fantasy, take control of them. Do not the recent Chaplins betray the desire to construct a simplified setting which no overprecise detail can localize (Charlie Chaplin being universal, the locations he performs in could be anywhere)—and also the preoccupation with creating a dream atmosphere which is believable and makes possible the extraordinary gestures of this unfortunate with the little mustache and big feet? Remember the strange chapel with its strange congregation in *The Pilgrim,* where Charlie, the bogus pastor, delivers that strange sermon; and in *Payday* Charlie, the mason in his cups, returning to a far-off lodging house that proves impossible to get to, and that nightmarish rain, and those futile, unreal attempts by the drunk to get on a tram which has no destination and will always escape, full of eternal commuters, back into the anonymous night.

Besides this burlesque Marvelous, Charlie's unique atmosphere, there is a place for that faerie [*féerie*] Marvelous certain films have already brought us, the essential elements of which would be the *geometry of line* and the *illogicality of detail.*

The Marvelous in the cinema, unable to utilize the infinite resources of color, must count above all on the resources of lighting and line. Just as in the world we inhabit no line is absolutely geometrical, so a resolutely geometrical stylization creates a surprising atmosphere.

In *The Thief of Bagdad,* for instance, two details strike the spectator forcibly: the gate of the town that opens and closes through the connecting and disconnecting of identically formed panels, and Douglas Fairbanks soaring above the unreal clouds on his scleroid horse. These two images have the admirable manifest artifice of the dream.

In the same film, on the other hand, the heavy-handed Americans, wanting to show us a monster, have laboriously sought verisimilitude and concocted a sort of enormous lizard, instead of painting in, in broad strokes, a clearly fantastic creature of geometrical cardboard. The Germans made the same blunder when they sought to represent Cerberus guarding Brunhild's castle (in *The Nibelungen).* They constructed a complicated, naively realistic mechanism needing sixteen men to make the huge thing move. What effort and money expended, not necessarily in vain, but they missed the whole point!

At least we have a success in the laboratory set F. Léger designed for Monsieur L'Herbier's *L'Inhumaine.* The effect of the machines used to bring the loved woman back to life is striking, the cubist décor coming alive and moving in a clever frenzy.

Let us quote Monsieur A. Breton again: "No matter how charming they may be, a grown man would think he were reverting to childhood by nourishing himself on fairy tales, and I am the first to admit that all such tales are not suitable for him. The fabric of adorable improbabilities must be made a trifle more subtle the older we grow, and we are still at the stage of waiting for this kind of spider." It is the fineness of this fabric we think of when calling for the *illogicality of the detail*. It is not without unparalleled sorrow that humankind, crushed by a thousand years of logic, will renounce the principle of identity. The American faerie that we find in this same *Thief of Bagdad* (flying carpets, flames, monsters) is not much more courageous than Perrault's, whose fairies didn't go quite so far as to change a pumpkin into a horse or a rat into a coach, but prudently changed an animal into an animal, an object into an object. "There are," adds Monsieur A. Breton, "fairy tales to be written for adults, fairy tales still almost blue." Who will write these tales if not the cinema?

The preceding pages, we repeat, aim only at suggesting one possible direction for the cinema.

As for the concessions needed to suit public taste, we do not think it useful to insist on them. There will always be enough industrialists to keep up the old traditions, to go on adapting novels to be acted out by boxing champions and France's most beautiful *midinettes*.

What the cinema has produced over a quarter of a century justifies all our hopes. One does not fight the forces of the spirit.

First published in *La Revue hebdomadaire* (Paris), February 1925. Reprinted in Alain and Odette Virmaux, *Les Surréalistes et le cinéma* (Paris: Seghers, 1976), 305–317. Although Goudal was not a Surrealist, Breton referred approvingly to this paper in "As in a Wood" (q.v.).

Introduction to
black-and-white magic

Albert Valentin

For some of those who belong to that generation whose appearance coincides with the appearance of a century that must still have several surprises in store for us, the birth of the cinema is contemporaneous with the arousal of curiosity that accompanied the return of Halley's Comet. One wonders what the compass of the years 1908 or 1909 would have been if they had not had, on Sunday evenings, the alfresco projection of films of black-and-white magic and, after the show, the promenade on the ramparts where you had recourse to a complicated system of opera glasses and some dubious notions of astronomy to persuade yourself you weren't telling tales about celestial phenomena. Two phosphorescent tails divided space at that time, though you observed the one that brought the end of the world with it without seeing that the other, which came out of the lens of a magic lantern, had arrived before us full to bursting with a humanity that flows over us today on every side. Today we must dream of regulating this fabulous circulation of images that holds sway at every crossroads on earth. It must be said that, if you thought about it a bit, you would not cross the threshold of a cinema without a feeling close to the one you get going into a church: a mixture of a humility of sorts before the deception you are the object of, and an admiration for the quality of the trap set you. In both cases someone is counting on a weakness of ours to trick us: in the temple, on the feebleness of our understanding; in the darkened theater, on a defect in our retina that delights in visual puns and cannot succeed in isolating the succession of forms moving at speed. Consequently, it seems extremely reckless to define the future of cinema, since a more evolved race than ours may emerge that will no longer yield to optical illusion and whose more sensitive eye will easily perceive the dead time that joins one frame of film to the next. Surely the idea of such a possibility distresses nobody, for it would be well within the tradition of cinema, whose whole development bears the mark of the provisional and the ephemeral. Up to now it was thought the chanson de geste revealed a certain form of lyricism: actually, it is only today that the verse chronicle comes of age; it comes to us via that great white window opening onto space. This fictional or, to be more precise, poetic aspect of the cinema is even more obvious to us when we recall that the poetry of a few years ago sought its inspiration in a "machinism" from which it hoped to borrow its line and rigor. Doubtless there was something too presumptuous in this project, because reality came to the aid of imagination, so that today poetry gets out alive from a moving machine through which slides a ribbon charged with a human, inert substance that comes to life when in contact with those wheels, gears, and sparks. The miracle is within reach of all eyes, within reach of every pocket. Above our heads the projector generates a transparent cone in which electrical atoms are suspended, a sort of seed, a kind of pollen that precipitates and starts to blossom on the rectangular surface of the screen. Still lives are still no longer, a universe crystallized in the film and reduced to its simplest expression is suddenly torn from its slumber, separated from its husk and, regaining its original dimensions, enters into our existence, our thought. It's here that every surface in the world and every land on earth is reflected; it's here, on this quadrilateral of white sheet, like a flag of surrender, that their images meet. America has sent us the effigy of its young women and men, straight out of the prospectuses that beauty schools and colleges of physical education put out. You might take them for brilliant automata of nickel or steel whose every pawl is easily gauged, so well does the play of their joints seem regulated by a system of motors. They don't waste their time with arbitrary or complicated sentiments, reply with a "yes" or a "no," never a "maybe," and so they go, across a planet docile to their will, with a magnificent lack of fussiness, reticence, and mystery. We have been torn between this insolent healthiness and that air of decomposition we have inhaled in the German films that blackmail us with a misery we have so readily given in to. They have transported us through a poisoned climate where an odor of the surgery reigned that soon merited our every resistance. The screen covered us like a hospital sheet and the nightmare led us along corridors laden with traps, along Expressionist streets where a dust similar to cocaine filled the air, where with every step you sensed crime, despair, suicide, the fairground sideshow—in a word, the balefulness of the postwar period. One would have sworn these tragedies had been made in the well-used, affected hothouses of the studios. Their scenarios renewed an acquaintance with the ancient law of "unity of time": one day sufficed to reduce all the actors to corpses and, for several years, they were without equal for ending in mourning in twenty-four hours. We're really sorry that these improvised films, about which it will someday be rather casually asserted that they represent a whole era, have given way to others in which all research is oriented toward the perfection of technical means. We regret this because we see in it a sign that the prodigy is little by little losing its exceptional character and that our passion for cinema is turning into a habit. One is busy taming the still half-wild animal and, while today its capriciousness surprises us less than it used to, one finds time to define, as for lovemaking, the thirty-six positions of a camera no longer content with embracing the scene it wants to master face to face, but insinuating itself into it, penetrating it from all angles, and finally abandoning to our gaze the vanquished, transfigured quarry. It has not been said often enough that the cinema, like the automobile, owes a part of its interest to a taste of recent origin which it flatters and maintains in us: a scorn for timetables. One comes and one goes, one enters and exits when it suits. All we have to do is push open the door and we are immediately conversing with phantoms: the introductions are quickly made. No curtain here, as in the theater, where the real is separated from the imaginary: you are on the same plane as the fiction, you treat it as an equal. In his aerial cabin the projectionist agitates his crystal and metal goblet like a barman, he pours a cocktail of images for our eyes, which would not drink it in without getting dizzy if they didn't have that straw one's brothers detect so easily.[1] Besides X-rays, which only retain death's image, only describe the secret skeleton, here are other rays that recognize and restore life, bodily appearance, and décor. A law of enlargement whose repercussions we still don't know how to assess seems to determine the cinema's fate, and it is not just film subjected to the lens's

---

1 [Valentin often mixes metaphors. Here straw means both "drinking straw," to drink the cocktail of images with, and "mote," a reference to the biblical adage: "Why beholdest thou the mote that is in thy brother's eye, but considerest not the beam that is in thine own eye?" (Matthew, 7:3) —*Trans.*]

action that obeys this frantic rule, but everything that from near and far participates in the existence of the film. Typists the world over have not stopped crying over the disappearance of Rudolph Valentino. Charlie Chaplin has the whole universe interested in his divorce. Charles Ray has been ruined by *The Girl I Loved*. Griffith had to work for five years to make good the losses of *Broken Blossoms*. Erich von Stroheim gave in to the deepest despair after *Greed* was mutilated. All things considered, one asks oneself if the cinema is not an enormous news item worthy of our time. Doubtless it is something else besides, though we leave it to the theoreticians to determine what. But even if it were no more than we've just said, we would not have been cheated one bit.

From René Jeanne, ed., *L'Art cinématographique* IV (Paris: Librairie Félix Alcan, 1927), 109–116. Albert Valentin's Surrealist life was brief. A new recruit in 1929 after the regroupment following the *Second Manifesto,* he worked with Breton on a screenplay of Barbey d'Aurevilly's *Crimson Curtain.* (Artaud was working independently on the same project at the same time in Nice.) Valentin signed the "Manifesto of the Surrealists Concerning *L'Âge d'or*" (q.v.). He made his exit in December 1931, after Paul Éluard and René Crevel accused him of working on a "counterrevolutionary film," Clair's *À nous la liberté,* in the pages of *Le Surréalisme au service de la révolution* 4. "Introduction to Black-and-White Magic"—this excerpt is about one quarter of its total length—has a distinctly Desnosian tone to it. It also predicts some of Breton's concerns in "As in a Wood" (q.v.).

Crossing the bridge

Jacques Brunius

René Clair raised an important objection in an article called "Surrealism and Cinema" (1925), putting the possibility of spontaneous expression on screen in doubt:

> What interests me about Surrealism are the pure, extra-artistic values it discloses to me. To translate the purest Surrealist concept into images means submitting it to cinematic technique, which runs the risk of making that "pure psychic automatism" lose a large part of its purity. . . . Even if the cinema cannot be a perfect means of expression for Surrealism, it nonetheless remains an incomparable field of Surrealist activity for the spectator's mind.

This reservation might seem strange coming from the man who made *Entr'acte*. I myself believe one cannot subscribe to it without calling into question the part inspiration plays in all the other arts, particularly painting. Indeed, over the centuries only poetry, spoken or written, has shown itself extensively privileged to espouse directly all the wanderings and unconscious movements of the heart and mind, because the intermediary it uses—words—is, of all techniques, the one that seems most intimately a part of ourselves. But the "pure psychic automatism" defined by Surrealism does not operate in the abstract, in a vacuum. It can be set in motion—and this is generally the case—by the bringing into play of any of the tools that serve to transcribe its dictation in words or images. Surrealism has always admitted this interaction between conscious and unconscious thought and the implement. In the *First Manifesto* there are instructions about the technique of automatic writing, and later on the "inspiration aids" of Max Ernst.

In the case of the dream, the objection applies even less. It is only possible in effect to note down the description of a dream on waking. There can be no more question of fixing the dream directly on film than of writing it down as it happens or of painting it automatically on canvas.

99

It is, therefore, only through memory rising to the surface of thought that the dream will be voluntarily and consciously objectified. Beginning there, the work of the artist in no way differs from the work of reconstructing external reality as faithfully as possible. For the filmmaker reality itself does not entirely imitate nature. In both cases the staging of memories is involved. This restitution is conditioned by the artist's gift for observation, lucidity of vision, and memory. There is little chance of it losing more of its purity here than in writing or painting.

It remains to be seen if the camera as a tool is as satisfactory as language or the brush.

During its first twenty-five years the cinema was so totally incapable of realism (in the sense of *an illusion of reality*) that any faithful representation of the dream was as impossible *voluntarily* for it as the faithful copying of the external world.

On the other hand, film, even at that point in time, especially at that point in time, frequently arrived at an *involuntary* simulation of the dream. The darkness of the auditorium, tantamount to the closing of the eyelids on the retina and, for thought, to the darkness of the unconscious; the crowd that surrounds and isolates you, the deliciously crass music, the stiffness of the neck necessary for the orientation of one's gaze, provoke a state like being half-asleep; on the screen are inscribed *white letters on a black background,* whose hypnagogic quality is obvious. At the time of silent film these titles, through the inattention of the projectionist, sometimes appeared *the wrong way round,* adding a further reminder of eidetic images. When at last the dazzling, window-like screen lights up, the very technique of film evokes the dream more than waking. The images *fade in* and *fade out,* dissolve into each other, vision begins and ends in an *iris,* secrets are revealed through a keyhole, the mental image of a keyhole. The disposition of screen images *in time* is absolutely analogous with the *arrangement* thought or the dream can devise. Neither chronological order nor relative values of duration are real. Contrary to the theater, film, like thought, like the dream, chooses some gestures, defers or enlarges them, eliminates others, travels many hours, centuries, kilometers in a few seconds, speeds up, slows down, stops, goes backward. It is impossible to imagine a truer mirror of mental performance. Despite the wishes of the majority of filmmakers, the cinema is the *least realistic of the arts,* even when photographic reproduction succeeds in creating an illusion of the concrete reality of each separate element. All the more before photographic technique permitted it.

But machines are perfected and audiences develop.

On the one hand, the improvement in material techniques and the mollifying of cinematic language augment the camera's acuteness of perception and its ability to depict a likeness of the real on screen.

On the other hand, the public's familiarity with the visual conventions of film gradually enables it to better imagine, by a sort of mental transposition, a reality that cannot be reproduced on screen as an absolute likeness.

For the spectator the mental representations elicited by the images on screen tend to get mixed up with the usual representation of the external world he develops from his perceptions. He is henceforth in a position to carry the fiction on the screen over into reality.

The cinema, then, has become more or less capable of realism, as far as any means of expression can be, with all reservations made about the generally ambiguous meaning one accords this term. Nevertheless, it remains, for the reasons suggested above, the *least realistic of the arts,* the art in which the mechanism of formation of the images gives them as concrete a character as possible, but in which the disposition of these elements is as distinct from temporal and spatial reality as it is possible to be.

It is then, only then, that one can try *voluntarily* to transcribe dreams without relying too much on chance. But from this moment on, the cinema has become the best tool for this transcription. At each stage, from the objectivization of ancient myths to the creation of new ones, from the reverie of awakening or half-sleep to the nocturnal dream, passing through entoptic lights and hypnagogic visions, from hallucinations brought on by hunger, fatigue, drugs, or mental alienation to the most complex and dramatized forms of the marvelous and the fantastic, this transcription is the real domain of the cinema, the one in which no other form of so-called artistic expression is to be found. In this domain—though all media can practice it—none other benefits from so many resources, so much liberty and prestige, none can nourish the imagination with so many images at once and, because of the time factor and the ellipses that are peculiar to film, still leave it hungry and anxious to pursue the creation of images.

The cinema is provided with enough weapons to rival the theater on the plane of normal psychology, but one can barely see what, of the characters' conscious psychology, the dramatist, stage director, and actor could not succeed in expressing with words, however poor in visual resources the theater may be. (We mustn't forget that this art blossomed before gas and electricity enabled the stage to be lit up.) At most, cinema provides, or can provide, another way of saying the same things, although few people think of using it for this: facility demands that it be used more for the well-tried formulas of theater, to which one restricts oneself to superposing a few close shots and camera movements which add almost nothing.

On the other hand, the cinema can reign supreme in that enlargement of reality which is the marvelous, in that prolongation of psychology that dream is. There is no need to oppose the two aspects, as certain short-sighted and emotionally stunted critics do. Only within the devout concept of realism, or in the devotion to the *unreal,* which both finally exclude from reality its highest forms on the pretext that they baffle the senses, are they opposed. Surrealism long since went beyond these attitudes in which man himself mutilates one or other of his faculties, and threw a bridge between the seemingly most distant activities of understanding, between action and speculation, common sense and utopia, psychology and the dream. One would like not to have to return to the above, but it is still fitting to repeat that film enjoys an incomparable facility for crossing the bridge in both directions, thanks to the extraordinary and sumptuous solidity it attributes to the mind's creations, objectifying them in the most convincing manner, while it makes external reality submit in the opposite direction to subjectivization.

From Jacques B. Brunius, *En marge du cinema français* (Paris: Arcanes, 1954), 107–115. Courtesy Anne Cottance Brunius. Translator's title.

Sorcery and cinema

Antonin Artaud

We hear it endlessly repeated that the cinema is in its infancy and that we're only witnessing its first stammerings. I confess to not understanding this way of seeing things. The cinema arrives at an already advanced stage of development within human thought and it benefits from this development. It is, to be sure, a means of expression that, materially speaking, is not yet completely perfected. We may imagine a certain number of advances capable of giving the camera, for instance, a stability and mobility it does not possess. One day soon we will probably have cinema in three dimensions, even cinema in color. Yet these are secondary resources that cannot add much to what is the bedrock of the cinema itself and which makes a language out of it, as music, painting, and poetry are a language. In cinema I've always been aware of a virtue proper to the secret movement of images, to their matter. There's a whole element of contingency and mystery in cinema that isn't found in the other arts. Indeed, any image, even the slightest and most banal, is transfigured on the screen. The smallest detail and the most insignificant object take on the meaning and the life that pertains to each of them. And this, in addition to the value of the meaning of the images themselves, in addition to the thought they express, the symbol they constitute. Due to the fact that it isolates objects, it endows them with a second life, one that tends to become ever more independent and to detach itself from the habitual meaning these objects have. Foliage, a bottle, a hand, etc., live a quasi-animal life which asks only to be utilized. There are also the distortions of the camera itself, the unexpected use it makes of the things it is asked to film. At the moment the image disappears, a detail which it was thought wouldn't particularly stand out takes leave of the expression chosen for it. Then there's the physical intoxication of sorts that the rotation of the images communicates directly to the brain. The spirit is moved, whatever the representation. The kind of virtual power images have goes rummaging in the depths of the mind for hitherto unused possibilities. In essence, the cinema reveals a whole occult life, one with which it puts us directly in contact. But we have to know how to divine this occult life. There are better ways of divining the secrets that stir in the depths of our consciousness than the simple play of superimpositions. Considered as such, in an abstract way, cinema in its raw state [*le cinéma brut*] emits something of the atmosphere of trance conducive to certain revelations. To use it to tell stories, a superficial series of deeds, is to deprive it of the finest of its resources, to disavow its most profound purpose. That's why the cinema seems to me to be made, above all else, to express things of the mind, the inner life of consciousness, not so much through the play of images as through something more imponderable that restores them to us with their matter intact, without intermediate forms, without representations. The cinema arrives at a turning point in human thought, at the precise moment in which an exhausted language loses its power as a symbol, in which the mind is sick and tired of the play of representations. For us clear thinking is not enough. It defines a world exhausted to the point of collapse. What is clear is what is instantly accessible, but the instantly accessible is what serves life as an outer shell. We begin to perceive that this over-familiar life, which has foregone all its symbols, is not life in its entirety. And it's a wonderful time, right now, for sorcerers and saints, more wonderful than ever before. A whole insensate substance takes on form, strives to reach the light. The cinema brings us closer to this substance. If the cinema isn't made to express dreams or everything that in waking life has something in common with dreams, then it has no point. Nothing differentiates it from theater. Yet the cinema, a direct and rapid-fire language, has no need of a certain slow and ponderous logic in order to subsist and prosper. Cinema will bear a greater and greater resemblance to the fantastic, that fantastic of which it is increasingly observed that it is really the real in its entirety; otherwise, it doesn't exist. Or cinema will ultimately come to the same end as painting, as poetry. What is certain is that most forms of representation have had their day. It's been a long time since good painting serves for anything other than to reproduce the abstract. It's not just a question of choice, therefore. There won't be a cinema that represents life, on the one hand, and another cinema that represents the functioning of thought, on the other. Because life, what we call life, will become increasingly inseparable from mind. A certain profound domain tends to blossom on the surface. More than any other art the cinema is capable of expressing the representations of this domain, because stupid order and habitual clarity are its enemies.

The Seashell and the Clergyman belongs to this research into a subtle order, into a hidden life I have wished to make plausible, as plausible and real as the other life.

In order to understand this film it will be enough to look deep within ourselves. To submit to the kind of plastic, objective examination that's attentive to an inner *self* that's hitherto been the exclusive domain of the "Illuminati."

Written circa 1928 and only published in part in 1949. First printed in full in Antonin Artaud, *Oeuvres complètes,* tome 3 (Paris: Gallimard, 1961). Copyright © 1961 Éditions Gallimard.

The screen's prestige

Jacques Brunius

I n the last analysis, what has always seemed to me to justify the lively attraction the cinema has for the majority of our contemporaries is, on the one hand, the promiscuity of hundreds of human beings enclosed in a darkened room with all that that entails for the play of imagination and for erotic chance—the fascinating prestige of the luminous screen—and, on the other hand, the mark of authenticity the photographed document impresses on the whole spectacle.

When, at the end of her "Pirate Jenny" song, the prostitute in *The Threepenny Opera* fluttered her eyelids as if "coming out of a dream," Margo Lion's face faithfully reproduced the trauma of awakening, the dazed expression the spectator has on leaving the cinema.

And those small Moroccan children I saw in 1928 in the front rows of the Renaissance cinema in Rabat were spontaneously attesting to the intense credibility the concrete realism of photographed form brings to film when they clambered up on the seats to see what was happening below the bottom edge of the screen during a showing of *Captain Salvation*, in which Pauline Starke and Lars Hanson purveyed a cheap puritanism.

From Jacques B. Brunius, *En marge du cinema français* (Paris: Arcanes, 1954), 11–12. Courtesy Anne Cottance Brunius. Translator's title.

Remarks on cinematic oneirism

Robert Benayoun

Every means of expression has, at one phase or another of its development, found itself faced with the dilemma its creative potential imposed on it: to represent nature in all its nakedness or to rise above it, in
one or more stages, through the power of illusion. Barely pubescent, the
cinema found itself facing the same choice: under very different names,
both possibilities opened up before it, thus dividing its forward thrust.
And yet the very essence of its power ought to have enlightened it: was it
merely a registering device, the more developed first cousin of photography, the perfected tracing of a simple image? Or was it not, rather, the
open sesame of a universe until then cloistered from view? Might it not
unveil, through picturing them, the truths an overly jealous nature fixed
in stone, truths the poets alone had ever really grasped? Might it not, lastly,
extend the Word by a parallel Vision more revelatory than any other?

The screen, we have to admit, communicates a reality beyond its flat
surface. But on the strength of the varied artifices of lighting, of framing,
of the very *choice* of its various elements, this reality can only be attained
in its contingent aspect, one practically impossible to reproduce system-
atically. Re-created by technical means, it is therefore by definition artificial. It also seems vain to try and typify its more readily external features in
order to indulge a public ever fond of conventional images. Just as one
sees tonsured pates nodding before the starkness of certain still lifes, so
one invokes the word "truth" when faced with any pictorial or mobile
reproduction of gestures consecrated by habit. The world remains Narcis-
sus-like, even in its least important concepts: denying itself any in-depth
exploration of the mechanisms of internal life, it prefers to endlessly blunder through the same old alphabet. In fact, the naturalist craze, which
compels certain directors to improvise the filming of passersby in the ac-

tual street, doesn't restitute a part of the real, the least manifestation of which touches on the impalpable. And what is more, this craze denies the very principles of cinematic language, the most obvious characteristics of which appertain to the domain of the unreal [*l'irréel*].

The spectator, one of the two poles of the cinematic experience, participates in an eminently subjective "spectacle," in fact. Caught up in a series of deeds that is foreign to him (but elements of which he recognizes from time to time), an invisible witness of the projected drama, he momentarily identifies with one actor or another, repeatedly interchanging his personality for that of the various protagonists.[1] Despite himself, he follows the action whose principle he has accepted, though not in all its details: this action is technically as well as psychologically disconnected; its concatenation, via montage, has nothing really logical about it. Chronology is not even respected: the narrative may be parallel, as in *Manèges*; alternated, as in *Citizen Kane*; back-to-front, as in *Thomas Garner*: it may be, and this is the most common, that these various procedures coexist. In the last analysis, the spectator gives in to this action without being able to influence it: he becomes the plaything of an uncontrollable rhythm that carries him along to the dénouement, the sudden rupturing of his dependency, the genuine reawakening of freedom. Are not these different phases, in their most subtle nuances, the directly perceptible ones of a dream?

An equally striking similarity enables us to discern the ideal complexity of cinematic language: unreal by nature, its only function should be to seek satisfaction in the unreal. It is in oneirism, then, that it can rediscover the veritable essence of human beings; the dream, an element common to all authentic individuals, the reassuring measure for man of his own interior richness, offers a much more revealing symbolism than that of fixed things. Turning their back on simple appearances, dream films penetrate to the very depths of the human being and touch upon that "potential grandeur" of which Thomas de Quincey speaks. The director reveals himself entirely, but by and large he presents a vision of the salient world that each of us can submit to with full knowledge of the facts.

1 The technique known as "subjective camera," which encourages the shooting of "first-person" films, doesn't authenticate the personal impressions of the viewer in the least. Aside from the flagrant oneirism of this partly assumed personality, how great is the shock of the camera-actor when, passing in front of a mirror, he discovers that he has the features of Robert Montgomery, for instance!

Two procedures are offered him, then: the first consists of integrating his dream in a real series of events, by transposing facts from one to the other. Examples are *Ballerina, Lady in the Dark,* and *Tom, Dick, and Harry.* If the film is well done this ambivalence, justified from the rational point of view, can preserve the specific integrity of both worlds. On the other hand, the ambition of certain filmmakers is to somehow emphasize the interpretation of the dream and of reality. An example is *A Matter of Life and Death.* The pretext for this is often psychoanalytic, and thus it is only valid as a pretext. What's more, it would be far too easy for any civilized viewer to rediscover the director's complexes through his films. It's not important to us if Hitchcock is a paranoiac or not, as long as we can read the subconscious beauties of his language. Neuroses are for psychiatrists; we'll make do with *art brut.* As for films about psychoanalysis, there are some very bad ones whose sole interest resides in the occasionally delirious atmosphere of certain imaginatively worthwhile images that touch upon creative automatism. Their medical justification bores us, but their unbridled discursiveness (in which the director's fantasy, justified in everything, is given free rein) puts us in touch with our true inner depths.

The second procedure, more delicate still, calls for genius: it consists in constructing a dream which nothing will explain, and this for the beauty of a purely gratuitous oneirism alone. However calculated the dosage of effects may be, however premeditated the disordered concatenation of events, an organic rhythm is created that extends beyond the creator's intentions or the tyrannies of his subconscious; it is the rhythm of the dream, a complete freedom of expression, the genuine automatism of visual writing, such as can be fleetingly glimpsed in a few rare successes: *La Nuit fantastique, Dead of Night,* etc. The sextants go wild, the vision of the world goes all to pieces, the delirious and aberrant nature of the images brings the beauties of total poetry to the viewer. In its highest manifestations, it is the frankly surreal language of certain visionaries like Buñuel, Richter, Man Ray, W.C. Fields, etc.

This doesn't mean that oneirism is only present in dreams. Aren't objects also endowed with symbolic life? There are a certain number of films, usually taken to be realist, in which a total gratuitousness of event, a constant arbitrariness of situation, cloaks everything in hallucination. Who can deny the purely oneiric qualities of *Night and the City, Le Jour se lève,*

The Big Sleep, or *Odd Man Out*? These films are only concerned at a secondary level with telling a story, they seek to attain a poetry drawn for the most part from everyday unreality, their narrative follows no logical convention and unfolds according to the rhythm we were speaking of above, one which doesn't submit to the slightest law. They transgress the current state of things due to the ability, conscious or not, of their creators: the latter intervene creatively in their own oeuvre, instead of making themselves the slaves of a one-off entertainment. These films are not, finally, the outcome of an accident, since authentic nature does not foist itself on the lens. A veritable surpassing of being, nature reveals herself to a few rare creators, who transfigure her by endowing her with the profundity that semblance itself never elicits. The rhythm of the dream, it has to be said, is that of life itself. This is why the idea of neorealism is a fraud: a real setting brings nothing to the director that he doesn't already possess deep within himself.[2] Certain constructed sets (those in *Les Portes de la nuit*, for instance) prove this, much more so than the impersonal ruins of a Rossellini or a De Sica. On the other hand, the exteriors rendered by Jules Dassin or Elia Kazan may possess the suggestive power of a nightmare. For the filmmaker, as for the painter, décor must be a state of mind. He can only recreate it, then, by bringing his personal dynamic to it; and the surreal vision will stand more chance of emerging here than in the passivity of simple transcription: a dream landscape is more readily remembered than a tourist postcard. When all is said and done, to refuse oneself the riches of transfiguration in the name of realism is to regress because of snobbery, lack of imagination, or penny-pinching.[3]

Time alone will tell when it comes to the merit of the differing statements of today: will future generations know more about us from our docu-

---

2 "If one finds something without looking for it, it's because one had searched for it without finding it," Egger wrote. Elia Kazan has described how, with the notion of realism in mind, he filmed an actual stunted tree: he'd had to search for this tree among many others because he knew this choice was to express a reality transcending the object itself. His genius having got the better of him, he believed he'd encountered the real, while in fact he'd re-created it according to his own lights. Likewise, every worthwhile utilization of a real setting presupposes an act of selection revealing an intention or an occasionally subconscious state of mind.

3 "To unduly mistrust, as people do, the practical virtue of imagination is to seek to deprive yourself at all costs of the assistance of electricity in the hope of reducing hydro-electric power to its absurd waterfall consciousness." (André Breton, *Il y aura une fois*.)

mentaries or from our works of art? I incline, and not from any spirit of paradox, toward the second. When it aspires to objectivity a visual statement ends up as mere abstraction, in the sterile sense of the word. Any purely documentary means of expression has its limits, extremely destructive ones at that.[4] The dream, on the other hand, does away with boundaries; far from being an end, it embraces in the complexity of its hidden workings the limitless solutions of an entire universe. It is a language superimposed on all the others, and directly linked to each of them.

Every film, then, ought to be a dream, coherent or not, that may, like automatic writing, reveal the creative imagination of its author. We would run the risk, at such a time, of having a cinema devoid of ambiguity, in which the contribution of genuine talent would be readily discernible, and in which the intricate expedients of the peddlers of celluloid would become what they deserve to be: lamentable failures which no amount of artifice can disguise.

From *L'Âge du cinéma* (Paris) 2 (May 1951): 3–6. Courtesy Robert Benayoun.

---

4 Roberto Rossellini is proof of this: seeking to move from the document to the surreal message, he gives us *Saint Francis, Fool of God,* a mammoth neorealist offering full of Saint-Sulpicien poesy.

The cinema, instrument of poetry

Luis Buñuel

The group of young people who make up the Committee for the Diffusion of Culture approached me and asked me to give a lecture. Although I was duly grateful for the attention they were focusing on me, my
reply was no: aside from the fact that I don't possess any of the qualities a
lecturer needs, I feel a particular sense of modesty about speaking in public. Inevitably, the person speaking attracts the combined attention of his
listeners, feels himself to be the target of all eyes. In my case I can't avoid a
certain confusion to do with the fear that I might be thought somewhat
exhibitionist, let's say. Although this idea of mine about the lecturer may
seem exaggerated or false, the fact of feeling it to be true obliged me to beg
that my period of exhibition be the briefest possible, and I suggested the
setting up of a round table at which a number of friends, coming from
different artistic and intellectual persuasions, could discuss *en famille* some
of the problems concerning the so-called seventh art: it was agreed, then,
that the theme would be "the cinema as artistic expression" or, more particularly, as an instrument of poetry, with all that this word possesses of a
liberating sense, of a subversion of reality, of a threshold at the marvelous
world of the subconscious, of a nonconformity with the mean-spirited
society surrounding us.

Octavio Paz has said, "It suffices for a chained man to close his eyes for
him to have the power to make the world explode," and I, paraphrasing
him, add, it would suffice for the white eyelid of the screen to reflect the
light proper to it to blow up the universe. But for the moment we can sleep
in peace, since the light of cinema is being conveniently meted out and
enchained. In none of the traditional arts does there exist a disproportion
as great as in the cinema between possibility and realization. In acting in a
direct way on the spectator, presenting him with human beings and con-

112

crete things, in isolating him, thanks to the silence, the darkness, from what we might call his psychic habitat, the cinema becomes capable of captivating him as no other human expression can. But it is capable of brutalizing him like no other, too. Unfortunately, the vast majority of current cinemas appear to have no other mission than this: their screens wallow in the moral and intellectual vacuity on which the cinema thrives, a cinema that limits itself to imitating the novel or the theater, with the difference that its means are less rich when it comes to expressing different psychologies; they repeat ad infinitum the same stories the nineteenth century grew tired of telling and that are still being repeated in the contemporary novel.

A moderately cultured person would fling aside in disdain the book that contained any of the plots the major films relate to us. And yet, seated comfortably in the darkness of the cinema, dazzled by a light and movement that exert an almost hypnotic power over him, attracted by the interest of the human face and ultrarapid changes of location, that same more or less cultured person placidly accepts the hoariest of clichés.

By virtue of such hypnagogic inhibition the movie spectator loses a high percentage of his intellectual faculties. I'll give you a concrete example: the film *Detective Story*, or *Hell's Antechamber*. The plot structure is perfect, the director magnificent, the actors extraordinary, the realization inspired, etc., etc. Fine, all that talent, all that savoir-faire, all the paraphernalia that the machinery of the film entails have been put at the service of a stupid story notable for its moral baseness. This puts me in mind of that extraordinary Opus II machine, a gigantic piece of equipment, manufactured from the finest quality steel, with a thousand complicated gears, tubes, pressure gauges, dials, as precise as a wristwatch, as imposing as an ocean liner, whose sole purpose was to frank the mail.

Mystery, the essential element of any work of art, is for the most part lacking in films. Scriptwriters, directors, and producers take a lot of care not to disturb our peace of mind by opening the marvelous window of the screen onto the liberating world of poetry. On that screen they prefer to depict issues that might be an extension of our ordinary lives, to repeat the same drama a thousand times, to make us forget the long hours of our workaday world. And all this, as is natural, fully sanctioned by conventional morality, by governmental and international censorship, by religion, presided over by good taste and embellished with white humor and the other prosaic imperatives of reality.

If we wish to see good cinema, rarely will we encounter it in major productions or in those others that come sanctioned by film criticism and the backing of the public. The personal story, the private drama of an individual, cannot, I believe, interest anyone worthy of living his era to the full; if the spectator shares something of the joys, sorrows, or anxieties of a screen character, it must be because he sees reflected therein the joys, sorrows, or anxieties of society as a whole, and therefore his own as well. The lack of work, insecurity of life, fear of war, social injustice, etc., are things that, in affecting all people today, also affect the spectator; but that Mr. X might not be happy at home and so seeks a woman friend to distract him, a friend who he will finally abandon in order to go back to his altruistic wife, is doubtless all very moral and edifying but it leaves us completely indifferent.

At times the cinematic essence gushes forth unwontedly in some anodyne film, in a slapstick comedy or poverty-row serial. Man Ray has said, in a phrase redolent with meaning: "the worst films I might have seen, the ones that send me off to sleep, always contain five marvelous minutes, and the best, the most celebrated ones, *only* have five minutes worth seeing; that is, in both good and bad movies, and over and above, or despite, the good intentions of their makers, cinematic poetry strives to come to the surface and show itself."

The cinema is a marvelous and dangerous weapon if a free spirit wields it. It's the finest instrument there is for expressing the world of dreams, of the emotions, of instinct. Because of the way it works, the mechanism for producing film images is, of all the means of human expression, the one that is most like the mind of man or, better still, the one which best imitates the functioning of the mind while dreaming. J.B. Brunius draws our attention to the fact that the darkness that gradually invades the auditorium is the same as closing the eyes: next, on the screen, and within man, the darkness of unconsciousness begins to make inroads; as in the dream, the images appear and disappear by means of dissolves or fades-in and -out; time and space become flexible, contract and stretch at will, chronological order and relative values of duration no longer correspond to reality; cyclical action may elapse in a few minutes or in several centuries; the movements speed up; the time lags.

THE CINEMA, INSTRUMENT OF POETRY

The cinema seems to have been invented in order to express the subconscious life that so deeply penetrates poetry with its roots; despite that, it is almost never used for such ends. Among the modern tendencies of cinema the best known is the so-called neorealist one. Its films offer up slices of real life to the eyes of the spectator, with characters taken from the street and even with authentic buildings and interiors. Aside from a few exceptions, and I cite especially *The Bicycle Thief,* neorealism has done nothing to emphasize what is particular about cinema; namely, mystery and the fantastic. What use are all those visual trappings to us if the situations, the motives that drive the characters, their reactions, the plots themselves are modeled on the most sentimental and conformist literature? The only interesting contribution that not neorealism but Zavattini personally has made is raising the anodyne act to the level of a dramatic category. In *Umberto D.,* one of the more interesting films neorealism has come up with, a domestic servant takes a whole reel—ten minutes, that is—to perform actions that until quite recently would have seemed unworthy of the screen. We see the servant go into the kitchen, light her stove, put a pan on it, repeatedly splash water from a pitcher onto a line of ants marching in Indian file toward some food, give a thermometer to an old man who isn't feeling well, etc., etc. Despite the triviality of these situations, the action is followed with interest and even with suspense.

Neorealism has introduced into cinematic expression a number of elements that enrich its language, yet nothing more. Neorealist reality is incomplete, official—reasonable, above all else; but poetry, mystery, that which completes and extends immediate reality, is completely absent from its productions. It confuses ironic fantasy with the fantastic and black humor.

"The most admirable thing about the fantastic," André Breton has said, "is that the fantastic doesn't exist, everything is real." Speaking with Zavattini himself a while ago, I expressed my nonconformity with neorealism: we were eating together, and the first example that occurred to me was the glass of wine from which I happened to be drinking. For a neorealist, I said to him, a glass is a glass and nothing more: we witness how they remove it from the cupboard, fill it with drink, take it to the kitchen to be washed, where the maid servant breaks it, for which she could be dismissed from the house or not, etc. Contemplated by different people, that same glass can be a thousand different things, however, because each man charges what he is looking at with emotion, and nobody sees it as it is but how his desires and state of mind wish to see it. I advocate a cinema that makes me see that kind of glass, because such a cinema will give me an integral vision of reality, augment my knowledge of things and of people, and open up to me the marvelous world of the unknown, all the things I cannot read about in the daily papers or encounter in the street.

Don't think from what I've been saying that I'm only advocating a cinema devoted exclusively to the expression of the fantastic or to mystery, an escapist cinema that, disdaining our everyday world, would seek to submerge us in the unconscious world of the dream. Albeit very briefly, I indicated just now the crucial importance I give to the film that tackles contemporary man's major problems, not considered in isolation as a unique case, but in his relations with other men. I make my own the words of Engels, who defines the novelist's function thus (for novelist read filmmaker): "The novelist will have acquitted himself honorably if by conscientiously describing the real mutual relations he breaks down the conventionalized illusions dominating them, shatters the optimism of the bourgeois world, causes doubt about the eternal validity of the existing order, and this without directly offering a solution or even, under some circumstances, taking an ostensible partisan stand."

This text was first published in *Cuadernos de la Universidad de México* (Mexico City) 4 (December 1958) and appears in J. Francisco Aranda, *Luis Buñuel. Biografía crítica*, 2d ed. (Barcelona: Lumen, 1975), 385–391. Copyright © Herederos Luis Buñuel. Courtesy Juan Luis Buñuel. Much of Buñuel's argument echoes the *L'Âge du cinéma* line (1951–52) as well as the ideas developed by Jacques B. Brunius in *En marge du cinéma français* (Paris: Arcanes, 1954).

Malombra, aura
of absolute love

The Romanian Surrealist Group

Malombra or love and nothing else.
The convulsion of beauty, the feebleness of memory, the color of regret, the charm of life, the mediumism of motion, the rarity of love, the madness of the senses, the beauty of madness, the sadness of lakes, lunar influence, life after death, the nobility of lust, the burning of a glance, the memory of madness, the future of the past, the somnambulism of thought, the death of the landscape, action at a distance, skimmed sleep, the lived dream, the arrogance of sacrilege, the lust of hysteria, the refusal to live, the beauty of hysteria, the beauty of beauty: in Malombra.

Never has the difficulty of raising revolution to the heights of poetry so confounded us, seduced us so. Never has it been so obvious in our eyes that in the flashing beauty of the woman destined for love there resides the concentration of the universe's most restless dialectical moments. Never, finally, has the thread which passes through beings seemed more slender to us, more fragile than when it ran through those bits of lace, movements, glances, in which the very power that animates the world has come to make its peace in the irony of passion.

"Do you recall that evening, Renato? The lake, the lanterns, the far-off sounds. . . . It's strange what happens to me, I don't belong to this world. You haven't understood me, you don't understand me because you don't know. Today I depart for an unknown destiny, unknown reader, goodbye."

So brief the eye was blinded by it, like an edgy scorpion for all that, the shadow passed through the gray diurnal light like a wound, a ruin, a sleepy waterfall. The air filled with terrible animals, and violet seas far beyond the safe limits of the globe were rocking their entrancing excrescences; the madness of being in two places at once was instantly broken in that era so favorable to triumphs of the imagination, and with it the moorings chaining reason.

The dinner on the revolving table, the murder without wound, the magnetic waterfall, the mystery of the figure eleven, the ship bed and the lily, the underbelly of the storm, storms everywhere, the limitless parks, deferred conversations.

The scenes in which Malombra gives herself to her lover at night by the lake's edge, in which she crosses the water filled with a hostile coldness toward the man awaiting her, in which she gives in to a lucid hysteria beneath the gray winds that put the torches out, are the triumph of what we like to call absolute love.

The burn and the search for the burning.

A character, hand bloodstained, has thrown himself into that immense pallor, and beneath the melancholy genitals the fodder crops were propagating, embalmed like the piddocks the ocean habitually visits, among so many superstitions, determinisms, errors, and origins, among so many accusations and so many symptoms of rage. This hand is the burning lymph, the Nordic sand momentarily solidified by the magic lines of the mirrors, in their conversations about the stars.

"Do you remember everything? Everything. I don't remember a thing. But I know that moment had to come, Cecilia. What a world you lived in. I'm suffocating. The lake can only be seen from the left wing of the chateau."

In the object Malombra: interrogations by the lake, fragile movements in the shadows, games as symptomatic provocation, disgust for everything that isn't love, the encounter in the present of the past.

And, unable to move or speak, she lies on a litter, covered in lace and veils. The only things on the vast manège were hypnotized horses that leapt over obstacles, and lakes extending over thousands of leagues were making their necks transparent; so close were the fires of our nerves the woman was touching them with the tips of her eyelashes: they were entering her eyes and exiting in her tears.

"Cecilia, I, Cecilia, have come with my lover to see you die, to see you die, see you die. There is so much darkness in my soul, so much sadness. I'm on the point of turning into stone, colder than stone."

Alongside the love of the heart, the love of the senses, relative love, there is also that sort of love in which absolutely everything withdraws, is concentrated, in which life is only the auxiliary wave of this invincible passion. After Nadja, Dora, and Matilda, Malombra in turn enters the eternal regions where desire, poetry, and chance restore the passage from life to an entirely dialectical, inevitably sensible life.

Obscure oppression was to announce its return before the curtain fell: but the unshakable atheism of any hysterical horror of living rejects the religious idea (which tries vainly to worm its way into passion) previously reduced to dust.

The pure love of absolute essence is consciousness become foreign to itself. It remains to be examined more closely how the quality of being the other is determined, and one must consider it solely in conjunction with that other. At first sight, pure love appears to have only the world of the effective for itself, but being itself an escape from this world and having the determinable character of its opposition as well, it bears this effectiveness in its bosom.

Lilium tigrinum can only grow on perfectly even ground, ideally the fine sand of a beach. Her laterality is at once gauche and inferior, her amorous thoughts underline the striking homology of the Serpent and hemlock. Her pulse is feeble, her nails are blue, she usually lies on her back, head thrown back, eyes closed. When she emerges from her moral torpor and reopens her eyes, she strikes down all who surrounded her with their wily indifference. Where the separation of human beings according to the violence of their desire meets the black secrets of the spagyric,[1] the gaze of this woman—whose rare incarnations still guide us toward precipices of velvet—stamps love with its unalterable call.

Keen nerves, flashing cats, solar migraine, cries, twisted arms, the reeling step on waves of crystals, explosive stammering, anguished cries, bottomless sighs, occult rage, the horror of living, raucous cries, bloody hair, dresses cut by a razor, the suicide exhibition, the speed of crazy glances, arrogant imposture, murderous scandal, lost cries, voluptuous spasms—all this and the pallor of silence too will never be enough to express the intractable defiance of all that is not shot through with the magnetism of eternal love.

O Malombra, *mal d'ombre.*

---

1 [The spagyric: alchemical methods of producing transmutations, mainly into gold or silver. —*Trans.*]

Inspired by the involuntarily Surrealist film *Malombra* (Mario Soldati, 1942), drafted by the Romanian Surrealist Group—Gherasim Luca, Gellu Naum, Paul Paun, Virgil Teodorescu, and Trost—and published in Bucharest in 1947. Reprinted in *L'Âge du cinéma* (Paris) 4–5 (August-November 1951): 34–36.

Data toward the irrational enlargement of a film: *The Shanghai Gesture*

The Surrealist Group

With the participation of Jean-Louis Bédouin (JLB), Robert Benayoun (RB), Georges Goldfayn (GG), Adonis Kyrou (AK), Gérard Legrand (GL), Benjamin Péret (BP), Bernard Roger (BR), Jean Schuster (JS), Anne Seghers (AS), Toyen (T), Michel Zimbacca (MZ)

I n its anguished abandon poetic thought comes up against the object, the line between the external and the internal is blurred, the screen separating them, furiously lacerated, goes by the board. Everything encourages the belief that the objectification of desire has taken place. This was made clear by the experimental researches on the irrational knowledge of the object undertaken in 1933.[1]

It seemed feasible to us to extend this experiment to a cinematic plane. This time it was a matter of jeopardizing the very notion of the world of art by revealing how it might be emptied of subjective content, further elaborated, and advantageously replaced within an objective compass, subsequently being integrated within the universal rhythm of time and space.

By a simple strategy of poetic thought the object,[2] freed of its rational characteristics, begins to assume the multiple reflections of the perceptible world, is set, not at all disoriented, in all the rings of reality, suffers, if it is a chair, from the haughty indifference of garnets, grips the seaweed bouquet abandoned by the cormorant, and perhaps will eventually die in a Dutch kitchen when by a remote chance we are no longer able to dream. Never, I maintain, has what depressing good sense calls the impossible

---

1 Cf. *Le Surréalisme au service de la révolution* 6.
2 Or the work of art considered as an object.

seemed more normal, more REAL to us; never have standards, weights, and measures, the "I call a spade a spade" mentality been invested with so much derisory impudence for us as today.

I must point out that the responses below are spontaneous, if not completely automatic, the circumstances in which the various experiences took place precluding almost all formal research. Nevertheless, we have agreed to suppress replies which from this point of view seemed of a doubtful character. This was our sole criterion for elimination.

1. What ought to happen when Mother Gin-Sling comes down to the gaming room after the revolver shot?
Fire breaks out in a mountain hut (JLB). Loaded revolvers are passed around (RB). Mother Gin-Sling masturbates ferociously over the suicide's corpse (GG). Boris's revolver appears on the dish of a pair of scales (which one does not see) (GL). A lion drops from the ceiling on to the gaming table (BR). Everyone drips and melts like candles (AS). The gaming room becomes a diamond worn by Ouspenskaya in her youth (MZ).

2. In what form and at what moment in the story does the coolie appear?
He was the owner of the forge the favored woman approached to make the Iron Mask (JLB). He raped Messalina at Suburre (RB). In the guise of the Divine Marquis he worked out plans for the destruction of Carthage (AK). He was the man from Varennes (JS). He contributed to the abolition of slavery in Egypt (MZ).

3. What dress would Mother Gin-Sling have worn if she had been the Princess of Lamballe about to be executed?
Her dress would have been black; she would have worn a wig that bore a second reproduction of her face (RB). A very simple dress made from Poppy's hair which she would have cropped close (AK). From greenish veils of water, with a belt of white hair (BR). A dress of shed rattlesnake skin, transparent, with gray eyelets where her breasts and genitals are (JS). A cloak of feathers (AS). The robes of an English magistrate (MZ).

4. At what moment should a snowfall take place?
It should happen upside down, from bottom to top, at the moment the

women are hoisted up in their cages (RB). At the moment Omar uncovers Poppy's shoulder (AK). During the final long shot, but the snow melts immediately (GL). During Poppy's jealous outburst about the powder puff to Omar (JS). As Dixie waits for food (AS). When the black swan breaks its two black eggs (T). When Omar removes Poppy's shoulder strap (MZ).

5. When is a river seen in the film?
When Omar lowers then raises the dress at Poppy's shoulder (JLB). At the moment Omar expresses the desire to see Poppy's hair down (AK). As Sir Guy Charteris is about to replace the fur on Poppy's shoulders (GL). When Omar opens the door, it rushes across the gaming room (BR). As Mother Gin-Sling goes down to the gaming room, a river, which she holds firmly in check, follows her (AS).

6. Whose dream does Maria Ouspenskaya belong to, and what is this dream?
Omar's dream. He finds himself in a cable car and sees this person behind a window (JLB). She is part of Charteris's dream; in it she represents the mother of all the petite Chinese women serving at the dinner table whom the worthy functionary raped (AK). A coolie's dream. In the midst of numerous broken windows Maria Ouspenskaya leads the Chinese maids toward an immense wicker cage (GL). It is the pianist's dream. He dreams that his game leg has run away: this is it (BR).

7. Who was Omar's mother?
The last of Bluebeard's wives (GG). Obviously, Matilda (from *The Monk*)! (AK). The female shark Maldoror made love to (JS). Mother Gin-Sling (GL). A telephonist from Breslau (BP). Mother Gin-Sling (MZ).

8. How does Omar exist outside of the film?
He moves around a lot, takes care to dress differently in each town, borrows only sailing boats whose compasses he sets out of true (JLB). He spends vast sums on the clothes of unknown females who abandon him almost immediately. Later on, they all become famous (RB). He passes the greater part of his time trying to ascertain the exact age of Chinese eggs (GL). He gets drunk every Saturday, plays tennis, snores, and has a cantankerous personality but is dominated by any woman he gets to know (BP). By prostitution (MZ).

9. What was on Mother Gin-Sling's menu for dinner?
It's obvious the week's suicides were cannibalized; seaweed enlivened many
of the dishes. There were brimstone candies, too (RB). Lacquered duck;
swallow's-nest soup, black eggs, shark fins with California wine. For des-
sert, babies' fingers with stewed strawberries (BP). Headless birds, a green
velvet butterfly with watery eyes, three antelopes which fled the table (BR).
Alligator eggs in rum, earlobes of children from the European Concession
in Shanghai; the juice of elephants' livers solidified by the gusts of wind
collected in the sails of all the junks of the Blue River, sautéed potatoes,
swallow's-blood wine (JS). A tongue two meters long (T).

10. What does the outside of the casino look like?
A grotto stuffed with stalactites and stalagmites on which petrified and
luminous seabirds are perched (JLB). The Palace of Versailles (with a dungeon for the Dragon) (RB). The casino, bang in the middle of a gas plant,
must have primary access via a steep stairway spiraling in the interior of a
pit, and secondary entrances decorated with colonnades and surrounded
by cypress trees (GG). A building whose upper story (comprising a chapel
in Portuguese style) has been completely burnt out, leaving only a black-
ened but intact iron framework (GL). The façade is sculpted of dragons
with real feathers changed daily, spitting real fire which is kept going in-
ternally, making the access paths soft (BP). Twisted columns climb the façade
and are hidden by hair; no windows (BR). It reproduces the outside of the
Comédie Française as seen from Alfred de Musset's statue (IS). The trunk of
a baobab tree (AS). A monk's cell (T). The Himalayas (MZ).

11. What should the casino chips be made of?
The breasts of pygmy women like the Jivaros (JLB). Hosts consecrated to
Satan during extremely lubricious black masses (GG). Black, yellow, and
white men's ears for the large amounts; teeth for the smallest and nails for
the middling sums (BP). Red nails (BR). False mustaches; brown: $1000,
red: $100, blond: $10, white: $1 (JS). Hosts (T). Burglar alarms (MZ).

12. What should the door Omar opens at the beginning of the film reveal?
An aquarium at the bottom of which lie Spanish galleons and bishops'
crosses (JLB). An arid desert of violet sand dotted with Greek temples dedi-

cated to love (GG). A seabed abyss in which people move slowly like divers (AK). A small and bare room wherein Omar would pass several minutes a day meditating (GL). A laundromat where women gossip in front of the washing machines (BP). A boat in flames out at sea (BR). A labyrinth (AS). A stove (T). The Forty Thieves' cave (MZ).

13. Between who or what should an accidental encounter occur at the gaming table?
The Princess of Clèves and M. de Nemours (JLB). A feather from the bird of paradise and a whip that once belonged to a follower of Cleopatra (GG). The pearl necklace Poppy is selling and Mother Gin-Sling's neck (AK). Dixie Pomeroy's powder puff and an enormous poppy seed that engulfs everything in black and white dust (GL). The first Montgolfier balloon and a first edition of Erasmus' *In Praise of Folly* (JS). A piece of paper in flames and a box of matches (T).

14. Where is the opium den to be found?
At Sir Guy Charteris's, but without his knowledge (GL). On the terrace, with musicians below within earshot of the smokers (BP). Behind Omar's bedroom, the entrance hidden by the cushions he lies stretched out on (BR). Under a gaming table, between the croupier's feet (JS). In Charteris's office (AS).

15. What is the dominant color of the gaming room?
Flesh-colored (JLB). Scarlet and black (RB). The color of Violette Nozière's eyes (GG). A dazzling gold (AK). Blue-green (GL). Violet (BP). Gilt and dark red (BR). Yellow ochre (JS). Melted gold (AS).

16. In what location outside of the action does the film take place?
In the petrified forest, the courtyard of the old Hôtel de Sens (JLB). On an oblong beach, dotted with totem poles and without an ocean (RB). In the Facteur Cheval's Palace (AK). In Paris, in front of the Panthéon (GL). At the base of the Pyramids (BP). Beneath the Sphinx (BR). In a poor village in Savoy, accessible only on donkey-back (JS). The Place du Tertre (AS). In a mouth (T). In the east (MZ).

17. How and when did you come into the film?
At the moment the curtain is raised, to stop it from being completely lifted
(JLB). In the form of a carved animal by the door; I blew with all my might
so that the revolver sitting on the polished table pointed in the right direction (RB). I cut the wires that hold the girls' cages shut (BR). During the
board meeting I gave Charteris a light which blew up the room (JS). As the
baskets went up I took the money they held (T).

18. What are the obligations of a doctor of nothing?
To search out the tangential point of the asymptote and the coordinate for
as long as he lives (GG). To resuscitate Saturday evening suicides for a short
time (GL). To dream the film (BR). To predict the past (JS). To roll and
unroll himself in a carpet (T). To make things turn that don't turn (MZ).

19. Who is found inside the dragon on Chinese New Year?
Madame Putiphar (JLB). Savonarola (RB). The Hindu policeman from the
beginning (GL). Me (BR). Benjamin Péret (JS). Lacenaire (AS). Two lovers
(T). A real dragon (MZ).

20. What is Poppy's perversion?
Clasping an octopus between stocking and thigh (JLB). Stretched full length
on the gaming table, she detaches pearl after pearl from her necklace (RB).
She has no sexual perversions, simply an intense sensuality (AK). Sodomy
of a self-confessed, mildly masochistic nature (GL). Purposeless masturbation (MZ).

21. Where did Charteris and Mother Gin-Sling meet?
In fact, they never did meet; all the rest is a misunderstanding (RB). On a
high mountain in the corner of a glacier, Mother Gin-Sling being chipped
off the glacier (BR). In a Buddhist temple where she was a bronze Shiva. By
lightly stroking the bridge of the statue's nose up and down Charteris transformed it into a woman (JS). In a fairground flea circus (T). Their meeting
caused the famous Japanese earthquake of 1923 (MZ).

22. How might the film be symbolized ?
By a salamander, the one Benvenuto Cellini saw (RB). A giant nettle in

flower (GL). A steel blade protruding slightly from a window (BR). By premature baldness (JS). By a snail (AS). By a town inhabited exclusively by hands (MZ).

23. Who is the deserter?
Obviously, Charteris (Mother Gin-Sling is his accomplice) (BR). The Russian barman (GG). Sir Guy Charteris and, if you like, the barman (AK). The barman (GL). The man with the crutch (JS). The barman (MZ).

24. What don't we see?
The scene deep in the forest, even though it is the one that determines all the others (JLB). The death of Mother Gin-Sling, who ultimately lets herself be swallowed by the dragon (AK). The flight of swallows and the swimming of sea cucumbers above and below the sea, far from Shanghai, over which Poppy's plane returns behind time (GL). The sea (BR). The Dunsinane Forest (MZ).

25. What is the pearl thief's role?
He writes the verses Omar recites (JLB). He serves Mother Gin-Sling as a bedside mat (in any case, he can't dive any more because of his lungs) (RB). The pearl thief (who deflowers Poppy Smith) is the somber, bearded man who passes before Van Alst and looks scornfully at him (GG). He sculpts the three women he had gone to find in a place he cannot name (AK). He knows that Poppy is Mother Gin-Sling's daughter, but it is in vain that he tries to get into the casino: he is of dubious origin and doesn't know Chinese (GL). He is the one who gives the order to execute a number of men in the streets of Shanghai (cf. the newsreels of two years ago) (JS). He is the caged girls' lover (AS). He massacres no one, he is at a show (MZ).

Notes
The mystery of the coolie whose brief appearances add still more to the enigmatic quality of the film is obviously revealed. He is a violent person (JLB, RB, AK) and his immediate past is marked by a revolutionary activity (AK, JS, MZ) which is openly declared.

The last image the world had of the Princess of Lamballe was, as everyone knows, of her long hair. It is surprising that hair should come four times into the makeup of the dress Mother Gin-Sling would have worn in the above circumstances (RB, AK, BR, MZ (1)). This relation seems too indirect not to be unconscious.

Snow must fall when eroticism becomes manifest (RB, AK, JS, MZ). Note the clearly symbolic "inversion" of Benayoun's, which considerably reinforces the eroticism of the sequence. As for the appearance of the river, the same observations apply (JLB, AK). It is obvious that Anne Seghers was much taken with Mother Gin-Sling, whom she considers as the grand organizer of unnatural forces.

Ouspenskaya is intimately linked with transparency, glass, diamonds (JLB, GL, MZ, question 1).

Paradoxically, Omar, beyond the film's confines, is the victim of women (RB, BP).

The meal offered by Mother Gin-Sling is anthropophagic (RB, BP, JS).

The outside of the casino is, or was, prone to fire (GL, BP). For some, it has the appearance of a natural phenomenon (JLB, AS, MZ); for others, it draws something from known architecture (RB, JS).

Human anatomical parts are recommended as casino chips (JLB, BP, BR), together with hosts (GG, T).

The door Omar opens at the beginning of the film generally reveals a liquid (JLB, AK, BR).

The encounter is fortuitous in only four cases (GG, GL, JS, T), but erotic for Bédouin, Kyrou, and Legrand.

The setting beyond the film is a strange landscape (JLB, RB, AK). It is characterized by a well-known monument (AK, GL, BP, BR); Péret and Roger situate it in almost the same place, in Egypt; Anne Seghers and I see it somewhere high up; while Toyen and Zimbacca have only an imprecise idea of its position.

Within the possibilities for intervention each one consents to, a desire for occultation becomes obvious (JLB) but also a tendency toward terrorism (RB, JS), theft (T), and struggle against repressive forces (BR).

The obligations of a doctor of nothing revolve, as one might have foreseen, around a quest for the impossible (GG, GL, JS, MZ).

A poet is inside the dragon (BR, JS, AS); its end is tragic (RB, AS). Toyen and Zimbacca, doubtless reacting against the artificial side to disguise, insist on its authenticity.

The meeting of Charteris and Mother Gin-Sling somewhat overthrows the established order. Three replies prove they lived for *amour fou* (BR, JS, MZ). For Benayoun and Anne Seghers the film is subsumed under animal symbolism, for Legrand vegetable symbolism. Roger and Zimbacca assign it a perfectly oneiric symbol.

The majority identify the barman as the deserter (GG, AK, MZ). Nevertheless, Kyrou's reply is ambivalent and concurs with Benayoun's in designating Charteris.

What we don't see happens in a forest (JLB, MZ) and in the sea (GL, BR). We do not see much of the pearl fisher who nonetheless plays an extremely important role in the lives of the principal protagonists (JLB, RB, GG, AK, AS).

In all honesty, it would be false to bring the creative re-creation of a film to a conclusion. Our only aim was to implement a modern critical attitude (objective-internal,[3] affective, dialectically opposable to creative intent thanks to the unlimited exchange of perceptible values over and above traditional critical attitudes, which are subject to aesthetic and technical reference).

In this aim, may it please the professional skeptics, we think we have succeeded.

Jean Schuster

From *L'Âge du cinéma* (Paris) 4–5 (August-November 1951): 53–58. *The Shanghai Gesture* was directed by Josef von Sternberg in 1941.

---

3 To the notion of objectivity remains associated the (Jesuit) one of impartiality. On this count objective criticism clips its own wings through compromise, the gravest and commonest consisting in rescuing certain debased subjects from disfavor under the pretext that their artistic manufacture is skillful. One has heard it all before; the beautiful cathedrals, the talent of Rouault, the cinematic genius of Milestone. No, no, and no. Once again form is separated from substance to legitimize the reactionary work (from Christian exegesis to socialist realism), enabling it to accomplish its putrescent ends. We believe that the "better" a film is made the more dangerous it becomes. It is essential constantly to put the spectator on his guard so that his admiration for this successful traveling shot or that well-staged crowd scene does not for a moment prevent him from discerning the spidery shadow of the Vatican or Stalinist mercenary in the background.

So-called objectivity, which is only the so-called synthesis of contradictory opinions, is an attack on the security of the spirit. It is a form of expression opposed to authentic subjectivity. Real critical objectivity is what is produced spontaneously when a number of people who share certain fundamental beliefs are led to judge a spectacle or an activity, artistic or otherwise. It is the third term which results from the objective-subjective opposition. This is what we mean by objective-internal.

The film and I

Ado Kyrou

When watching a film I inevitably perform an act of will on it, hence I transform it, and from its given elements make it *my* thing, draw snippets of knowledge from it and see better into myself. Certain films (it doesn't matter what kind, only a detail, an atmosphere, a feeling of déjà vu comes into it) are especially mine. I could take them as they are and just add my signature. Few people would understand these "ready-made" films, the perturbation my sensibility brings to them being wholly personal. One of Harry Piel's old films set in Spain, Anatole Litvak's tearjerker, *The Sisters,* Herman Shumlin's pretentious *Watch on the Rhine,* Helmut Käutner's *Auf wiedersehen Franziska,* these are some of my ready-mades. I could not begin to explain the reasons why since, contrary to Duchamp's objects, I am not at all sure that these films, generally extremely bad ones, can have an objective value; or then I would have to work on them, make some changes in the montage, cut, accentuate, or tone down the sound track, finally *interpret* them before my subjective vision could be objectified.

. . . .

In cases like this nothing differentiates the *beautiful* from the *ugly,* and I'd go as far as to say that nowhere else does the *ugly* (or what passes for it) come so close to the sublime. The *unheimlich,* the uncanny, has some dazzling surprises in store, and objective chance arranges for the most exalting encounters between screen and spectator. Subterranean air currents blow through the cinemas.

Through interpretation new films could be born that render their mystery visible to all, and this would prepare the films for further interpretation. The experiment would be thrilling. A single film would be entrusted to many people, each of whom, seeing it a different way, would transform it so as to underline *what they see in it,* and this new vision would be entrusted to another person, and so on. These liberated images would fill up the world and finally pulverize all antinomies. The efforts of Paul Gilson and, more recently, Heisler and Goldfayn, bring together the *interpretation* and *re-creation* of a new film from disparate elements.

The transformation of a film can be obtained in different ways. Man Ray has told me that if a film bores him he spontaneously transforms it by blinking his eyes rapidly, by moving his fingers in front of his eyes, making grilles of them, or placing a semitransparent cloth over his face. In these ways—and dozens of others—characters on screen who lack all mystery acquire a supplementary dimension, and the mechanical perturbation of their existence becomes a powerful stimulus for the imagination. For my part, it has often occurred to me during the showing of a displeasing film to call recollections of another film or novel to the rescue and to willfully mix characters and intrigues together. The result is always extraordinary, and in the encountering of two contrary elements new and magnificent images are created. It must be said that the darkness of cinema auditoriums, the obviously unusual atmosphere of people of shadow speaking and living for immobile people of flesh and blood, creates an ambiance particularly propitious for this kind of outstripping of the cinematic spectacle, and hence of life itself.

Like all Surrealists, André Breton could not but be sensitive to the magical specificity of the darkened cinema: "With Jacques Vaché we would settle down to dinner in the orchestra of the former Théâtre des Folies-Dramatiques, opening cans, slicing bread, uncorking bottles, and talking in ordinary tones, as if around a table, to the great amazement of the spectators, who dared not say a word" (*Nadja*). The intrusion of a novel sense of the strange into the strangeness of the cinema acquires unsuspected and enormous dimensions. The film that powerlessly attends Breton and Vaché's meal or that unwillfully mingles with the spectator's imagination and his life cannot but take on a Surrealist aspect.

. . . .

Critics of manifest reality are journalists. It's useless to dwell on this profession. . . . Critics of latent reality (and therefore much more than critics) are poets. Going beyond the journalist stage, cinema critics must become poets. The manifest aspect of films rarely being the occasion for the exaltation of the spirit, it is their latent content that must be prospected. Let's see the most popular films with new eyes and find the most unexpected riches there, let's be carried along as much by the machinations of the

131

Black Dragon (*G-Men vs. The Black Dragon*) as we are by the festivities in R. Roussel's *Impressions of Africa*.

The poetic, frenetic kind of criticism that takes into account everything invisible, everything mysterious in a film is the only one in which necessity must surface. The critic must begin with his fiercely personal impression, the shock produced by the encounter of the film-object and the self-subject, in order to objectivize its hidden beauties.

The first part of this process, the subjective-Surrealist form of criticism, holds considerable interest, not so much as criticism but as a means of personal knowledge. Often, when leaving a film that has set something off inside me, I sit down at the first café table I come to and write down, automatically, my impressions. Without searching for ideas or a logical sequence, I fill page after page. Extremely curious relations are established between the film and myself, unexpected, dazzling explanations offer themselves, precise details are given about problems going beyond the film and my manifest life as well. Unknown sources of illumination shed light on shadowy regions. Knowledge, the supreme form of all activity, seems within our grasp.

I consider this practice to be as important as the transcription of dreams on waking. In its raw state such criticism can only be of relative value for a public that demands enlightenment about a film, not the personal impressions of the critic, but such texts would be of capital importance for the improved comprehension of certain people who particularly interest us. What a film brings to the surface, as does a dream, are elements for the understanding of our friends as much as for ourselves. Furthermore, I think that all true criticism interesting itself in the secret aspect of a film must begin by making a personal, automatic critique. Based on such a text, it would have the necessary guidelines for the objectivization of impressions and for the analysis of the total film.

Surrealism seized on objects and events to draw enrichment and light from them. Words have lost their restricted sense, they "make love." There is still a lot of work to be done on the cinematic fact. Images can make love, too.

From Ado Kyrou, *Le Surréalisme au cinéma*, 2d ed. (Paris: Le Terrain Vague, 1963), 271–272, 279–280. Courtesy Joëlle Losfeld and Le Terrain Vague. The Paul Gilson film is *Manières de croire*, "film de montage" (1930). Gilson wrote the delightful memoir, *Cine*magique* (Paris: André Bonne, 1951).

Cinemage

Man Ray

The worst films I've ever seen, the ones that send me to sleep, contain ten or fifteen marvelous minutes. The best films I've ever seen only contain ten or fifteen valid ones.

That observation, made on many occasions during my ten years' stay in Hollywood, never provoked comment there, was politely ignored, or simply misunderstood. When I repeated it for the first time in Paris, it cheered me to see several gentlemen take it seriously enough to comment on and analyze it. It is a caprice, of course, and my intention in making it was to provoke discussion. I think I've succeeded in this!

Whatever my convictions, they are obviously extremely personal, biased even; besides, like the prophecies an oracle makes, you can't analyze a caprice.

I referred to ten or fifteen minutes because the few films I made some years ago were never longer than that, and it's on that basis that I craved the indulgence of my audience, in promising not to inflict an excess of footage on it. Since two people rarely agree on the merits of a film, unless they share a similar point of view or have been influenced by an astute publicity campaign, I have long cast doubt on the value of all criticism.

As for being a purist to the extent of preferring old, silent, black-and-white film, this criticism is purely arbitrary because I insisted from the start on sound accompaniment, longed for the use of color and three-dimensions, even hoped for the addition of the sensations of warmth, cold, taste, and smell to film, so that the spectator, coming out into the fresh air at last, could be totally in enjoyment of all his senses, with the added advantage of being the principal actor!

One of my critics points out that the cinema is situated somewhere between literature and the plastic arts. I thought that today the cinema was unanimously recognized as the junction of the seven arts, an opinion I share as well. The critic also states that I was a photographer before being a Surrealist which, he says, explains everything. Excuse me, but that explains nothing unless it be that it is possible to explain an explanation. In fact, I was a Surrealist before being a photographer, and I flatter myself in having remained a Surrealist in the profoundest sense of the word, as defined by those who so admirably set out its principles, including the one which makes of Surrealism a product of every age.

If my quarrel with films seems principally founded on their length, as my critic-accountants suggest, it is simply because almost without exception these films cannot be seen twice over without giving rise to the nostalgic sensation that emanates from an old, yellowed photograph. At least, you can instantly rid yourself of that photo. Perhaps it is too early to expect a film to take its place beside a book or a painting and continue for all time to give lasting pleasure and inspiration as they do. Any form of art that is mainly resolved in a finance operation, or in a means of propaganda, must stand in for the immediately depleted money, which is replaced by fresh funds. Permanent values, then, are the last thing to be desired.

From *L'Âge du cinéma* (Paris) 4–5 (August-November 1951): 24–25. Courtesy Lucien Treillard and L'Association des Amis et Défenseurs de l'Oeuvre de Man Ray.

Another kind of cinema

Marcel Mariën

Every one of us today has the opportunity to burgle a jewelry store, to drive a truck filled with nitroglycerin, to assassinate with scrupulous care his mistress or his wife, to foment a mutiny of sailors, to command a squadron of bombers. This is not the limit of our power, which is infinite. We can discover America with Columbus, the rabies vaccine with Pasteur, a new way of painting with Toulouse-Lautrec and Van Gogh. This is not all. We can wander about the ocean depths, breathe the air of Thebes in the company of pharaohs, and have the overall view of Waterloo that Stendhal's Fabrice despaired of knowing and of which Napoleon himself was deprived. Finally, nothing prevents us from seating ourselves at a table of the Moulin-Rouge in 1900 or, more modestly, from getting into the beds of the most attractive males and females (suit yourselves) in the world.

Thus, in our time, the cinema accomplishes what a hundred religions dare not hope for, in spite of their untiring efforts: to transform real life into myth and to substitute for it the illusion of a reality so powerful, so insidious, that real life becomes colorless by contrast.

In truth, we must confess that the majority of us maintain with our parents, children, and friends—even with our own wives and husbands—psychological rapports less profound, less rich, and thus, ultimately, less "real" then those bonds that tie us to the all-powerful phantoms of the cinema, whose violence, tenderness, and grace penetrate and stir us with a hold more powerful than that of our daily relations. Perhaps nothing enlightens us more on this point than the cheap literature of the movie world wherein the epistolary relations of thousands of people with the stars of the moment provide evidence of the stupefying emotional transferences of which we are capable.

What is true of our feelings is even more true of the surroundings in which we live. If we were to travel, there is every likelihood that we would experience fewer aspects and learn fewer facts of, for example, Italy or

Africa, than he who, without stirring from his town (or even his room, with television), witnesses the unfolding of a film made in the same regions.

In the end, only small compensation is afforded the traveler: the fact (or, more exactly, the remembrance) of having been on that spot in actual flesh and blood remains. But nothing is more temporary than the "permanence" each human being feels of himself, so well do we remain aware at every moment that our sense of ourselves is subject to change. Thus, as time passes, what becomes of this flesh, these bones, and these transient sensations? We are forced to admit that the memory of our travels dims rather quickly, that the travelers we were become mere ghosts to the men that we are in actuality. Undertaking to remember what we once said and did at some remote time and place, we evoke ghosts as intangible as those of the screen and even, perhaps, less privileged. For at one point or another, each of us finally dies, whereas the smiling and talking phantoms that the cinema preserves of us lend themselves complacently to living again, to reproducing untiringly these ageless smiles and words.

Analysis thus reveals, when we pause to contemplate ourselves, that we living men are not very different from these ethereal ghosts on the screen who seem undying; that the only difference is in the area of our misery; and that, in sum, it is to this difference alone, to the implacable necessities and obligations of everyday life, that we must give thanks for not yet being completely dominated by the narcotic properties of the cinema.

One senses the economical reasons that cause the flowering of this surprising double of human life, the cinema, motives that are responsible for its elaboration and its dogged continuation. The mind abdicates and bows to the rudimentary manipulation of emotion that defines cinema. The mechanics of evoking feelings are exploited to prevent man from passing on to acts other than those that are permissible and prescribed. For example, we are trained in the virtue of toiling with good grace so that we will pay, beyond our means, for our nourishment in dreams.

Thus, the cinema does not hesitate to attempt the impossible of eliminating the last barrier between the spectator and the illusory life on the screen. Cinema seeks to perfect its resemblance to reality. Cinema employs words, sound, color, almost three dimensions. And if, someday, the cinema succeeds in provoking gustative, olfactory, and even tactile impressions, would that be so surprising?—since from the beginning of time our most commonplace waking and sleeping dreams succeed so perfectly in these manifold sensations? Already, television spares us the need to cross the street. We no longer need to go out except to acquire through labor the means to meet the expenses of this second life, which relieves us so perfectly of the need to live. But there will soon be found also a remedy for this aforementioned labor, so that all the unhappiness of man will come eventually from only one thing, from staying—contrarily to Pascal—at ease in a room.

To this end of a totally cinematized universe, the filmmaker works within a rhetoric and a refinement of means such that in knowing intimately his business he can obtain automatically, from no matter what given subject, the engagement of the spectator and his identification with the spectacle. This has been well illustrated with Renoir's *French Cancan*. Henceforth, it will suffice to assemble all the banalities and all the clichés, to blend in assorted out-of-date situations involving the most grotesque characters, and to dress the whole in color and noise in order that the critics nod in admiration, thus affirming that they are incapable of reflection and of escaping the spell.

If such is the empire of modern cinema, can one then speak of a seventh art? Is not film actually a synthesis of all the other arts? Is not film indeed a universal art that can take the cleverest advantage of its predecessors, encompass, transcend, and force them toward its singular ends? Film takes from literature, from music, and from painting in multiplying the powers of the writer, musician, and painter. Film uses elements of dance and theater more effectively than these arts know how to, if we except their immediate *imaginary* presence, rather questionable as soon as it is scrutinized with attention. Finally, oriented toward didactic ends, the cinema teaches or corrupts more effectively than does the savant, the politician, or the priest.

That such a perfection in the reproduction of life, in the imitation of life, serves in the final reckoning only to hobble the mind of man can scarcely be surprising. The means of the cinema, by their complexity and their amplitude, depend strictly on the industrial powers whose ends are to feed the cultural market with an adulterated food and to forestall an eventual lassitude by trying continually to make the merchandise ever more appetizing.

It is certain that the care to surpass this sterile perfection preoccupies many filmmakers. They are not unanimously animated by the foolish preciosity that now characterizes, for example, Hitchcock and Clouzot. But the better filmmakers are nonetheless caught up in this race, hoping that their salvation will come from technique. When an invention appears in film, it sets off no fundamental changes in the art form. The enlarged screen, the development of three dimensions, and stereophonic sound serve only the sempiternal repetition of the same nonsense, the same adulteries, the same fist blows. The enrichment of technical skills has no other effect than to restrain further the chances of the spectator to free himself from the cinema's oppression and to sap his last resistance when, the séance over, he is thrown out, dazed and stupid, onto the street.

The outcome of it all, however, is not very difficult to forecast. After all, there is no critic who is not pleased to remind us periodically of the parable of sound, no history of film that does not mention it with insistence.

The mediocrity of the cinema, this mediocrity that goes hand in hand with the always growing perfection of its technical resources, appears due largely to the appearance of "talking" films and to the incapacity of the filmmakers to discipline the new means that were imposed on them.

We know how filmmakers responded to the first sound. The necessity to record simultaneously with image forced them to return to the immobility of the origins of the cinema. Nothing unplanned could happen. This momentary necessity to integrate sound devices had the effect of conferring upon the screenplay a brazen power. For the great directors of silent films, sound signified a change of method so radical that with it all chance of discovery, proper to cinematographic language, was practically banished.

Whereas before sound, whatever the care taken with the preparation of the script, the film was made *after* shooting, today the film is made even *before* the shooting is begun. And the editing, which was first held to be the essential operation of cinematographic realization, is in our days relegated to the status of a minor craft.

Thus every precaution is taken so that the film will emerge from the theoretical schema precisely as previously conceived and that nothing new will appear under the sun. The director has become only the servile executor of this schema, even if it happens that he is also the author of it. Everything is carefully foreseen so that nothing can menace or corrupt the preliminary agreements. Everyone is at his post: director of photography, set designer, property man, wardrobe mistress, electrician, sound editor, and, finally, the script girl, the real Cerberus whose task consists of examining the smallest details, to prevent life from interfering at all cost. If an actor, in passing from one room to another, appears with a different tie or with his face darkened with ecchymosis that he did not have in the preceding shot, imagine the drama! This would be the end of the world! In truth, this would mean opening wide the door to this freedom from which one tries, by any means, to protect the mind.

Is it any wonder that under such conditions the cinema is reduced to being only a simple illustration, moving and boisterous, of romanesque literature, to endlessly rehashing the same petty situations, to offering and eternally re-offering the all-too-eternal triangle?

It would be unjust to incriminate here only the commercial producers. To tell the truth, the obstacle in question is the whole conception of the cinema and its present work methods. If, in spite of everything, an original script were somehow to be introduced, the method of realization would still remain unchanged, so that nothing would distinguish the realization of a film from that of a novel. The scriptwriter amply translates into the cinematic idiom situations and events conceived by the ordinary means of literature.

It is worthwhile to remember that cinematographic language is an accretion of editing practices, and that its most elementary aspects, such as the close-up, were the product of mechanical accidents, technical mishaps, that were almost always in opposition to the filmmaker's intentions. From Archimedes' bath to the discovery of penicillin by way of universal gravitation, accident has been a characteristic of human invention. Accident operates in almost all important discoveries.

It is evident that it is not in manipulating social ideas or in nuancing two or three emotional situations that we can hope to develop the resources of cinematographic language, and still less to overthrow it or to turn it to other ends. Such an extension, such a change or rupture, can come only from experimentation bearing on the images themselves, the isolated images wrenched from the eternal narration to which they are now constrained.

Faced with the menaces and wrongs that result from the bewitching power of the current cinema, we can only wish for a radical transformation in present working methods that inevitably engender this absurd, sterile perfection. Such an overthrow appears possible under only two essential conditions:

1. We must create means by which to rescue cinema from its present floundering, means that concern only the work itself, its conception, its realization, and its effects.

2. We must oppose the economic, material forces that forestall any enterprise—whether the means of production be the property of only a few individuals or of the State—so that it would become possible, under capitalist or socialist regime alike, for any amateur, like Lenin's woman cook, to create a film.

The first point above, presupposing some favorable circumstance that would ensure the success of the second, offers possibilities sufficiently vast to arouse eager hopes. If, however, it were necessary to endure longer the conditions of work currently in effect, then it seems that the translation into images of certain situations—different from those we are accustomed to seeing—could be effected by means of a preliminary script. In short, it is possible to obtain satisfactory results by means of an invention anterior to the realization. For that, it would be appropriate first of all to reject the literary, theatrical, and historical rubbish that now encumbers the cinema. No more of Stendhal or Tolstoy, or of detective stories! No more life of Caesar, of Beethoven, or no matter who, unless it is to try everything possible to betray them, to disfigure them, to contradict their routine portrayals. For, of course, it always remains possible to draw from *any subject* an honorable film—subversive, or at least comic.

But what seems most important for film is to break the thread that has led men by their noses since the time novels were first written and read, and of which the cinema is content to be a grandiloquent illustration. A certain psychological attitude, after several centuries of dullness, has come to be so encrusted in our minds that it seems to be one with life; this embedded attitude is such that no one today, excluding perhaps the insane, can pretend not to *romanticize* his existence. It is possible then, in departing from the mental habits now in force, to try to break this cursed thread by preparing scripts in which self-romanticization is held in check, scripts which then need only to be converted into images.

Such an enterprise doubtless offers considerable possibilities for film, but here again the economic barrier is so well fortified that such films could be realized only under exceptional circumstances, on which it would be too naive to rely.

As toilsome as this path appears, a sustained drive is not thereby condemned to ineffectiveness.

Let's look more closely at the task of revitalizing film.

We recall that the cinema owes its crucial resources to chance; furthermore, that it owes its present distress in large part to radical changes in working methods that came with the invention of "talking" films. Thus nothing would appear more salutary than to return to former methods whereby the editing played a decisive role and the film was built after its shooting. In effect, I propose that we take up where we left off. As it is necessary, however, to progress even as we return, it is well to recall that the utilization of editing such as we find in, for example, the best days of Soviet cinema, was nonetheless prisoner of a certain aestheticism that over the years was subject to further degradation. Most often, Soviet editing functioned only to underscore some intention of the director, to reinforce some idea; in brief, Soviet editors were still captives of the narrative frame, which was purely descriptive. It was the abandonment of this rhetoric of images—which were rendered superfluous in almost every case by the sound films which caused so many tears over the tomb of silent pictures, which forced Chaplin into a long silence, and which made more than one person think that the cinema was dead. And actually, the cinema, as an autonomous art, died with sound; and its cadaver is still being fed upon by a gigantic industry, where the results are as small as the efforts are huge.

But whatever the degree of abjection into which the cinema has fallen, this misery is still preferable to that fastidious aestheticism that was partially revived under cover of shorts such as *Crin blanc*. But it is not the revival of art that matters today; still less that of "true cinema."

In any case, admitting that it is necessary to pursue research in editing, the obstacle of film economics remains no less awesome.

If it is true that for the cinematic experiences we are seeking the best method of realization is that which operates *after* the shooting of the film, why not simply ignore this latter stage altogether by eliminating the shooting? Why not take all of the existing cinematographic productions as the primary material of such a cinema and work directly from it, taking a shot here, a scene there, a fragment of this or that, at our will? The original *ends* (the old films)

141

would become *means* (raw material for reediting), and we would need only to disarticulate this subtle texture of images, sounds, gestures, and words. We would deliver these millions of stock emotion-stimulators from their petrified affectation and, by creating a new sequence, we would express fresh emotions. It would be quite acceptable to reshoot, here and there, an original scene in order to effect a more harmonious accord.

Such a method has the added advantage of reducing almost entirely the expenses of realization, if not doing away with them. For everything is useful, *everything is good:* fragments of newsreels, documentaries, previews of coming attractions, amateur films, cartoons, commercials, and finally the "works" themselves, in their entirety. Just as the *same words* appear in *Les Fleurs du Mal* as appear also in the most banal prose, so, we have reason to think, the *same images* can serve in the composition of a mediocre or of an excellent film. It is only a question of assemblage, suppressions, and inversions.

Thus all that remains is to transform into gold all the base metal that for more than a half century has accumulated in film at great expense and uproar. The new alchemy may be reduced to its simplest expression: the raw material may be purchased secondhand and refined at need (as Vesalius did with his skeletons) with the Moviola and the sound recorder. And, lastly, we need a pair of scissors, that traditional weapon of censorship now become a tool of liberty in our hands.

Certainly, such attempts have already occasionally been made, but never in a systematic fashion, while conceivably an intensive exploitation of such possibilities, in a sense altogether different from the limited efforts to this date, might lead to the most astonishing discoveries.

I remember an American film in the original version of which diverse characters underwent difficulty to regain a wallet that had been stolen by a pickpocket. This wallet contained microfilm on which appeared some new discovery in nuclear physics and accordingly was coveted by foreign spies. The entire film had a character that was clearly anti-Soviet. In the dubbed French version, the dialogue was transformed so that the document in question now interested only the narcotics racket. Some man made an infinitesimal modification, involving only a few words in the dialogue, but this was sufficient to transfigure completely the film's intentions and to put it in the category of the traditional gangster film. We could elaborate at length on this small example. Scholars would find it an unparalleled source of fruitful meditation on substance and form. But, for the moment, it is enough to exemplify the possibilities of creating new films from the simplest alterations of original material.

The point of departure could be simply any film, banal or not. Stripped of the sound track, each one of the film's visual elements would be studied in silent projection, particularly those sequences conserving emotional residues or charged with intellectual significance. From this operation a new script, modifying the interrelationships of people or objects, could be elaborated. The new continuity could then be enriched with appropriate dialogue. But this is only one of thousands of possible interventions. We can also proceed inversely from the dialogue and sound track, whose succession would be kept more or less rigorously intact, matching with new visual images, borrowed from other films. It would probably be necessary at the outset to avoid comic or purely queer effects that risk shackling us by their mechanical facility. The danger here, however, might be to bar ourselves from access to unsuspected domains, perhaps more fructuous.

It is truly a question of approaching an unknown world, of inventing *a new type of man*. This intention inclines us to think that the most difficult obstacle to surmount would be the traditional concept of the narration, that it would be important to cut the story-line thread while retaining the emotional effects.

The point is to deal a mortal blow to present notions of personality such as we know it from historic reality and from film's infantile and miserable representation of this reality. Nothing could be of greater help to us here than the star cult to which the cinema has sacrificed almost everything. The prestige acquired by this or that face over the years has actually tended toward the decomposition of the human person, leaving only the guise of a single familiar and fascinating face. One thinks of Garbo's face, borrowed from its diverse films and engaged in some poignant adventure of our invention, so that the face recolors a little the simple-minded mystery that has contented us until now.

Various possibilities suggest themselves to us: the destruction of a given character's identity by constant modifications of voice and dialogue over his visage in a single shot; or a rigorously invariable voice issuing from ten different mouths. As complex and delicate as such efforts would appear, they are quite feasible technically. And further, these new films are a means of finishing with the poor ghost we submit to so completely that in the long run we and the ghost are one.

We could start with a classic triangle rivalry, tragic or vaudevillian, and play adroitly on the original sound tracks of two or more films, using two characters distinctly differentiated by situations, sentiments, and words, but each character played by the same actor, putting them in relation to a third character, an actress, who always knows, supposedly, what is going on. In other instances, we would alternately put feminine voices and masculine voices in the mouths of men, taking care, however, to counteract as much as possible the immediate reactions of the public, the imbecilic laughs, the eventual confusion with known situations, like the existence of twins and doubles, which are now abundantly exploited by the cinema. We could evoke surprises by a film composed of diverse cinematographic illustrations of the same historic myth, like that of Joan of Arc. From a deliberate entanglement of diverse Joans—Falconetti, Morgan, Bergman—we could draw effects sometimes dramatic, sometimes comic. The same thing goes for other puppets: Napoleon, thanks to the collaboration of his multiple interpreters, would begin his coronation over and over again; or we would have a half-dozen Jesuses entangled in an inextricable Passion, continuously climbing as many Golgothas. What better way, in this domain, of denouncing the imposture? Repetition, when forced, is of a nature to produce, without any doubt, singular effects, when one insists cleverly. These effects are all opposed to this other multiplication that is imposed on us today: people lighting twenty cigarettes in the course of a film or ringing at thirty doors—"punctuation" that isn't less frequent in literature, where Simone de Beauvoir, for example, thinks it is legitimate to show us, in almost each of the six hundred pages of her *Mandarins,* one or another of her creatures gulping a whisky.

If you remark, and quite justly, that these guides to another kind of cinema are valuable only in so far as they may be realized—and realized in a convincing manner—you can see, however, that on this path we should rediscover the spirit of cinematic inventiveness. And we would simultaneously rediscover something about the mind, the mind that *romanticizes,* that turns itself, without ceasing to be "itself," into one or the other character, into hate or love, victim or executioner.

Still another aspect of such a cinema awaits our attention and, furthermore, it is one that will reassure us. This aspect concerns the legal involvements entailed in this new cinema, involvements that cannot fail to weigh upon such experiments. Let us not forget that we are pitting ourselves against the sanctity of private property, and against its intellectual and moral armament, and against the sacred personality of the actor and of the director, and against this professional vanity that inflames and consumes all filmmakers. This vanity plays, however, a role as transitory and vile as that which money plays in the economic world: crude sign, ephemeral convention more elusive than anything else in the world.

We can assume the juridical risks of such a cinema to be inevitable, so well do we know from past experience that nothing great or valuable is created that does not place itself in violent opposition to the established order; this order that must always be upset from top to bottom. This obligation to rebel will probably be more urgent than ever in the perfect societies that we are going to know before long. And so we can laugh beforehand at the vehement protestations to be heard at forthcoming trials, protestations from conservatives "in the name of liberty and of culture." Censure never fails to accompany the approach of innovation in the arts.

But whatever the results of such an enterprise, we can already underline the fact that, in spite of the barricade of money that prevents "everyman" from the realization of his own film, little is needed to liberate possibilities more extensive than those available to all the Hollywood powers together. Hollywood, having enormous resources, is enormously handicapped. The greatest magnate, dependent upon contracts, the day's caprices, and his own fortune, is reduced to hopelessly rehashing the same, monotonous tale. Today it is enough, and will always be enough—once the crack is discovered—to pry open and disembowel the Holy Inquisition—that is, not to respect the rules of the game.

An experimentation that bears on elements as concrete as images and sounds need not concern itself with a given philosophical context. We can see that the experiment's chances of accomplishment will be all the greater if it can thwart the hold of such a context. However, it is perhaps useful to think at this point of the teaching of Pavlov, of the theory and experience of reflex conditioning.

We know, to give a precise example, that in the time of Rameau the minor chord did not at all prevent dancing. But, principally since Beethoven, and because of several marches termed funeral, the minor chord has been so intimately associated with feelings of sadness that it is no longer possible, whatever is tried, to dissociate them. We are now at a state where we see, everywhere, idiots of all hues proclaiming seriously that the minor chord *expresses* sadness, or solitude, or death. We know that such a transformation of the affective signs is only the product of slow conditioning, of a secret and obscure crystallization that is but an invention of man, an experiment of man on man.

Rather than utter interminable asininities on content and form, as has been done incessantly from Aristotle to Zhdanov, what is important is to till the affective field, lest all that is attempted today only succeed in filling it in with sand. What better means than the cinema to help us in this task, since it constitutes the chief means of all means, since it permits all the resources of expression to be tempered into a single weapon.

However one tries to resist them, the images of the cinema, studded with words and sounds, interlace themselves insidiously with the images that people our minds, that govern our lives, that *are* our lives. These images reveal themselves thus as the most efficacious of all the relays given to our senses and to our sentiments. Their powerful organization in the cinema composes a sort of satellite of our existence, a strange mirror where the shadow of who we are is written, grows, and stays, curiously stagnant. It is important to try to make new reflections in this film mirror other than those of the execrable Narcissus. We need new reflections which, far from reproducing our appearance, would seek instead to trouble the pool's surface and to transfigure their model, which is ourselves.

A revised version of a text from *Les Lèvres nues* (Brussels) 7 (December 1955). This translation, by Beth Roudebush, first appeared in *Film Comment* 1, no. 3 (1962): 14–19. Courtesy Marcel Mariën.

Intention and surprise

Nora Mitrani

In a little Mexican village near the American border a man is stretched
out in a hammock. It is siesta time, that most accursed hour as far as the
monasteries are concerned, when the thousand and one demons of lewd-
ness, pride, and madness assail the imprudent sleeper.

The demon—a brown girl with clear eyes—*fish in hand*, silently approaches the sleeper—James Mason—lifts the hat shading his face from
the sun and wafts the fish two or three times right under his nose. Mason
wakes, leaps on the temptress, but he is so clumsy that he falls and pulls
her down with him. The spectator is left to guess the outcome, as if he had
already felt the clammy touch of the fish between his hands.

Such is an unusual sequence in an otherwise mediocre film: *One Way
Street*, directed by Hugo Fregonese.

One can say, then, that the sequence avoided Hollywood's puritan censorship completely, in the sense that its insolence and freshness situate it
beyond the level of compromise between bourgeois virtue and pornography, the level of most current commercial film.

If the objection is raised that the symbolism of this scene is too obvious
or too Germanic, or even that the director has only conformed to the taste
the public has for risqué situations, we will retort that fortunately a director is not always the master of his intentions that he would like to be, that
it is very rare in even the most willful film for at least one of its sequences
not to break free and, unknown to itself, reveal an intense reality.

What does this mean?

That this sequence is not entirely announced by the previous one, just
as it remains without finality in the general architecture of the film, which
is the progressive encounter of a man with his fate.

It is more common, more tasteful, for a girl to stroll along with a flower
in her hand, for decorative or for amorous ends; but should the flower
become a fish, that leads to sudden disorientation and scandal for the spec-

tator: between this man and this woman it is not a question of whispering sweet nothings; their relationship is a carnal one, burning and icy at the same time, free from sentimental ambiguity, the fish, a small piece of cold, still flesh, becoming the very symbol of this purity.

So if this sequence profits from such forcefulness of meaning, it is because it is unforeseeable and shocking at the same time.

A supposedly perfect film would have rejected it precisely because it smacks of incoherence or vagabondage of the imagination. So it is with certain "good" American thrillers whose scripts and direction, logical and absolutely coherent, reject any image that does not bear its burden of light and shade within the general comprehension of the action.

It is the same with "good" French films which, even more than the others, offend by their excess of rationalism: films too well constructed, in which every image, to the extent it has been deemed necessary, becomes foreseeable, even when it forms the "suspense" that anticipates the action.

Yet if one is surprised, it is only within an intellectual anticipation already accessory to one's surprise, and not on the poetic plane where the authentic image arises, negative and upsetting in the first place, because it has to be, because appearances falter and fall apart when the subterranean life reaches their level.

It is a question, we think, of liberty.

It pleases us that from time to time characters live according to *their* will, obeying *their* imagination more than the director's intelligence. A sticky problem, perhaps, for the latter to reckon with the imagination of his own characters.

Success comes on two levels, one beyond talent, the other this side of it:

—If the director is endowed with an imagination "surprising" for him.

—Or if he is not complete master of the situation and his logical intelligence occasionally fails him.

The poets of the screen get rarer and rarer. For that reason it's the inferior sort of film that stores up for us the greatest number of liberty's *flagrants délits*.

From *L'Âge du cinéma* (Paris) 4–5 (August–November 1951): 50.

The ideal summa

Petr Král

Even though generally speaking it's by far the deadest Fellini, with its tricks and cultural references, *Satyricon* contains an isolated sequence which is, in itself, one of the director's purest: straightforward serendipity suddenly intrudes into the stagy setting, an aesthete and window dresser's notion of antiquity. It is nightfall, and two young pilgrims are wandering through the rooms of a farmhouse, from which we've just seen the masters dismiss their hired help, and chance upon a "forgotten" servant in the act of bathing in a pool. A chase ensues, occasionally punctuated by echoing trills of laughter. Finally, they catch the girl and lead her into a bedroom. She laughingly agrees to join in their game, when all of a sudden she spots that their interest lies elsewhere: the men beside her are kissing each other. Her laughter becomes all the more beautiful, but just as quickly gives way to silence: something is happening out in the courtyard. Intrigued, the two men and the servant girl go out into the corridor. Through the doorway, under the blackest of night skies, they see burning in the yard a straw-filled cart on which some never-to-be-identified person is cremating two bodies: the owners of the house, who had sent everyone away so they might commit suicide together, unwitnessed, on their very own doorstep. . . .

This sequence is in itself a magnificent film, incomparably more important to me than the film it comes from. Like *Satyricon*, many works contain such "films within the film," especially magical sequences that become even richer when taken on their own. Indeed, this is the way they wish to be taken. Most escape from the linear logic of the plot, substituting a truer story of our own devising; or better still, our own "peregrinations."

In Antonioni's *Zabriskie Point* a single sequence, as dense and opaque as the rest of the film is candid, defines in just a few images the entire mystery of America. The heroine, who is, I think, trying fruitlessly to telephone some remote town, wordlessly quits a diner situated in the middle of an arid landscape, leaving behind the doddery old men at the bar, literally caught up in their own solitude behind the windowpane. Distressed, she takes a few steps on the dusty ground before reaching a sort of platform on the boards of which an old grand piano, resting on its haunches, agonizes. All at once she finds herself surrounded by a host of children who've appeared from nowhere and who wordlessly press themselves against her with scabrous insistence. Increasingly disconcerted, she manages to tear herself away, descends from the platform, and runs back to the diner: the old men under glass have not budged an inch.

In *The American Friend* Wenders creates a similar sequence in a single dolly shot. Watching a behatted Dennis Hopper jaywalking along the old highway in front of an apartment house, an anonymous gangster, twirling a long plastic tube that emits a lugubrious drone, turns from the window to the interior of this brick building somewhere in New York, while murmuring something like, "Watch out, cowboy." Advancing slowly into the far reaches of the apartment, we in turn discover a horrible porcelain bulldog, a gang leader of waxy complexion, cigar in his mouth, midway through hearing by telephone of an accomplice's murder in Paris, then, in the very background, a couple obviously taking up their positions—in a draped bed—for the shooting of a porno film. Here, to be sure, the mystery partly comes from the context: the sequence is in fact a chance encounter, in the midst of the chaos existing in the world, of protagonists who without knowing it are participating in the same drama, Hopper being directly implicated in the Paris murder. As well as being a "minifilm" condensed into one shot, the dolly also creates a striking spatial telescoping.

There's a pure "film within the film," too, in W.C. Fields's *Never Give a Sucker an Even Break*. The comedian, grumpier than ever, enters a modest milk bar and orders—just for a change—a milk shake. Manipulating two straws as if they were chopsticks, he fruitlessly tries to hoick out the cherries. Each time he gets them up to his mouth the straws bend under the weight and the fruit falls fatefully into the glass. And all this under the fascinated gaze of the barman, whose attention is from time to time distracted by an invisible fly, at which point, grabbing a bottle, he takes a huge swipe at the air. Otherwise, he does nothing but drum on the counter. The plainness of the bar, where for the whole scene we stay rooted in one corner of the counter facing a cash register, doesn't make this face-to-face encounter any the less oppressive. When, dumbfounded by his customer, the barman involuntarily presses the key of his cash register—triumphantly ringing up "No Sale"—he actually materializes the silence reigning in the room. Finally, Fields gives up. Setting down the milk shake, he crushes an invisible crumb with one of those *impossible* gestures he alone was master of, declares he'd be better off in a real bar, and leaves. The only comment that could follow this is something we've heard said about him at the beginning of the film: "He's as strange as an alarm clock." Here's the proof.

From Petr Král, *Private Screening* (London: Frisson, 1985), 32–33 (translation slightly revised). Courtesy Petr Král.

Turkey broth and unlabeled love potions

Gérard Legrand

First, let's understand one another. A film, like human life, can be Surrealist by moments. However, it can be wholly so without its author (let us generalize and define him as that two-headed monster, the scriptwriter or storyteller and the director) having expressly set out to make a Surrealist work. Involuntary Surrealism? Well yes and no, since he may or may not be aware of its real nature at one and the same time.

The expression "commercial film" is not exempt from the converse ambiguity: it does not necessarily involve the notion of financial success. Besides, whatever its redemption has been, it could not be associated with that long and glorious series of productions in which the symbolism and expressionism of the greatest directors was given free rein by a process tangential to Surrealism. The most recent marvel issuing from this current, Clouzot and Ferry's *Manon,* constitutes in my opinion the *accomplishment* of a revolt singularly close to our own in spite of its marginally documentary quality. But when I see Maurice de Canonge directing Pierre Brasseur in *L'Homme de la Jamaïque,* I fear the worst. And I am wrong to do so because in this desert picture through which the great actor prowls like a lion we will not forget the last two contrasting shots: "hope"—that nocturnal road along which a young woman trudges while neither she nor the spectator knows if the man she loves awaits her.

Here is a typical example of the windfall, the "gag" which can sometimes be enough to save an evening's viewing for the lover of films. It can grab us by the throat as here, or *liberate* the intellect from its moorings by pushing vacuity and foolishness as far as they can go, to the point where they outstrip themselves. In *Aladdin and His Lamp,* a puerile Technicolor B movie, we suddenly come upon the following scene: the genie of the lamp, a ravishing young girl in love with her master and invisible to all but him, descends the immense palace staircase side by side with the thronging courtiers. Suddenly we see her take the steps three at a time with ease, go back to the top, and begin all over again, while the cortege continues its descent with suitable solemnity.

Is it to be satisfied too easily to see therein the germ, albeit sterile, of the "Neronian dream of always claiming the most beautiful feasts for one-self"?[1] It is this desire which totally animates the sumptuous, often successful, "musical" and sexual productions the puritans, dotards, and champions of "proletarian" art hold in contempt: one thinks of *The Ziegfeld Follies,* the pseudoclassical ballet in *Tonight and Every Night,* and even the completely gratuitous return to the oneiric musical hall sequence at the end of *Up in Arms.*

On the contrary, present-day Westerns and exotic films exhibit numerous traces of usury and a touch of rationalization. The Italian cinema, however, alongside the lyrical and courageous tragedies ("realistic" in the way Aeschylus or Euripides are) of De Santis (*Bitter Rice*) or Lattuada (*Senza Pietà*), has surrounded the traditional exaltation of the lover of justice who is outside the law with an extremely perverse, decorative aura. It isn't by chance that the hero here is a painter (Blasetti's *Un'avventura di Salvator Rosa*) or a director of symbolic ballets (*I Pirati di Capri*). Through so many banquets, grottoes, and openly erotic tortures, the principle of identity, civil status, is constantly and happily undermined. Thanks to masks and mirrors, the young male lead suffers the fascinating ups and downs of a traitor, all for the greater good of heroine and people.

It isn't enough just to accumulate unusual objects to make a Surrealist film. *Tumak,* of course, has no interest save its fine lizards. But in *The Thief of Bagdad* the tempest and the immense beach where the wreckage lies, the flight of the doves at the instant the blind man reopens his eyes are as moving as the genie in the bottle and the temple scenes. And I'm tempted to believe that the merit of *La Nuit fantastique* is situated *somewhere beyond* its mummies, playing cards, and tricks. In any case, it seems to me that on a filmic plane you can't easily attain the subjective richness Ofterdingen's blue flower or Duchamp's *Bottle Racks* have.

Do we arrive at the paradox of a poetic cinema in which the "surreal"

---

1 André Breton, *Anthologie de l'humour noir.*

would count for little? There is only one *Nosferatu,* and one alone. The horror film is no longer feasible in the same shape as in the silent film days. Phantoms smile readily (*Blithe Spirit, The Ghost and Mrs. Muir*). The authentic humor, black and cold, of *Kind Hearts and Coronets* is clouded by post-Romantic charms that only accentuate its merit. We are far from the cruelty of films by Tod Browning like *The Unknown,* in which Lon Chaney as an "armless" man, a circus attraction, has his arms really cut off to satisfy the whims of his mistress. Should we see in this the signs of a suspect vitality, of a purely formal diffusion of cinematic poetry? In reality, it is the conditions of this poetry that have changed, and it is through their latent content, let us call it their *ethic* even, that some films I want to consider more fully rejoin Surrealism.

To what extent are their authors responsible for or conscious of this? We are often forced to remind ourselves of the historical and industrial process of cinematic development so as to weigh impartially those admirable works whose authors may have nothing revolutionary about them, especially on the social plane. I would not dream of comparing *The Big Sleep* to *L'Âge d'or,* but from Raymond Chandler's masterpiece Howard Hawks has adapted a film of "quotidian mystery" (Laverne Terrace, the bookshop, the final trap), of a long amorous maturation which, aided by excellent acting, constitutes a sort of epic about *fated people* (as we say: a fated conclusion). Howard Hawks had already given us *Scarface.* Chance has it that the three recent "commercial" films whose content seems to me to correspond closest to the main preoccupations of Surrealism are the work of directors who are less in the public eye. One of them is totally unknown even. Must we refuse them every favorable prejudice?

In *Laura,* Otto Preminger invites us to contemplate the liquidation of time, in a less simply magisterial way than Sjöberg does in *Miss Julie,* but to the profit of an audacious innovation: the concept of eternity which alone explains this film and thanks to which *Laura* makes an appearance in the history of ideas as decisive as its allegorical appearance must have been in 1926 in André Breton and Louis Aragon's *Le Trésor des Jésuites.* The screen is black, a voice is heard: "I'll always remember the day that followed Laura's death. . . . " A retrospective vision. But this vision dovetails into another in which the heroine finally appears in the shape of Gene Tierney. Each mention, each image of Laura is underlined by a subsequently well-known refrain which retains its inexpressible magical power here. Finally it comes into the "story" during the only "false" cinematic dream I know, the triumph of a lonely man's obsession in front of a portrait. The story unfolds in reverse to meet up finally with its protagonist. At the same time as it proclaims on the radio the brevity of all love, the voice from the beginning of the film dies down, mumbling, "Forgive me, my love. . . . " And the spectator is forced to see into the "beyond," where he will try to pigeonhole this specifically surreal pathos, a "beyond" without transcendental justification covering the whole plot and disarticulating his memory. The film ends on the clock that concealed the weapon of an *impossible crime:* the clock is broken.

If such a structure seems artificial, extreme simplicity presided over another sublime film: *Gun Crazy*.[2] After the Encounter of an exemplary couple nothing more happens for, say, another hour. The sensuality, grace, and marvelous edginess of Peggy Cummins, of whom John Dall is not in the least unworthy, enliven a rigorous love poem. Nothing prevents the heroes getting away from a society in pursuit of them, but they cannot separate, even for a prudent two months. There is the extraordinary moment when, as if by common accord, two cars driving off in opposite directions turn back toward each other after going a few yards. And the overpowering smile of Peggy Cummins is there to prove to us that they aren't going to perdition blindly or under duress: there's nothing here that recalls the "fetters" dear to preachers and "concerned" *chanteuses.* (Well! Well!) Some honorable sentiments are exhausted along the way: for the young girl it's all a question of living "without working," of doing your nails in the very kitchen where a mother busies herself, a mother capable, nevertheless, of the worst betrayal. Before they reach the symbolic "Mexican border," children are only good for hostages. So much cynicism begs for punishment. But their death at dawn in the ignoble swamp of "real life" surrounded by cops, including two "old" (that is to say, false) friends, has nothing in common with the miserable union, with its mystical stench, of the fugitives in *Odd Man Out.* The film as a whole, made by Joseph H. Lewis with a technical brio equaled only by his openly subversive intentions, adds up to a song of triumph.

---

2 The American title, *Deadly Is the Female,* is an abominable swindle taken from a biblical source, for which Joseph H. Lewis does not seem responsible.

As for *Dark Passage,* here it's a question, you could say, of a multilevel masterpiece, the last, most beautiful level of which was completely over-looked by critics and domesticated public alike. We may be surprised that from David Goodis's worthy novel the ordinary Delmer Daves has created a firework of such splendor, a progressive plot of such vigor (as for this aspect, I think only *Gilda,* an absolutely scientific masterpiece I cannot analyze here, is comparable to it). *Dark Passage* has for its ideological theme nothing less than a man's discovery of his "definitive" face, this going hand in hand with the discovery of real love. There are three stages in this adventure: the subjective camera; the scenes where the masked man, his head bandaged, lost in the immensity of San Francisco, is suspected of a second crime; and in the end the search for the real guilty party who will finally take from Humphrey Bogart, more striking here than ever, all means of proving his innocence. Up to this point the film remains accessible. As for adventure, the public must have noticed the beauty of the vast urban skies pressing in on the quarry, the iron fire-escapes, the crests of waves indifferent to the human drama. It must have admired the nightmare se-quence of the surgical operation to modify the hero's physical identity: a sequence almost as brilliant as the one in Edward Dmytryk's *Murder My Sweet.* But the epilogue disconcerts it. . . . Because it can *only* be justified from the Surrealist point of view.

Unable to demonstrate his innocence in court, the hero "flees." To the woman he loves, the last being he has confidence in, he gives the most fragile, whispered rendezvous, and disappears.

An enormous dark wave, standing for the whole of the Pacific Ocean, breaks on a small beach. Humphrey Bogart has kept his freedom, he has "rebuilt" his life. . . . But suddenly Lauren Bacall appears. He takes her in his arms without a word and, smiling, they lose themselves in an endless dance. And this is not a dream! Actually, this happy ending is in fact the most revolutionary challenge to the improbable, to sordid renunciation, émigré romance, the comfort of all those with an interest in the failure of love. *Dark Passage* definitively displays the lights, murmurs, and nocturnal tropical flowers Breton evokes in *L'Amour fou,* vertiginous "as the approach to the Sphinx." But here the enigma, completely clear, resides nowhere save in the glance exchanged by the now unbandaged man and the woman who has always believed in him. Doubtless, it also resides in the unforgettable power of these images displaying a *new optimism* in the way Lautréamont's *Poésies* do, enough at present to reanimate our confidence in the cinema's Surrealist destinies.

From *L'Âge du cinéma* (Paris) 4–5 (August-November 1951): 17–20. Courtesy Gérard Legrand.

The fantastic – the marvelous

Ado Kyrou

O nly with "the transcendence of the anecdote" can I bring my attention to bear. Many roads meet in this transcendence which, in its
simplest form, results in the fantastic. It is there one meets the *marvelous*,
the crux of Surrealism.

Before looking at what the cinema holds for us in this enchanted domain, let's clear up a misunderstanding some people cultivate with a passion for the rewards it brings them. *Everything fantastic is not marvelous.*
The fantastic without the marvelous (in which case the fantastic becomes
the enemy of the marvelous) does not belong here: I gladly leave it to the
priests, Cocteau, and the spectacular revues. I don't confuse monstrances
with lanterns and I don't get ecstatic about *every* vampire or *every* apparition; there are phantoms that belong to the lowest strata of commerce,
phantoms which have their place in the bedrock of respectability.

Fear, the unknown, mysterious forces, predestined places, ghosts, the
magic of love find themselves on the other side. "As soon as Hutter crossed
the bridge, the phantoms came to meet him" (*Nosferatu*). The crossing
cannot be made in carpet slippers and many are the renunciations, falls, or
searches for other, safer bridges which lead to the fantastic without the
marvelous, since (in the majority of cases) they are without an earthly
basis. To speak of angels is simple, you can lift their robe up to see what sex
they are if you like; a life after death is reassuring to a degree, and stories of
bearded old men entertain weak children, but these idle tales divert the
mind from the unceasing quest for the authentic marvelous, and it should
be noted that "spiritualists" are in general the fiercest adversaries of the
marvelous.

It's as a frantic materialist that I love the impossible. Things and people
are immensely rich and secret, the marvelous explodes *on earth*. Magi of
"uncivilized" lands and alchemists attain the marvelous only when they
destroy (often without wanting to) *every* idea of god, supreme power,

otherworldly forces, sin. A Christian (to take the simplest example) has no merit if, through prudence, fear of death, or need for tranquillity, he believes in apparitions; there is nothing marvelous in a man who thinks his mother is a virgin. On the other hand, the glance of a woman who loves is the bridge leading to the forces on the other side, and these forces are as *worldly* as that glance. Therein resides their magic which, instead of reducing man to the level of a kneeling domesticated animal, lifts him up, makes him aware of the power of revolt, and puts him in touch with the treasures he refused to see surrounding him. So-called supernatural phenomena are only unknown human forces or the magnificent symbols of terrestrial power. Any religious, esoteric (in the theological sense), mystical interpretation of these phenomena can only diminish their liberating significance. That famous "reason" perturbed by the fantastic and immersed in surreality attains the authentic sense of materialism, which is not limited to its manifest content.

Everything I know, everything I can find, everything that can move me, everything that exists is found on earth. This *everything* is endless, and the marvelous it conceals accepts no idealistic, deistic, or in any way nonexistent accretion that destroys it.

Let's take as an example an Italian film, Vittorio de Sica's *Miracle in Milan.* From the first moments we are gripped by the whimsical freedom of the images; the most exquisite poetry tears down the veils of reality one by one to introduce us to the purest kind of marvelous. In his grandmother's absence a child watches the milk boil over and form a long stream on the floor. The grandmother enters and not only does not scold the child but places around the lengthening white line some little wooden houses, trees, and gates, thereby transforming the sad room into a landscape with all sorts of resonances. They admire the curious river that waters this countryside. A little later the sun goes down, its rays get longer, while the cold has been defeated by games that are no longer infantile. Everything is transfigured, the setting of the sun becomes an exceptional *spectacle,* balloons become Montgolfiers of the marvelous. By his simple, *total* presence, man opens up the horizon, life's latent content colors the least act with its profound poetry, love can only emerge victorious in this universe where the refusal to consider the earth a vale of tears opens up the floodgates of human revolt. Then suddenly things deteriorate because De Sica and his scriptwriter Zavattini cause an otherworldly marvelous to intervene: angels in body stockings, a miraculous dove, miracles owing nothing to man. The fall is vertiginous; conformism, poverty of imagination, betrayal of the power of love (the dove chosen by the beloved woman cannot replace the dove from heaven) undermine the fantasy, and this new kind of fantastic, poor and miserable, worthy of Cocteau, draws us toward Mussolinian paternalism and the evasion of "liberating" death.

The man who dreams is unaware of his condition, he believes he lives, *he lives*. At the moment of dreaming, the fantastic does not exist, it is real. To accept that reality, to make it his own by discovering the point where haunted castles and lakes full of monsters open their secret doors to us, is the first duty of the cineaste who doesn't create the fantastic because the tricks please him or on the orders of the church. Monsieur Cocteau creates the fantastic because for him it signifies facility, evasion, the abandoning of reality, a turning away from urgent problems, the illustration of narcissistic and pederastic themes. No, thank you. I prefer (and how!) the ghosts of De Chirico which, as Breton says, can "come in no other way than by the door." I believe in the unusual, the impossible, I believe in the absolute reality of the marvelous; those who don't and who nonetheless, through aestheticism or stupidity, lay claim to it are simply pathetic fools who will never meet Melusina and Frankenstein in the middle of the Place de l'Opéra.

From Ado Kyrou, *Le Surréalisme au cinéma*, 2d ed. (Paris: Le Terrain Vague, 1963), 63–65. Courtesy Joëlle Losfeld and Le Terrain Vague.

Concerning *King Kong*

Jean Ferry

We are a long way from the waters I've navigated in. . . .
—The Captain

I had so definitely given up the idea of seeing a poetic film that, any attempt at criticism aside, I cannot help reporting the appearance of that rare phenomenon, greeted as you would expect by howls of derision and contempt. I hasten to add that what gives this film value in my eyes is not at all the work of the producers and directors (they aimed only at a grandiose fairground attraction), but what flows naturally from the involuntary liberation of elements in themselves heavy with oneiric power, with strangeness, and with the horrible.

Allow me to point out right away the most flagrant elements of absurdity in this admirable film, and not just for the increased amusement of the crowd who noticed them before I did in laughing (to cover up their fright, in fact) at these "grotesque and serious" images.

(Let me say briefly that *King Kong is* the grandiloquent story of an enormously tall ape who seizes a white woman; he is recaptured and, taken to New York, escapes from the theater where he is on exhibition. He makes off, carrying the woman to the very top of the world's highest building, where he is vanquished by a squadron of planes.)

(a) It's absurd that on board ship a director should be making a screen test of the actress accompanying him (to appear in a documentary, what's more!). Since he takes her on such a long voyage, the screen test must have been made already. Furthermore, it would be impossible for him to develop, shoot, and project this film on board a tramp steamer.

(b) It's absurd to think that various defunct species, of pseudoscientific form, among them a gigantic ape that comes from who knows where, can reproduce themselves on a Pacific island; it is even more absurd to draw attention to this, seeing that it is the very basis of the film.

(c) It's absurd for the Europeans on King Kong's trail to think that he can hide himself in a lake, and that they build (too easily) a raft to continue the hunt.

(d) It's absurd to have a liana hanging from a promontory in the cavern, enabling the young girl and her rescuer to get away down the abyss; it's absurd to think they can find their way through the jungle back to the gate and safety so easily.

(e) It's absurd to show us King Kong suddenly smashing down the gate that till then separated him from the rest of the island.

(f) It's absurd to ask us to believe that King Kong, anaesthetized by gas grenades, could be so easily taken on board a raft and chained up for the rest of the voyage.

(g) It's absurd that King Kong, escaping from the theater where he is on show, so easily rediscovers the woman he seeks.

(h) Last but not least, it's absurd that King Kong perpetually changes size; one minute his hand is big enough to seize an underground train, the next it only goes round the torso of a woman we see waving her arms and legs about.

I think you begin to see what I'm getting at, and will not be surprised to find me on the beaten tracks of the dream, the dream in which, pursued by too pressing a danger, we create the elements of our salvation (d) without being able to escape (e–g). Around the age of ten or twelve I was struck more than anything by "The Murders in the Rue Morgue," and the fear of seeing a gorilla appear at the window haunted my childhood insomnia for a long time (at the age of three I had been extremely frightened of a small marmoset which suddenly leapt up at the window; it is perhaps the only precise memory of my earliest years). Finally, I am not calling on particularly complicated reminiscences when I ask that you bring to mind the countless dreams based on this theme: you are being pursued by some animal or monstrous danger and all of a sudden you cannot run a step farther; the thing approaches; you are consumed by anguish and it is impossible for you to cry out or to lift your feet. For me there are two ways out: either I can cry out, and my cry awakens me, or I manage to flee and in the second part of the dream I hide in the most inaccessible places where the monster rediscovers me. For a long time the monster was a raging bull which, contrary to all expectation, opens doors, climbs stairs; as often as not it is some wild beast or other which, of ten doors, always beats down the one where I am concealed and unhesitatingly pulls aside the tapestry behind which I am hiding, choking with terror.

I find all these elements in *King Kong,* and this is one of the reasons why the film affects me so deeply. In the episode in the theater I rediscovered bit by bit a striking detail from my personal nightmares and all the anguish and atrocious malaise that goes with it. A member of the audience, extremely ill at ease, would like to leave but is chastised for his pusillanimity, and sits down again. This spectator is me; a hundred times in my dream, at the catastrophic moment when the invisible crocodile, the plaster man, or the bull surge into the room, I curse myself for not having left the instant I spotted the danger which the other spectators seem ignorant of.

It is unnecessary to dwell on the apocalyptic grandeur of some of the scenes, particularly the battle in the cavern between King Kong and the enormous serpent; the quality of the sets at this point seems strictly Maldororian to me; maybe American professors of paleontology designed the models of the prehistoric monsters for Hollywood; their spiritual father is none other than Max Ernst. But I would like to insist on the absolutely equivocal side of the story, because in the last analysis why does King Kong carry off this white woman instead of devouring her, why does he tear off her clothes then sniff their perfume, why does he defend her against the other monsters, why does he pursue her when she is ravished by him, finding the strength to break down a gigantic gate which till then isolated him from the rest of the world, what power (and I am no longer speaking of absurdity) makes him rediscover the woman's refuge among the thousand rooms of a skyscraper, why does he let himself be gunned down by airplanes to keep her? As one of my neighbors said: "In any case, he can't do anything with her." That remains to be seen.

I come now to the serious folk who have claimed to see in it only a trick film which does not satisfy them one bit. Let us note in passing that the dubbing, which even in the best of cases is still the worst of a bad job, has been magnificently bungled this time; you can barely understand the murky dialogue which never holds the attention. I will be pitied perhaps for having first seen *King Kong* in an empty cinema in the company of some technicians who from one end of the film to the other were explaining to each other how it was made. It appears, finally, that the tallest King Kong, for there were many of them, as you may have guessed, was but a meter high. But, you see, we knew it already. And this is why I think the inept laughter of the public is only a defense mechanism to force itself to think that this is only a mechanical toy and, having succeeded in this, to escape the feeling of *unheimlich*, of disquieting strangeness, that we cherish and cultivate, for our part, so carefully, and which nothing brings to life as readily, and rightly so, as being in the company of automata. I think that the film would be no less moving, no less frightening, if it was not about a supposedly living beast but an automaton of the same height making the same movements. In any case, whether the monster is real or false, the terror he provokes takes on no less a frenzied and *convulsive* character through its very impossibility. Suppose that you, sitting on the metro, suddenly see his head appear over the trees on the Boulevard Barbès, would you ask yourself whether this is a machine before feeling frightened?

To sum up, through the absurdity of its treatment (an inept script with numerous incoherent details), its violent, oneiric power (the horribly realistic representation of a common dream), its monstrous eroticism (the monster's unbridled love for the woman, cannibalism, human sacrifice), the unreality of certain sets—or, if you are incapable of letting yourself be taken in by all that, by the acute sensation of *unheimlich* with which the presence of automata and trickery imbues the whole film—or better still, in combining all these values the film seems to correspond to all that we mean by the adjective "poetic" and in which we had the temerity to hope the cinema would be its most fertile native soil.

Note A. In this film the Europeans show themselves, as is usual, particularly repugnant where the natives are concerned. This must be most noticeable in the dialogue, and this detail escaped me. King Kong, however, reestablishes a sense of equilibrium by eating both races without prejudice.

The people who think the film reminds them of *The Lost World* need only draw a comparison between the verisimilitude of the prehistoric animals in both productions.

Note B. The quality of the trick work is extremely uneven. Often the animals display a painful stiffness, all the more inexplicable because certain movements are strikingly true (I am thinking of King Kong's action in exploring the rocks and receiving a knife wound in his hand.) As for the back-projection effects, if they fit in with the rest of the film with surprising virtuosity, the least skilled eye will not fail to be troubled by the confusion in perspective ignored by the cameramen during shooting. The first prehistoric monster killed, for example, sweeps away the hunters and a good part of the audience with its tail. Nothing of all this, by the way, worries me.

First published in *Minotaure* (Paris) 5 (1934): 5, under the title, "King-Kong" and signed "Jean Lévy." During the Occupation the Jewish author changed his name to Ferry, the name by which he is now known. Ferry, a prominent member of the College of 'Pataphysics and an expert on Raymond Roussel, would later co-script Buñuel's *Cela s'appelle l'aurore* (1955) with the director. Courtesy Mme. Lila Marcelle Ferry.

Larry Semon's message

Petr Král

The human countenance, "the most engaging—and disquieting—of landscapes," shone no doubt with an altogether singular light in some of those pale meteorites which crossed the screen in the magical quiet of the silent age of cinema, the most mythic period of this modern mythology. I'm thinking of the flickering faces of the earliest stars whose clarity coincided unforgettably with that *rediscovery of man* we owe to cinema. In the gallery of noiseless apparitions, whose look, after half a century, has lost none of its magical hold on us, it is the genial masters of the alchemy of the gag, the comics of American slapstick, who hold the place of honor.

Few have confronted contemporary man with his fatal *solitude* as often as the cinema hero, particularly the strange hero of that precious genre of poetic film known, inadequately, as "burlesque." Like the writer, of course, the reader of a book gives himself over to his solitude. But the solitude of a cinema spectator, face to face with an actor on the screen, is even more pressing because the innate "reality" of the film, set against a background of the most concrete images of the external world, brings this out; reflected in indifferent objects the gaze of the solitary human is *naked* once more. Rarely has man's face been so actively illuminated from within by essential human anguish as in the films of the Sennett school (the humor of which is only a magical exorcism of this anguish). Despite their apparently epic character, these films have but one center of gravity: the countenance of the hero as the *lyrical subject* of all the fantastic catastrophes by which he settles his score with objective reality, catastrophes whose explosions color his cheeks with a reflection of *inner* fire.

Every face is pale in silent cinema. In some ways, this makes you think of some miraculous flour mill: the style of makeup then, of course, but also those swirling clouds of "flour" which the projection of old, worn-out prints calls forth on the screen. The ones whose pallor was not a quality but the very *essence* of their personality, the palest of all, were two in number: Harry Langdon and Larry Semon, who share with Fatty Arbuckle the role of being the most *suspect* heroes in burlesque. Fatty's mystery barely extends beyond the limits of his ambiguous *appearance*; Harry and Larry, on the other hand, are suspect in everything. Not only in their disturbing behavior, on the screen and off, in the obscure character of their inner (sexual) bents, in the atmosphere of inevitable *tragedy* they bear with them: even the universe they move through is created in their image, completely impregnated by the uncertainty that is special to them alone.

Unfortunately, the *obscure* aspect of silent burlesque continues to be unjustly neglected, even by its most inspired disciples, like Raymond Borde. It seems the interpretations that actually consider the *subversive* nature of the orgiastic humor of Sennett & Co. cannot rid themselves of the simplified, idyllic conception of that epoch as our century's "lost childhood," still characterized by its primordial purity and harmony: for the most part, the humor of burlesque is considered an expression of the healthy optimism and vigor of the young American civilization (or even young American capitalism), so sure of itself it can laugh at its own expense. Indeed, it isn't just by chance that the end of the "golden age" of silent cinema, the 1920s, with its flappers, burlesques, and "Yes, We Have No Bananas," coincides with Wall Street's "Black Friday." But this health and insouciance represented only one face of that intoxicating—and intoxicated—period, whose euphoria was of an extremely apocalyptic kind to begin with. To the parade of legs dancing the Charleston must be added another, altogether more fascinating one, the parade of bags under the eyes. Today the perfidiousness of the whirlpools of private life which those bright young things tried to navigate, while all the time touting the official screen doctrine "Keep Smiling," is no longer kept secret. And the comics of the period, however exceptionally favorable it was for them, often lived out the same bitter, tragic destinies: think of Max Linder's suicide, Keaton's confinement, Arbuckle's brush with the law, Langdon's bankruptcy.

Now, it is on this *hidden side* of the 1920s that Larry Semon has his place, which undoubtedly counts as one of the reasons he is so scandalously forgotten. The little one knows about his life suggests an existence as bizarre, perhaps, as Langdon's: a marvelous infantilism through which, during the shooting of the exteriors for *The Sawmill,* he squandered a large part of the budget building absolutely unnecessary luxury cabins for himself and his colleagues, suggests an inability to come to terms with the American law of *enterprise,* an inability comparable to the one that also brought down Langdon. Today, of course, it is mostly through the intermediary of his films (the ones that remain, that is) that we can speak of the disturbing mystery of Semon's personality. Therein as nowhere else—except in Langdon's work—do we find the embodiment of everything that, in burlesque, formed a romantic, introspective, nonconformist, in a word, *nocturnal* countercurrent to the healthy, classically balanced *white* humor whose purest—and often most conformist—strain is represented by the two most marketable products of the Hal Roach studio:[1] Harold Lloyd, and Laurel and Hardy.

Semon is Mack Sennett's most important disciple in what I would call the *concrete* gag, the one that, in contrast to the abstract gag founded on an intellectual plane, aims first of all at the material, tangible effect of filmic action. Toward this kind of gag, whose prototype is the classic custard pie, there unfortunately exists, even in our own day, considerable prejudice, influenced by the spiritualistic interpretation of burlesque coming from the avant-garde of the Dellucs, Clairs, and Cocteaus who saw in it just a vulgar sort of humor vastly inferior to the "absolute values" of filmic rhythm and "photogenia." It needed somebody like Salvador Dalí to set a new tone in the debate about burlesque, to rehabilitate the "materialist" gag as the supreme form of "concrete irrationality" ("Abstract of a Critical History of the Cinema"). One can only regret that Dalí didn't know about Larry Semon—he would not have been blind to the irrationality in Semon, which is as highly developed as the kind he revealed—within the framework of sound cinema—in the Marx Brothers.

In the shorts produced by Mack Sennett a liberating, *quantitative* squandering (entire companies of cops and bathing beauties chasing solitary heroes, not to mention the cataclysmic accumulation of catastrophes) is dialectically linked to a sense of the singular *quality* of certain elements and objects which perform a relatively constant role in Sennett's variable

---

1 It is obviously significant to the part Hal Roach plays in the history of cinematic humor that his "laugh factory" perhaps finds the greatest number of *consumers* during the 1930s when America, stabilizing itself—as Europe becomes more and more disordered—again loses, and for a long time, that sense of the *marvelous* found in the anarchic disasters of Mack Sennett and the fragile fata morganas of Buster Keaton.

universe and give it the quality of an irrational *system* (custard pies, false beards, Model T Fords, hoses). In Semon the imagination's inclination to systematize is taken to the point where it becomes a delirious interpretation of the world, completely conforming to the notion behind Dalí's "paranoia-critical" method: the universe is fearlessly and unconditionally *identified* with a mobile formation of many stable elements, no less alluring than a rhinoceros's body or a soft watch, even though now we're speaking of an empty barrel, a motorbike, an ax, a real monkey, rotten eggs, and clouds of feathers escaping from ripped pillows. These are the principal elements in this galaxy, whose general and perpetual center of rotation is formed by the pale sun of Larry's cunning face, producing a progressive succession of encounter, collision, and unexpected destruction of all the planets, ceaselessly, inevitably ending in total *cosmic disaster:* the majority of Larry's films[2] end in a *veritable* explosion.

A gag by Larry is a gag without a fall. To be exact, a "fall" is elementary physical violence if it is the work of the human hand, "blind" chance, or even—as happens in the majority of cases—the result of their involuntary collaboration: a stumbling, kick, punch, or blow from a thrown object (nothing less respectable, possibly, than a barrel or bucket), hurtling into the air, fallen to earth. The "spiritual," human sense of this pitiless "settling of accounts" in the name of repressed aggression, to which Chaplin's humanist coquetry is completely foreign, rests solely in the marvelous unexpectedness of the ways the action of the film is brought to a climax or end. Seldom do we find a gag so remote from the comic *anecdote* as we do with Semon; seldom is it identified in as coherent a way with the adventure of the free and disinterested play of the imagination. Nevertheless, his gag-image has nothing gratuitous about it. Even though the freedom he permits himself in the treatment of the external world comes close to that in comic strips and animated films, his real strength lies in the joining up of that freedom and a fine sense of the materiality of things, which makes it possible for him to profit from the singular facility cinema has of integrating the imaginary *directly* with the real, of insidiously *proving* the impossible through the intermediary of the possible. Semon's films are as

---

2 I have deliberately set aside the decadent, and short-lived, phase of his feature films and concentrated solely on his shorts.

convincing and concrete as the most "lifelike" of dreams. The *symbolic* character of objects, underlined by their exaggerated proportions (the monstrous planks crashing down on Larry in *The Sawmill,* and that blazon to his sado-masochism, the terrifying executioner's ax), does not in the least prevent them from performing their most ordinary, "civil" functions.

In *Larry en Méxique* there is a dismaying scene in which Semon, dragged out of a dining room still on his chair, hauls behind him a fully laden table to which he is united by the tablecloth, the corner of which he had shoved in his collar in lieu of a napkin; what's more, the chandeliers crash down on the table and set alight the uniforms of the flunkies, before whom this fantastic train passes. I think this scene is a sufficiently expressive example of that *insatiability* for exaggeration and the accumulation of objects that makes Larry the only legitimate ancestor among silent comics of the Marx Brothers. His films have none of the purism and geometric proportionality unique to Buster Keaton. They are dominated by the same unrestrained bad taste devoid of all "sense of proportion," taken as far as the nauseous and paroxysmal forms expressed in the Marxes by the disharmony of Harpo's shirts and ties and by the trio's obsessive predilection for violent scuffling in confined spaces (*A Night at the Opera*). Of all the 1920s comedians who rely to a large extent on a modern economy of means of "pure style," Semon is the least *cultural* to the degree that he is the closest to the marvelous impurity of the Art Nouveau of 1900. His interiors are littered with sumptuously decorated screens, heavy curtains, and bizarre vases. His heroines, with their complicated coiffures and tasteful dresses, often dripping with jewels, have no relation to the mass-produced young things of the Charleston era: here are the highly evolved female monsters who, in burlesque, prepare the way for the proud entrances of those queens-to-be, Margaret Dumont, Groucho's partner, or Mae West, W.C. Fields's companion in the unforgettable *My Little Chickadee.*

Finally, Semon is not inferior to the Marxes when it comes to the *aggression* with which he places the heavy burden of his personal obsessions on the spectator's shoulders. Like Harpo,[3] he does not hesitate to give his gluttony toward the objective world direct physical form: in *Zigoto dans les*

---

3 With whom he shares a happily only occasional weakness: the inclination toward a too clownish form of expression.

coulisses[4] he bites as avidly into a pom-pom as Harpo does into a bowl (*A Night at the Opera, A Night in Casablanca*) or a telephone (*Duck Soup*). To my knowledge, the culminating expression of this oral-sadistic attitude to reality, *cannibalism,* never reveals itself *directly* in him, but this is no more than the problem of dotting the "i." Furthermore, in the scene cited from *Zigoto dans les coulisses* the devouring of the pom-pom is obviously the fetishistic representation of the affinity Larry feels toward the cabaret star who left it on her dressing table.

The most suspect aspect of Semon's work is naturally its erotic content, overloaded like no other great comic's work with obscene meaning. Semon is ultimately too preoccupied with his obsessions and perversions to be able to devote himself to the problem of transcending sex through love as each of the other comedians manages to do: Chaplin like Keaton, Langdon as well as Lloyd. One of Larry's gags obliterated the frontier separating man from the object or animal and transformed him into a ghostly being, half animal, half wax dummy, about whom you no longer need have sentimental scruples. Semon gives no more important role to that black man present in all his films than the part of a no less omnipresent monkey; more than likely the opposite. When he escapes his pursuers, concealed under their very noses in a perambulating barrel or transformed into a monstrous urchin, Larry resembles not so much a human being as a *something* in search of its set of instructions or at least of a muzzle. Let's pass over the strange team into which the trio of flunkies (in *Larry au salon*) *is* directly transformed, having received such an artful kick that they push each other out of the room by the backside—with their heads. It is pointless, perhaps, to underline how many *insupportable* meanings are elicited by the relatively classic gag of the artificial leg mistakenly taken for a real woman's, when performed by Semon.

Of course, the same more or less elementary sexual *complexes* are to be found at the source of Semon's poetic courage, as with the other great "lyricists" of slapstick.[5] Especially the most fatalistic of all, the fear of im-

---

4 [I have been unable to discover an annotated Semon filmography. *Zigoto dans les coulisses* could be *The Stage Hand* (1920) or *Between the Acts* (1919). I don't know what *Larry en Méxique* or *Larry au salon* could be. —*Trans.*]

5 By "lyricists" I mean those comedians situated at the opposite pole from the sexually balanced, socially adaptable "realists" whose prototype is Harold Lloyd.

potence, expressed symbolically in the typical garment covering Larry's grotesquely small physique, for which every pair of trousers, every bowler hat is irremediably *too large*. But there, where others give in to their incapacity for "normal" erotic life to the extent of masochistic passivity (Langdon) or frigidity (Keaton), Semon, with wholly Dalíesque arrogance, gives credit to it. Wholly without sense of guilt, it is he, rather, who is the accuser when he unleashes in his films a totally fantastic orgy, the agenda of which misses nothing out that, as far as *valid convention* is concerned, is considered illegitimate in sexuality: from ritual and regular homages to masturbation (whose classical symbol, feathers, sooner or later speckle the draperies in his splendid drawing rooms with their sperm) to Larry's disturbing dance disguised as a woman (*Larry au salon*), the only drag number in the history of screen humor that does not disgust by its gratuitousness,[6] he gives the impression of *authenticity*.

Taking the natural unity of humor and poetry as far as it can go, Larry Semon's oeuvre is at once a magnificent and lasting manifestation of the unwholesome, indecent forces of the imagination. Again and again *real life* uses these forces to set itself against the divisions in the handsome, hygienic cages where all reasonable, discerning bourgeois of clear conscience and sound stomach and the technocratic apostles of "well-executed work," "the sense of proportion," or "pure cinema" would like us to be imprisoned.

From *Positif* (Paris) 106 (June 1969): 28–33. Courtesy Petr Král.

---

6 Only Jerry Lewis is an exception to this when, disguised as a kabuki actor in the last sequence of *The Big Mouth*, he is endowed with a surprisingly tender charm.

Hands off love

The Surrealist Group

Whatever may be invoked, whatever has brio in the world, whatever is worthwhile, worth defending above all else, at the expense of all else, whatever invariably involves some personal whim or other of a judge, and reflect a second on what a judge is, how at any moment in your life you are dependent on a judge to whom all of a sudden the merest accident delivers you up, in a word, whatever negates everything, genius for example: this is what a recent trial has stunningly brought to light. Both the nature of the defendant and of the charges brought against him make it worthwhile to examine Mrs. Chaplin's suit against her husband, as reported in *Le Grand Guignol*. It goes without saying that what follows is based on the belief that the documents are authentic, and though of course it is Charlie Chaplin's right to deny any of the alleged facts and remarks imputed to him, we have here taken their truth for granted. It is a question of seeing what has been dug up to set against such a man, of appraising the means used to diminish him. These means cast a strange light on everyday moral opinion in the U.S.A. of 1927, that is to say, one of the major human agglomerations, an opinion that will tend to spread and prevail everywhere, in so far as the immense reservoir clogged with commodities in North America is also an immense reservoir of stupidity ever ready to wash over us and, indeed, to totally cretinize the amorphous clientele of Europe, always at the mercy of the highest bidder.

It is truly monstrous to reflect that if a professional secrecy exists for doctors, a secrecy that is after all only a precaution against awareness of self, and which yet exposes any incumbent to relentless repression, there is, on the other hand, no professional secrecy for married women. Even so, being a married woman is a profession like any other, from the day the woman claims as her due her alimentary and sexual ration. A man whom the law saddles with the obligation to live with one woman has no alternative but to share his own morals with that woman, to put himself at the mercy of that woman. If the wife hands him over to public opprobrium, why shouldn't the same law that has given her the most arbitrary rights be turned against her with all the rigor that such a revolting abuse of confidence merits, a defamation so obviously linked to the most sordid self-interest? And, furthermore, why should morals even be the subject of legislation? What an absurdity! But to confine ourselves to the extremely episodic *scruples* of the *virtuous* and *inexperienced* Mrs. Chaplin: there is something comic in taking the practice of fellatio—for example—to be *abnormal, against nature, perverted, degenerate,* and *indecent.* (*All married people do it,* Chaplin rightly remarks.) If the free and frank discussion of morals is to be rationally undertaken, then it would be normal, natural, sound, and decent to dismiss the suit of a wife guilty of having *inhumanly* rejected practices so widespread, so utterly pure and defensible. And how can such stupidity make any appeal to love, as today this woman who at sixteen years and two months of age knowingly enters into marriage with a man both rich and in the public eye dares to do, with her two *babies,* doubtless born through her ear since *the defendant never had conjugal relations with her as is customary between man and wife,* these babies she brandishes as soiled Exhibits 1 and 2 of her own personal demands? The italics are ours, and the revolting language they emphasize is that of the plaintiff and her counsel who seek primarily to sully a living man with the most repugnant stereotyping worthy of mindless journalese, the image of a mother who calls her legitimate lover *Daddy,* and this with the sole intent of levying on this man a tax even the most exigent state has never dreamed of, a *tax* that burdens his genius most heavily, that even tends to dispossess him of that genius, or at very least to discredit its truly precious expression.

The five principal charges brought by Mrs. Chaplin are as follows: (1) the lady was seduced; (2) the seducer advised her to opt for an abortion; (3) he only agreed to marriage when coerced and with the intention of divorcing her; (4) for this reason, and following a preconceived plan, he behaved injuriously and cruelly toward her; (5) the proof of these accusations is demonstrated by the habitual immorality of Charlie Chaplin's speech and by the theoretical conception he had of all things held most sacred.

As a rule the *crime* of seduction is a difficult one to define since what constitutes the *crime* is merely the circumstantial side of the seduction proper. This outrage, to which both parties have consented and for which one alone of them is responsible, is further complicated by the fact that nothing can humanly prove the *victim's* part in provoking or initiating it. But in this instance the innocent party has indeed succumbed, and if the seducer did not intend to make an honest woman of her, then the fact is that it is she who in all naïveté has gained the upper hand over this demoniac being. Such perseverance and persistence is surprising in one so young, so defenseless. Unless, that is, she imagined that the only way of becoming Charlie Chaplin's wife was to sleep with him first . . . but then let's hear no more about seduction; this was purely business, with its various risks, possible desertion, pregnancy.

At this point, being pressed to undergo an operation she held to be *criminal,* the *unfortunate woman,* pregnant at the time of her marriage, refuses to do so for reasons that are worthy of examination. She complains that her condition would become public, that her fiancé had done all he could to render it so. An obvious contradiction: who stands to profit by such publicity? Who is going to reject any means to prevent what in California amounts to an outrage? But now the victim is well armed, she will be able to say, to put it about that abortion was demanded of her. This is a decisive argument, and not a word the criminal utters concerning the matter— which is *a great crime against society, both legally and morally, and therefore repugnant, horrifying, and contrary to the instincts of a mother* (the plaintiff's) *and to her sense of the maternal duty of protection and preservation*—not a word of Charlie Chaplin's will go unheeded. Everything will be noted, intimate daily phrases, circumstance, even dates; from the day the future Mrs. Chaplin first thought to make use of her *instincts,* to present herself as a monument of normality, and even though she wasn't yet legally married, she continued, she affirms, to love her fiancé despite his horrifying predilections, and so, a spy in the house, she assiduously keeps up her martyr's diary with nary a tear left out. Does not the third of the charges she brings against her husband apply to herself first and foremost? Did she not *enter into marriage* with the firm intent of emerging therefrom both rich and respected? As to the fourth charge, the treatment Mrs. Chaplin suffered during the marriage, once it is examined in any detail, does it register as a distinct attempt on Charlie Chaplin's part to demoralize his wife, or is it the natural outcome of the everyday attitude of a wife who amasses grievances, welcoming them, rejoicing in them? In passing, let us note one omission: Mrs. Chaplin forgets to give us the date she ceased *loving* her husband. Maybe she still loves him.

In support of her allegations she reports certain of Charlie Chaplin's remarks as if they were so many moral proofs of the existence of a premeditated plan attested to in the rest of the evidence, after which an honest American judge can no longer consider the defendant a man, but a scoundrel, a contemptible brute pure and simple. The perfidy of this maneuver and its efficacy will escape nobody. And thus the ideas of Charlot, as we call him in France, on the most burning issues are suddenly thrust before us, and in so direct a manner that they cannot fail to throw a singular light on the morality of those films from which we have derived more than mere pleasure, in which we have taken an almost unrivaled critical interest. A tendentious relation, given that state of acute surveillance the Great American Public likes to hold its favorites under and which, as we saw in the case of Fatty Arbuckle, can ruin a man in the space of one day. Our model wife has played her trump card; nevertheless, it transpires that her revelations have a worth she did not anticipate. She thought to denounce her husband, the stupid woman, the cow. But she only bears witness to the human grandeur of a mind which, clearly and correctly perceiving the welter of deadly forces in a society that cramps his life and even his genius, has found the means to accord his thought a perfect and vigorous expression without betraying this thought, an expression whose humor and power, whose poetry in a word, suddenly and before our very eyes takes a beating in the glimmer of the little bourgeois lamp held above his head by one of those bitches who, in every country, turn into *good* mothers, *good* sisters, *good* wives, these pestilences, these parasites on every kind of feeling, every kind of love.

Given that during the cohabitation of the plaintiff and defendant, the defendant declared to the plaintiff on occasions too numerous to be specified in minute and complete detail that he was not a partisan of the custom of marriage, that he could not tolerate the conventional restraint that marital relations demand, and that he was of the opinion that a woman could honestly bear children to a man outside of wedlock; given that he also ridiculed and mocked the plaintiff's belief and faith in the moral and social conventions pertaining to the state of marriage, the relation of the sexes, and the bringing into the world of children, and that he set little store in the laws and statutes of morality (regarding which he remarked one day to the plaintiff that a certain couple had had five children without being married, adding that "This was an ideal way for a man and a woman to live together"), we are thus alerted to the essential point about Charlot's much vaunted *immorality.* It is to be remarked that certain extremely simple truths still pass for monstrosities. It is to be hoped the idea gains ground, a purely human idea which here borrows from the man who manifests it in his personal prestige. Everybody, that is to say, everybody who is not a hypo-crite or a whore, thinks like this. Besides, we would like to know who would dare make claims for a marriage contracted under threat, even if the woman has borne her husband a child? Let her come and complain that her hus-band goes straight to his room, that once to her horror he came in drunk, that he did not dine with her, that he does not take her out in society. Such arguments are worth no more than a shrug of the shoulders.

All the same, it seems that Charlie Chaplin aspires in good faith to make their conjugal life possible. But no such luck: he comes up against a wall of stupidity. Everything seems criminal to this woman who believes or feigns to believe that the procreation of brats is her sole raison d'être, brats who will in turn beget brats. A noble idea of life. "What are you trying to do? Repopulate Los Angeles?" he asks her in exasperation. So she will have a second child, since she demands it, only now she must stop pestering him: he does not lust after fatherhood any more than he did wedlock. Then to please the lady he has to baby-talk the kids. But that isn't his way. He is seen less and less *around the house.* He has his own idea of existence; this is what is under attack, being diminished. What could possibly bind him to a woman who spurns all he holds dear, who accuses him *of undermining and perverting* (her) *normal impulses . . . of corrupting her sense of decency, of degrading her conception of moral values,* and all because he tried to make her read books in which sexual matters were openly discussed, because he wanted her to meet people who bring to morality a little of that freedom she is the inveterate enemy of. And again, what obligingness there was on his part just four months before their separation when he proposes invit-ing to their home a young woman who has a reputation for participating in *acts of sexual perversion,* saying *to the plaintiff that they might have a little fun together.* A last ditch attempt at acclimatizing the battery hen to the natural proclivities of conjugal love. Books, the example of others: he has tried everything to make the dimwit understand what she is incapable of doing so for herself. After all this she is surprised at the swings of mood in a man whose life she has made hell: *"Just mind I don't go crazy one day and kill you"*; she hasn't forgotten to enter this threat in the charge book, but on whom does the responsibility for it lie? For a man to become aware of such a possibility—madness, murder—doesn't this mean he has been subjected to such treatment that madness and murder might result from it? And during these months, when a woman's spite and the danger of adverse public opinion force him to act out an intolerable comedy, he remains a man in a cage whose vitality, whose heart, does not die.

"Yes, it's true," he says one day, *"I'm in love and I don't care who knows it. I'll go and see her when I want, whether you like it or not. I don't love you and I only live with you because I had to marry you."* This is the moral foundation of the man's life, this is what he defends: love itself. Throughout the whole affair Charlot is in truth the champion of love, uniquely so, purely so. He will say to his wife that the woman he loves is *marvelous,* he would like her to see him with her, etc. Such frankness, such honesty, everything that is admirable in the world, is now used against him. But the best argument is a brace of brats born against his will.

Here again Charlie Chaplin's attitude is clear. Both times he asked his wife to have an abortion. He told her the truth: it can be done, other women do it, *have* done it for me. *For me* means not for social gain, or convenience, but *for love.* But it was pointless appealing to love with Mrs. Chaplin. She only had her children to attest to the fact that: *"The defendant never manifested any normal and paternal interest, nor any affection"*—note the fine distinction—*"for the two offspring of the plaintiff and the defendant."* Ah, the little ones! Doubtless for him they are just an idea linked to his enslavement, but for the mother they are the basis for a lifetime's claims. She wants to build a wing for them on the family home. Charlot refuses: *"It's my house, and I don't want it spoilt."* This eminently reasonable reply, the milk bills, the phone calls made and those that weren't made, the husband's comings and goings, whether he sees his wife, whether he happens to see her when she's entertaining idiots who displease him, whether he has people to dinner, whether he takes his wife out or leaves her behind: for Mrs. Chaplin all this constitutes cruel and inhuman treatment, but for us it chiefly defines the desire a man has to obviate everything that is not love, everything that is its fierce, hideous caricature. Better than any book, better than all books, all treatises, this man's conduct puts marriage and the imbecilic codification of love itself on trial.

We recall an admirable moment in *The Impostor* when of an instant, during a social gathering, Charlot sees an extremely beautiful woman go by, as alluring as can be, and immediately abandons what he's doing to follow her from room to room and out onto the terrace until she disappears from view. At the command of love, he has always been at the command of love, this is what his life and his films constantly proclaim. Instant love, with its great and irresistible appeal. At such times all is abandoned, as for instance, at a minimum, the home. The world and its legal fetters, the housewife and her kids backed up by the policeman, the savings bank: it's these the rich man of Los Angeles is running away from, as is that other poor devil from the wretched suburbs, the Charlot of *The Bank Clerk* and *The Gold Rush*. Morally speaking, all he has in his pocket is a dollar piece of seduction that is forever getting lost. In *The Immigrant* we see it forever falling onto the café floor via a hole in his pants. Maybe it's only a semblance of a dollar, easy to bend between the teeth, a bogus coin that will be refused but which just for a moment enables you to invite to your table a woman like a tongue of flame, the "marvelous" woman whose pure features eclipse the heavens. This is how the morality constantly expressed in Charlie Chaplin's work finds an echo in his life, but with all the circumlocutions social conditions demand. And finally, when Mrs. Chaplin informs us—and she knows the kind of argument to use—that her husband, a most unpatriotic American, intends to export his capital, we think back to the tragic sight of steerage passengers labeled like animals on the deck of the boat taking Charlot to America, the brutality of the authorities, the cynical questioning of the immigrants, the dirty hands laid on the women on arrival in the land of Prohibition, under the classic gaze of the Statue of Liberty. What this Liberty's torch casts in Charlot's films is the menacing shadow of the cops, those bounty hunters of the poor, the cops who pop up at every street corner and are instantly suspicious of the tramp's miserable suit, his cane (which in a remarkable article Charlie Chaplin calls *his insurance*), a cane that's always falling from his grasp, the bowler, the mustache, right down to his fretful smile. Make no mistake, despite several happy endings, next time we shall rediscover him in misery, this awesome pessimist who today, in English and in French, has given new meaning to the saying: *une vie de chien,* a dog's life.

A DOG'S LIFE: right now this is the life of a man whose genius won't save him, a man on whom the world's back is about to be turned, who will be ruined with impunity, whose whole means of expression will be taken away, who is being demoralized in the most scandalous fashion, all for the sake of a dirty, spiteful petty-bourgeoise, the sake of the greatest public hypocrisy imaginable. A dog's life. Genius means nothing to the law when matrimony, holy matrimony is at stake. Genius is never ever anything to the law. But Charlot's experience marks, above and beyond public curiosity and the chicanery of the legal profession and the whole shameful divulgence of a private life henceforth tarnished by such sinister clarity, Charlot's experience today marks his destiny, the destiny of genius. Its role and its value are conferred more than by any single work of his. The mysterious ascendancy that an unrivaled power of expression confers on a man: now we can understand its full meaning. We suddenly understand the place genius has in the world. It takes hold of a man, makes him an erstwhile symbol and thus the victim of baleful brutes. Genius serves to signify moral truth to the world, which universal stupidity obscures and endeavors to undermine. Thanks be, then, for the man who, over there on the immense western screen, on the horizon where one by one the suns go down, projects his shadow, great realities of mankind, perhaps the sole realities, moral truths whose value is greater than the whole earth. The earth opens up at your feet. Thank you, victim from the other side. We declaim our thanks to you, we are your obedient servants.

Maxime Alexandre, Louis Aragon, Arp, Jacques Baron, Jacques-André Boiffard, André Breton, Jean Carrive, Robert Desnos, Marcel Duhamel, Paul Éluard, Max Ernst, Jean Genbach, Camille Goemans, Paul Hooreman, Eugène Jolas, Michel Leiris, Georges Limbour, Georges Malkine, André Masson, Max Morise, Pierre Naville, Marcel Noll, Paul Nougé, Elliot Paul, Benjamin Péret, Jacques Prévert, Raymond Queneau, Man Ray, Georges Sadoul, Yves Tanguy, Roland Tual, Pierre Unik

Largely composed by Louis Aragon, "Hands Off Love" first appeared in Nancy Cunard's idiosyncratic English in *Transition* (Paris) 6 (September 1927), and then in *La Révolution surréaliste* (Paris) 9–10 (October 1927): 1–6. The current translator has consulted Cunard and Richard Howard's version in Maurice Nadeau, *The History of Surrealism* (New York: Macmillan, 1965).

Chaplin, the copper's nark

Jean-Louis Bédouin

The very announcement of Charles Chaplin's official visit to Europe, given everything such an odious parade must by definition entail, was grounds enough for us to become alarmed about somebody one still took to be a free agent. In the last number of *Le Libertaire* our anarchist comrades drew attention to this man's bowing and scraping in public. But it wasn't yet evident just how anxious he was to debase, to deny himself; that it would take only a few days of social engagements for him to slough off the personification of the legendary tramp and reemerge as the crony of a Prefect of Police.

We condemn the behavior of a Chaplin who, of his own free will, proceeded to thank the Police Department for "having protected him so well" (against what?); the Chaplin who, by accepting a gold medal commemorating the 150th anniversary of said Prefecture, together with a keepsake presentation truncheon, is marked with infamy in the eyes of all those who had believed in the subversive nature of his work and who had accorded him all their affection, as to no other great artist. This essentially popular affection he now tramples underfoot, and all for a fancy dinner with Monsieur Auriol, a handshake with Monsieur Baylot, a reception at the Ministry of Trade.

It goes without saying that for us Chaplin's work must be reassessed the moment it is betrayed by the actions of its author. Drawn by him in the Police's "Visitors Book" (*sic*), photostatted and distributed in homage to the brutalizers of striking workers, Charlot's world-famous silhouette ceases to be an image of protest to become that of the buffoon capitalism claims for itself at our expense.

Le Libertaire (Paris), 20 November 1952. Reprinted in José Pierre, *Surréalisme et anarchie* (Paris: Plasma, 1983), 236. Courtesy Jean-Louis Bédouin. Bédouin's rubric, *Charlot policeman,* echoes the French titling of a typical early Chaplin short. A few weeks before this declaration, the International Lettrists—the future Situationists—had attacked the director in public; cf. Greil Marcus, *Lipstick Traces: A Secret History of the Twentieth Century* (Cambridge, Mass.: Harvard Univ. Press, 1989), 340–343.

Manifesto of the Surrealists concerning *L'Âge d'or*

The Surrealist Group

On Wednesday 12 November 1930 and on subsequent days several hundred people, obliged to take their seats daily in a theater, drawn to this spot by very different, not to say contradictory, aspirations covering the widest spectrum, from the best to the worst, these people generally unfamiliar with each other and even, from a social point of view, avoiding each other as much as they can, yet nevertheless conspiring, whether they like it or not, by virtue of the darkness, insensitive alignment, and the hour, which is the same for all, to bring to a successful conclusion or to wreck, in Buñuel's *L'Âge d'or,* one of the most extensive sets of demands proposed to human consciousness to this day, it is fitting perhaps, rather than giving in to the pleasure of at last seeing transgressed to the nth degree the prohibitive laws passed to render inoffensive any work of art over which there is an outcry and faced with which we endeavor, with hypocrisy's help, to recognize in the name of beauty nothing but a muzzle, it is certainly fitting to measure with some rigor the wing span of this bird of prey so utterly unexpected today in the darkening sky, in the darkening western sky: *L'Âge d'or.*

The sexual instinct and the death instinct
Perhaps it would be asking too little of today's artists that they confine themselves to establishing the brilliant fact that the sublimated energy smoldering within them will continue to deliver them up, bound hand and foot, to the existing order of things and will not make victims, through them, of anybody but themselves. It is, we believe, their most elementary duty to submit the activity which results from this sublimation of mysterious origin to intense criticism and not to shrink before any apparent excess, since above all else it is a question of loosening the muzzle we were

speaking of. To give in, with all the cynicism this enterprise entails, to the tracking down within oneself and the affirmation of all the hidden tendencies of which the artistic end product is merely an extremely frivolous aspect, must not only be permitted but demanded of them. Beyond this sublimation of which they are the object and which could not be held without mysticism to be a natural aim, it only remains for them to propose to scientific opinion another term, once account has been taken by them of this sublimation. Today one expects of the artist that he know to what fundamental machination he *owes* his being an artist, and one can only give him title to this denomination as long as one is sure he is perfectly aware of this machination.

Now, disinterested examination of the conditions in which the problem is, or tends to be, resolved, reveals to us that the artist, Buñuel, for example, merely succeeds in being the immediate location of a series of conflicts that two nonetheless associated human instincts distantly engage in: the sexual instinct and the death instinct.

Given that the universally hostile attitude involving the second of these instincts differs in each man only in its application, that purely economic reasons oppose themselves within present-day bourgeois society to whatever this attitude profits by in the way of other than extremely incomplete gratifications, these same reasons being themselves an unfailing source of conflict derived from what they might have been, and which it would be permissible then to examine, one knows that the amorous attitude, with all the egoism it implies and the much more appreciable chance of realization it has, is the one which, of the two, succeeds in best sustaining the spirit's light. Whence the miserable taste for *refuge* of which much has been made in art for centuries, whence the great tolerance displayed to all that, in exchange for a good many tears and much gnashing of teeth, still helps place this amorous attitude above all else.

It is no less true, dialectically, that either one of these attitudes is only humanly possible as a function of the other, that these two instincts for *preservation,* tending, it has been pointed out, to reestablish a state troubled by the appearance of life, creates a perfect balance in every man, that social cowardliness which anti-Eros allows, at the expense of Eros, to be born. It is no less true that in the violence we see in an individual's spirited amorous passion we can assess his capacity for refusal, we can, from a revolutionary viewpoint, making light of the fleeting inhibition in which his education may or may not sustain him, give him more than a symptomatic role.

Once, and this is always the case, this amorous passion shows itself to be so clear about its own determination, once it bristles the disgusting spines of the blood of what one wants to love and what, occasionally, one loves, once the much maligned frenzy has taken over, outside of which we, Surrealists, refuse to hold up any expression of art as valid, and we know the new and dramatic limit of compromise through which every man passes and through which, in proposing to write or paint, we are the first and the last to have, without more ample information—this more ample information being *L'Âge d'or*—consented to pass.

It's the mythology that changes
At the present, undoubtedly most propitious time for a psychoanalytic investigation which aims to determine the origin and formation of moral myths, we believe it possible, by simple induction, marginal to all scientific accuracy, to conclude in the possible existence of a criterion that would free itself in a precise way from everything that can be synthesized in the general aspirations of Surrealist thought and which would result, from the biological point of view, in an attitude contrary to that which permits the admission of the various moral myths as the residue of primitive taboos. Completely opposed to this residue, we believe (paradoxical as it may seem) that it is within the domain of what one is in the habit of reducing to the limitations(!) of the congenital, that a depreciative hypothesis of these myths would be possible according to which the divination and mythification of certain fetishistic representations of moral meaning (such as those of maternity, old age, etc.) would be a product which, by its relation to the affective world, at the same time as its mechanism of objectification and projection to the external, could be considered as an obviously complicated case of collective transference in which the demoralizing role would be played by a powerful and profound sense of ambivalence.

The often complete individual psychological possibilities of destruction of a vast mythic system coexist with the well-known and no less frequent possibility of rediscovering in earlier times, by a process of regression, already existing archaic myths. On the one hand, that signifies the affirmation of certain symbolic constants in unconscious thought and, on the other, the fact that this thought is independent of every mythic system. So everything comes back to a question of language: through unconscious language we can rediscover a myth, but we are very much aware that mythologies change and that on every occasion a new psychological hunger of paranoiac tendency overtakes our often miserable feelings.

One must not trust in the illusion that may result from the lack of comparison, an illusion similar to the illusion of the moving off of a stationary train when another train passes by the carriage window and, in the instance of ethics, similar to the tendency of facts toward evil: everything happens as if, contrary to reality, what is changing were not events exactly but, more seriously, mythology itself.

Sculptural reproductions of various allegories will take their place in a perfectly normal way in the moral mythologies of the future, among which the most exemplary will prove to be the one of a couple of blind people eating each other and that of an adolescent "spitting with pure delight on his mother's portrait," a nostalgic look on his face.

The gift of violence
Waging the most desperate struggle against all artifice, subtle or vulgar, the *violence* in this film divests solitude of all it decks itself out in. In isolation each object, each being, each habit, each convention, even each image, intends to revert to its reality, without materializing, intends to have no more secrets, to be defined calmly, uselessly, by the atmosphere it creates, the illusion being lost. But here is a mind *that does not accept* remaining alone and which wants to revenge itself on everything it seizes on in the world imposed on it.

In his hands sand, fire, water, feathers, in his hands the arid joy of privation, in his eyes anger, in his hands violence. After having been for so long the victim of confusion man replies to the calm that's going to cover him in ashes.

He smashes, he sets to, he terrifies, he ransacks. The doors of love and hatred are open, letting violence in. Inhuman, it sets man on his feet, snatches from him the possibility of putting an end to his stay on earth.

Man breaks cover and, face to face with the vain arrangement of charm and disenchantment, is intoxicated with the strength of his delirium. What does the weakness of his arms matter when the head itself is so subjected to the rage that shakes it?

Love and disorientation
We are not far from the day when it will be seen that, despite the wear and tear that bites into us like acid, and at the foundation of that liberating or somber activity which is the seeking after a cleaner life in the very bosom of the machinery with which ignominy industrializes the city,
LOVE
alone remains without perceptible limits and dominates the deepness of the wind, the diamond mine, the constructions of the mind, and the logic of the flesh.

The problem of the bankruptcy of feelings intimately linked with the problem of capitalism has not yet been resolved. One sees everywhere a search for new conventions that would help in living up to the moment of an as yet illusory liberation. Psychoanalysis can be accused of having created the greatest confusion in this area, since the very problem of love has remained outside the signs that accompany it. It is the merit of *L'Âge d'or* to have shown the unreality and insufficiency of such a conception. Buñuel has formulated a theory of revolution and love that goes to the very core of human nature, by the most moving of debates, and determined by an excess of well-meaning cruelty, that unique moment when you obey the wholly distant, present, slow, most pressing voice that yells through pursed lips so loudly it can hardly be heard:
LOVE . . . LOVE . . . Love . . . love . . .

It is useless to add that one of the culminating points of this film's *purity* seems to us crystallized by the image of the heroine in her room, when the power of the mind succeeds in sublimating a particularly baroque situation into a poetic element of the purest nobility and solitariness.

Situation in time
Nothing is more useless today than that a very pure, unassailable thing be the expression of what is most pure, most unassailable in man, when whatever he does, whatever we do, to insure his labors against injury, against misunderstanding—by which we mean merely to point out the worst that consists in the turning of that thought to the profit of another not on a par

186

with it—whatever he does, we say, is done in vain. At present everything seems indifferently usable toward ends we have denounced and reproved too often to be able to disregard every time we come up against them, for instance, when we read in *Les Annales* a statement in which the last clown to have done so indulged in some delirious commentary on *Un chien andalou* and felt qualified by his admiration to discover a link between the film's inspiration and *his own* poetry. There can, however, be no mistake. But whatever fence we put around a seemingly well-protected estate, we can be sure it will immediately be covered in shit. Although the means of aggression capable of discouraging swindling can hardly be contained within a book, painting, or film, despite everything we continue to think that provocation is a precaution like any other and, on this plane, that nothing prevents *L'Âge d'or* deceiving whoever hopes conveniently to find in it grist for his mill. The taste for scandal which Buñuel displayed, not from deliberate whimsy, but for reasons on the one hand personal to him that invoke, on the other, the desire to alienate forever the curious, the devotees, jokers, and disciples who were looking for an opportunity to exercise their more or less large capacity for airing their views, if such a mind has succeeded this time in the scheme it undertook, we could think he had no other ambition. It's up to the critical profession to look for more, and concerning this film, to put questions about the scenario, technique, use of dialogue. As long as nobody expects us to furnish them with arguments meant to fuel their debate on the expediency of silence or sound, for we maintain that this is a quarrel as vain, as resolved as the one between classical and free verse. We are too sympathetic to what, in a work or in an individual, is *left to be desired* to be very interested in perfection, wherever that idea of perfection comes from, in some progress it seems to initiate. That is not the problem Buñuel sets out to solve. And can one even speak of a problem in reference to a film in which nothing that moves us is evaded or remains in doubt? What do we retain of the interminable reel of film put before our eyes till today and now dispersed, certain fragments of which were just the recreation of an evening to be killed, certain others the subject of despondency or unbelievable cretinization, others the cause of a brief and incomprehensible exaltation, if not the voice of the arbitrary perceived in some of Mack Sennett's comedies, of defiance in *Entr'acte,* of a savage love in *White Shadows,* the voice of equally unlimited love and despair in Chaplin's films? Apart from these, nothing outside of *The Battle-ship Potemkin*'s indomitable call to revolution. Nothing outside of *Un chien andalou* and *L'Âge d'or*, both situated beyond anything that exists.

Let's give way, therefore, to that man who, from one end of the film to the other, passes through it, traces of dust and mud on his clothes, indifferent to all that does not uniquely concern the love occupying him, driving him on, around which the world is organized and rotates, this world he is not on terms with and to which, once again, we belong only to the degree we protest against it.

Social aspect – subversive elements
One would have to go back a long way to find a cataclysm comparable to the age we live in. One would probably have to go right back to the collapse of the ancient world. The curiosity attracting us to those troubled times, times similar, with certain reservations, to our own, would love to rediscover in that time something more than history. A Christian heaven, alas, has completely obliterated everything else, and there is nothing in it that one has not already seen on the ceilings of the Ministry of the Interior or on the rocks by the seaside. This is why the genuine traces left on the human retina by the needle of a great mental seismographer will always be, unless they disappear along with everything else when capitalist society is annihilated, of utmost importance to those whose chief concern is to define the critical point at which reality is replaced by "simulacra." Whether the sun sets once and for all depends on the will of humankind. Projected at a time when banks are being blown up, rebellions breaking out, and artillery rumbling out of arsenals, *L'Âge d'or* should be seen by all those who are not yet disturbed by the news which the censors still let the papers print. It is an indispensable moral complement to the stock-market scare, and its effect will be direct precisely because of its Surrealist nature. For there is no fictionalization of reality. The first stones are laid, conventions become a matter of dogma, the cops push people around just as they have always done, and, as always too, various accidents occur within bourgeois society that are received with total indifference. These accidents which, it will be noticed, are presented in Buñuel's film as philosophically pure, weaken the powers of endurance of a rotting society which is trying to survive by using the clergy and the police as its only buttresses. The ulti-

188

mate pessimism issuing from the very bosom of the ruling class as its optimism disintegrates becomes in turn a powerful force in the decomposition of that class, takes on the value of negation immediately translated into anticlerical, therefore revolutionary, action since *the struggle against religion is also the struggle against the world.* The transition from pessimism to the stage of action is brought about by Love, the root, according to bourgeois demonology, of all evil, that Love which demands the sacrifice of everything: status, family, honor, the failure of which within the social framework leads to revolt. A similar process can be seen in the life and work of the Marquis de Sade, a contemporary of that *golden age* of absolute monarchy interrupted by the implacable physical and moral repression of the triumphant bourgeoisie. It is not by chance that Buñuel's sacrilegious film is an echo of the blasphemies screamed by the Divine Marquis through the bars of his prison cells. Obviously, the final outcome of this pessimism in the struggle and triumph of the proletariat, which will mean the decomposition of class society, remains to be seen. In a period of "prosperity" the social value of *L'Âge d'or* must be established by the degree to which it satisfies the destructive needs of the oppressed and perhaps also by the way in which it flatters the masochistic tendencies of the oppressors. Despite all threat of suppression this film will, we feel, serve the very useful purpose of bursting through skies always less beautiful than those it shows us in a mirror.

Maxime Alexandre, Aragon, André Breton, René Char, René Crevel, Salvador Dalí, Paul Éluard, Benjamin Péret, Georges Sadoul, André Thirion, Tristan Tzara, Pierre Unik, Albert Valentin

This difficult text was published by the Studio 28 cinema, Paris, as part of the publicity brochure to launch *L'Âge d'or* in 1930. After two weeks on the marquee, the film was banned. A facsimile of the brochure forms a supplement to Jean-Michel Bouhours and Nathalie Schoeller, eds., *L'Âge d'or: Correspondance Luis Buñuel–Charles de Noailles, Lettres et documents (1929–1976)*(Paris: Les Cahiers du Musée National d'Art Moderne: Hors-série/Archives, 1993).

Zaroff; or,
The prosperities of vice

Robert Benayoun

Even if it facilitates the task of our educators, the forbidding of certain films to those under sixteen will complicate the lot of our psychiatrists. Few of our young scapegraces will have occasion to receive, as did your humble servant at the age of ten, the sexual shock of his pre-teen years at the showing of a serial as stupefying (let's be precise) as can be, Charles Brabin's *The Mask of Fu Manchu* (1932).

I still recall with emotion the sight of Myrna Loy, Fu Manchu's daughter, licking the wounds of the lover she has been whipping at length, an image that for the first time managed to suggest to me the aphrodisiac possibilities of a simulacrum of this order, in which violence cuts a figure of almost exotic sensual refinement. Since then I've seen *The Mask of Fu Manchu* two or three times: while the aesthetics and the décor have dated, the sadistic ritual remains precise and rigorous, effortlessly discountenancing the vulgar deviations the cinema tends to inflict upon it today. In *The Mask of Fu Manchu* the tortures Fu Manchu visited by turns and for his own pleasure upon each of his guests were doubtless far from effective (they'd have made a third-rate mercenary hoot), but they were undeniably *plastic:* torture by bell as in Mirbeau, an elevating swimming pool complete with crocodiles, an iron maiden the size of an armory; all these contrived to excite the imagination, to drive the senses wild through the workings of a machinery of Babylonian proportions. In the film, torture was hinted at, never seen, and erotic delirium, once attained, climaxed in the supreme orgasm of cataclysm.

And now we will speak of Sade. No occasion should be missed to speak of Sade, whose glorious name is today linked with ideas he especially abhorred. "Sadistic" is used increasingly to mean "torturer" (as in "Nazi"); "sadistic" is used to mean "neurotic" (*Le Sadique de l'autoroute*), while Sade himself, paying for his passion for liberty with twenty-seven years of imprisonment under three different regimes, dared even during the Terror to attack the principle of the death penalty, given that he was the most lucid, well-balanced, and most generous of moralists. Between Sade and gratuitous cruelty, between Sade and brute violence, between Donatien-Alphonse-François and pathological excess there exists the constellated space of a number of universal bridges.

For the first time in history, Sade, a true liberator of mankind (he created a veritable science of morals), gave us a total picture of human nature: to quote Maurice Blanchot, he rendered men "worthy of nature in the very deviations she inculcated in them." In a century in which the vilest arbitrariness held sway—"The idea of God is the only error I cannot forgive man for"—he conceived the idea of strengthening man by according him the unshakable, almost oneiric will to realize his *desires:* "You will know nothing if you haven't known everything, and if you are so timid as to stop with nature she will escape you forever." He created a new kind of man: the sadist is he who is capable of taking pleasure in *everything* on this earth: virtue (which he scoffs at), vice (which he assumes), and death (which he accepts).

And this concept, being assimilated in the most imprecise ways, has reached right into the darkened auditorium. Should we be surprised at this? In exalting the imagination, cinema liberates the spectator from all servitude, gives him a thirst for unwonted identification, the will to supersede the established order. By inventing "suspense," the cinema has us submit to a real *torture by hope.* The placid Louis Lumière had no idea that, with subjective delirium, he'd invented a new sensation.

The sadist is he who creates himself through new sensations, who equals God and scoffs at Him by proving there is *an order in evil.* In *The 120 Days of Sodom,* when the Duc de Blangis and his accomplices shut themselves away in Selligny Castle to set out their catalog of every conceivable passion, he commits a blasphemy of such enormity that Luis Buñuel, evoking it in his film *L'Âge d'or,* found no better solution, the perspicacious Sadean that he is, than to depict the Duc as having the features of Jesus Christ.

Let us, then, state our theme: in acting according to "the logic of fundamental pluralism," the sadists gather as a group to conceal their excesses in an inviolable obscurity. The secrecy of their debauches necessitates an abode of darkness: *the castle*. Zaroff's castle, situated on an island surrounded by reefs; Count von Bruno's keep hidden in the deepest Black Forest (in Nathan Juran's *The Black Castle* (1953)); the Carpathian fortress "as strange as life and death" (in Edgar G. Ulmer's *The Black Cat* (1934)); the subterranean lair of Fu Manchu; the island laboratory of Doctor Moreau, etc. "You are shut away in an impenetrable fortress," counsels the Duc de Blangis. "You are dead to the world and henceforth it is only for our pleasure that you go on breathing. . . . "

What pleasures are they? Inconceivable pleasures, of course, concocted in the heat of desire by the lyrical imagination of the master of the house: Count Zaroff,[1] who claims "to live only for danger," has invented a game [*un gibier*] of a special kind, the most dangerous of all: held prisoner, a steady stream of shipwrecked survivors of both sexes are hunted over a period of three days. When this time is up he kills (or possesses) the victim: "The sex doesn't matter," observes Sade. "I don't look too closely." In *The Black Cat* Hjalmar Poelzig plays chess with the women he lusts after, hypnotizes and then shuts them in coffins made of glass. Count von Bruno sets a black panther on his guests lost in the fog. Through horrifying surgery Doctor Moreau[2] revives and conjoins various mythological hybrids: gorilla men, panther women, etc.

It is vital to add that the true sadist considers constraint not as an instrument of injustice or oppression but as a test of character. Constraint remains a sort of ornamental luxury in the appeasement of his pleasure. The protest, anguish, despair, and ultimate abandon of his victim will provoke his bliss. Except for a fatal error, say, it is impossible for him to submit to a mind as free as his own: he in turn would fall victim to such. Thus he will choose as his natural prey the anxious, the timid, the timorous, all those who expect from life a succession of bitter disappointments. They will satisfy his megalomania, inspire in him his most genial traits.

We are far, here, from the unfeeling executioner, the degenerate criminal: our hero is generally possessed of a broad culture, an insolent courtesy, more often a refined sense of humor, considers crime a work of art

---

1 *The Hounds of Zaroff,* aka *The Most Dangerous Game* (Shoedsack and Pichel, 1932). The subject was reprised in *Johnny Allegro* (Ted Tetzlaff, 1949) and *The Race in the Sun* (Roy Boulting, 1956).

2 *Island of Lost Souls* (Erle C. Kenton, 1932).

and a labor of love ("Everything Sade signs is love," says Gilbert Lely), and loyally accepts the rules of his own game to the extent of becoming its victim. Given his respect for the established rules, there can be no end more exalting than this, to die a victim to his own passion, to complete the destructive edifice he has invented by offering up his own life.

Count Zaroff loses the game once only: he honors the wager like a perfect gentleman.[3] Fu Manchu is blasted by his own death ray, Moreau vivisectioned by his own creatures. Beaten at chess, Hjalmar Poelzig gets flayed alive by his rival. The variants on this pitiless canvas count for little. They are to be found, pell-mell, in Louis Friedlander's *The Raven*, Roy William Neill's *The Black Room*, Ernest Schoedsack's *Doctor Cyclops*, in the recent *Castle of Terror*, and even in James Whale's *The Man in the Iron Mask*, in which the hero experiences the rare and equivocal delight of martyrizing his twin brother.

It is in these enclosed spaces, these hidden crypts and passageways which a fulgurating lighting endows with the most scabrous terrors that the cinema, following the Duc de Blangis, can be said to have orchestrated a *psychopathia sexualis* comparable in every detail to Krafft-Ebing's. The scandalous catalog of every kind of monomania, every type of paresthesia (let us reject, with Maurice Heine, the vague term "perversion") is revealed all but complete.

In *El* Luis Buñuel evokes D.A.F. Sade's intimate gadgetry, pressed here into the service of a passion exacerbated by titanic jealousy, while *Archibaldo de la Cruz*, inventor of the "intellectual" crime, furnishes his sex life with effigies more fatal than their model. The sardonic avenger in *Obsession* (Edward Dmytryk, 1951) confines his rival in a dungeon where for months on end he affably describes to him his imminent dissection. The torment of the enigmatic Paul Mangin, obsessed by women's hair, is reflected in *The Corridor of Mirrors* (Terence Young, 1947), wherein he conceals the sumptuously adorned flayed skins of his strangled mistresses. In *Night of the Hunter* Harry Powell has set up, given God's silence (seen as His tacit com-

---

3 "'I congratulate you,' Zaroff said. 'You have won. One of us will make a meal for the dogs. The other will sleep in this excellent bed. En garde, Rainsford. . . . '
"Rainsford had never slept on such a fine bed."
This is the marvelous ellipsis that closes Richard Connell's original novel, *The Most Dangerous Game* (1924).

plicity), a new religion founded on the murder of rich widows whose posterity he pursues with an almost elemental, Maldororian hatred.

In the odd film noir you get certain actors whose temperament, let us say, is particularly suited to evoking the genius of sadism: they are a mixed bunch and, aside from their simple physique, possess natures as singular as George MacReady's, Paul Henreid's, Lee Marvin's, Raymond Burr's, or Stephen MacNally's, actors whom scriptwriters never fail to oppose homosexually to the accomplished masochists, Burt Lancaster or Alan Ladd.[4] Just as to the insistent eye male sadistic traits are recognizable by their coldness, precision of gesture, their terrifying alacrity, and antarctic humor, so these traits are discernible in the fair sex by an ambiguity or slowness of movement, an exasperating talent for dissembling, and a malicious appetite for evasion, refusal. Marlene Dietrich, Ona Munson, Anita Björk, and the early Rita Hayworth all projected the cruel seductiveness of seasoned tormentors in *The Blue Angel, The Devil Is a Woman, The Shanghai Gesture, Miss Julie,* and *The Lady From Shanghai.* In the third film, Mother Gin-Sling, a female version of Blangis, officiates hieratically at a banquet of forbidden orgies. In Von Sternberg's masterpiece sadistic ritual attains a perfection that renders unbearable the rigidity of etiquette and costume, the baroque perfection of décor, the effect of close confinement, and the spectacular promiscuity of objection.

"Man's entire happiness is in his imagination," Sade tells us.

Authentic sadistic cinema is not that which, through a vulgar display of brutality, solicits the sadism *of the spectator.* It is a cinema in which discomfort, vague misgivings, a fascinated paralysis of mind, and a twitching of the limbs exceed the frontiers of expectation, a cinema whose elective, even ceremonious climate remains, venomous and intoxicating, that of total *perdition.*

From *Présence du cinéma* (Paris) 6–7 (December 1960): 7–12; special issue on "Sadism and Libertinage." Courtesy Robert Benayoun.

---

4 In William Dieterle's *Rope of Sand* (1949), Henreid tries out no less than fifteen different whips on the strangely splayed body of Lancaster. We know that according to certain press reports the latter insists on relative authenticity in his flagellation scenes. In *Kiss the Blood Off My Hands* (Norman Foster, 1948), he suffered a real cat o' nine tails.

Eroticism

Robert Desnos

O ne of the most admirable things about cinema and one of the reasons for the hatred shown it by imbeciles is its eroticism. These men
and women, luminous in the dark, make their moving gestures in a sensual way. Imagine it, their flesh becomes more real than living people's,
and while they move on screen toward an irrevocable destiny they are
taking part, for the sensitive spectator, in some more miraculous adventure. The cinema, then, becomes the most powerful of all cerebral drugs:
the dual scenario develops in an atmosphere superior to opium's while,
participating in two discourses, facts and gestures are suddenly illumined
as dazzling points of contact.

Kisses from horsewomen in the middle of prairies, the apparition of a
dancer's shoulder, an adventurer's proconsular neck, a white hand, long
and slim, "sliding toward a letter" or a revolver, eyes above all else, more
beautiful in the cinema's mysterious light, it's to you that this *Love* scattered throughout the movies comes back. Just as a cavalcade of cowboys
takes the spectator's breath away, so the vibrant life on the screen overex-
cites the imagination. Among the audience wholly drawn into the domain
of the tragic and the romantic, the elect are they who can admit you into
their life, virile or feeble heroines, seductive murderers! The old fogies and
eunuchs will join forces in vain, vainly will the cinema submit to more
censorship than the Ancien Régime once counted on; these details will
escape their shortsightedness. Today it is in this cinematic eroticism that
consolation for everything that is disappointing in artificial, everyday life
must be sought. An inborn poetry circulates through these luminous beams,
ready to be turned into halos. More supernatural than tongues of fire at
Whitsuntide these ethereal mouths speak across frontiers, to any mind
initiated in the dream. Throughout the world impassioned stares meet in
the person of the star raised to the inaccessible majesty of the gods and,
though her terrestrial image may be vulgar and despicable, she gains by

the illusion that she gave us an indefeasible right to our recognition.

It's because, despite everything, it is protected by an objective representation of reality that the cinema escapes the control of its legal guardians. It transforms external elements to the point of creating a new universe: this is how the slow-motion film of the Siki-Carpentier fight in fact simulates gestures of passion.

Discipline, which indifferently defines army and prison, the strap and the ideal of the mediocre rhetoricians who defend tradition, should not be applied to this perfectly new form of cerebral pleasure. (They haven't linked the cinema with Ronsard, but they're bound to soon.) The ones who were stupid enough to get hot under the collar about an anodyne novel like *La Garçonne* and who prosecute the most tolerable manifestation of French theater, the music hall, cannot fail but persecute the new art. The book Louis Delluc published recently (*Drames de cinéma:* his own film scripts, with photographs of the censored sequences) revealed that the incompetence of the cinema censors outstripped even that of their colleagues concerned with the novel. It is deplorable that film directors do not have every license in the making of their scenarios and that the nude and nearly nude in particular are severely proscribed.

Admitted by Nazimova and Pauline Frederick into an anxious and precipitate life, we shall no longer be satisfied with banal reality. During the intermission we will seek out the man or woman who will sweep us along in an adventure equal to cinema's twilight dream.

First published in *Paris-Journal,* 20 April 1923. Reprinted in Robert Desnos, *Cinéma* (Paris: Gallimard, 1966), 101–103. Copyright © 1966 Éditions Gallimard.

Eroticism = love

Ado Kyrou

Why the necessity to link love with eroticism when they are one and the same thing? Why must we always submit to the will of short-sighted old women and asexual censors? They are the ones who have drawn lines and erected seemingly insuperable barriers to underline the imaginary frontier between good and evil. The simplest solution would be to ignore them, take no notice, and rediscover the primary force of words without worrying ourselves about prohibitions. Unfortunately, that is very difficult, not to say impossible, for us to do since, though our instincts inform us of the unity of all physical and moral phenomena associated with "love," we find ourselves up against a kind of fragmentation, the pieces of which—desire, love, eroticism—we must collect to reconstruct the great puzzle.

Taken separately, each piece of the puzzle is inoffensive enough. Let us choose examples from the cinema (you could take them from any form of expression you like). We give the name "love film" to those affected stories whose frantic idealism induces a *tranquillity of spirit* in the spectator. Grand salons of the haute bourgeoisie, evening suits and gowns, "noble" senti-ments, bickering, sufferings in silence, silliness. The affair is king. The young girls blush; the young men, momentarily led on by the "bad side of their natures," get a grip on themselves and beg forgiveness. Order is restored, sacrosanct values have the last word, and loveless couples triumph over love thanks to their need for tranquillity and mediocrity. Some titles? There are too many of them. All the same, here are two: *Brief Encounter* and *Stazione Termini* (the first by David Lean, the second by Vittorio de Sica). In these two films the lovers stifle their love. We could say that they are only docu-ments and that the directors assume a critical stance vis-à-vis their charac-ters, their cowardliness, and their attachment to society's rules. Even if that were so, and I don't think it is, I don't see the need for this kind of film, though I understand only too well the infatuation of official criticism for it. To our misfortune we are surrounded by faint-hearted couples, love-less couples, couples who are the enemies of love. Why make a song and dance about them, why hold them up as examples? But my question is redundant since I've already answered it.

"Their" love without eroticism is an illusion, an intellectual game to be analyzed and dissected. They have their magnifying glasses and micro-scopes and patiently examine this idea so as to deprive it of any material insulation it may retain. In order to be taken seriously they borrow their arguments from "literature," the Bible, occult and esoteric texts, and cer-tain great experts on the subject, like Anouilh (love's most fanatical en-emy, the false witness of woman) and Cocteau. We are witness to this curi-ous fact: that the impotent become champions in the study of love. They lay down laws, delegate responsibility, give orders, scrupulously analyze our actions and feelings. They judge us and condemn us. Let's forget these "moralists," ignore them, not let ourselves be contaminated by the insan-ity of their emasculated theories. We must go one better: show them *our* conception of love, pin their arms behind their backs so they can't cover their faces and make them look at the beauty of the feminine body and the poetry of Eros. They will relieve us of their company in a panic. Love is sex. To separate love from the sex act is like cutting a printing press off from its fonts of type.

The other side of the coin is hardly more heartening. "Their" eroticism without love ignores every physical law. Obviously, I believe in degrees of the intensity of love, but to assume from this that eroticism has no rela-tion to love is a step I categorically refuse to take. Under the influence of certain great thinkers this step has unfortunately been taken by the major-ity of our contemporaries. In their adult life they practice the pernicious habit of fifteen-year-old boys who love a little cousin with the kind of "pure" love that does not stop them assiduously frequenting the brothel. Today supposedly erotic films play (in the majority of cases) the part of intellectual brothels, and supposed love films (again the majority of them) the part of the favorite little girlfriend.

Doubtless it would be possible for the spectator to make a synthesis of these two kinds of love and so have a complete image of it, an image that would give him a weapon for the passionate realization of his life, the only objective that interests me, finally. Yes, that would be possible if these films were authentic love films and authentic erotic films. In reality they are false witnesses, made even worse by their terrible quality. We give the name "love film" to stories about the evasion of reality, writs of execution, compensations, princes marrying shepherdesses (so that our shepherdesses carry on dreaming of the prince, in life, without coming out into the street, meeting him, and making love to him). We give the name "erotic film" to any film in which the occasion arises arbitrarily for a female character (rarely the heroine) to reveal a breast or thigh, any inept film that has a bath or dance sequence or an abortive rape in it. As a rule these sequences are "harmoniously" integrated into a story of traffickers, of peasant revenge, or of some musician coming to the capital to seek his fortune. As for eroticism, one looks for that in vain. . . . I have nothing against baths full of beautiful naiads (as they are called) or dances with naked girls—on the contrary! The hypocrisy of a great many of my peers who pretend to remain unmoved by the sight of a breast or a beautiful movement of the hips leaves me cold.

. . . .

I will content myself with briefly outlining what love is to me, since it is not enough just to protest the opinions of those one disagrees with. To be sure, my hopes and ideas for a sincerely erotic cinema are, given present conditions, only dreams. The censors . . . are there, polymorphous and all powerful.

I would like it if we could or would forget all prohibitions, all previously acquired conceptions, all advice, to make films in which love, seen normally and sanely, would no longer be conditioned by bourgeois mores, in which love, finally purged of the terrible notion of sin, will forcefully proclaim its name, bringing together within the same poetic image the magic of the encounter, the stars of concord, beyond time and place, and the splendid grandeur of the sexual act without which love is merely an idealistic gold-beater's skin. This love will be pleasure, knowledge, and a call to revolt, it will change the world.

From Ado Kyrou, *Amour-érotisme et cinéma*, 2d ed. (Paris: Eric Losfeld, 1967), 13–15. Courtesy Joëlle Losfeld. Reading this essay, it's droll to consider the accuracy of Louise Brooks's ungracious and homophobic dubbing of Kyrou as "that Greek pansy."

Au repas des guerrières

Nelly Kaplan

Love is a word that must be used very carefully. In certain cases it has a
sexual meaning.
    —*The News of the World*

A specter is haunting the world—the specter of eroticism. To subdue it
the Holy Alliances are ceaselessly in action, O paradox. But nothing is
harder to destroy than a specter, nothing less annihilable than this "assert-
ing of life up to the point of death." And then the Holy Alliances begin to
get anemic.

If in this domain the cinema has already performed miracles, one facet
is absent, nevertheless. Is there anything as exciting as a beautiful woman
knowingly caressed by the caprices of a lens? Yes, the sight of a beautiful
young man captured by a heterosexual camera. "These fauns, you want to
perpetrate them, hoofs turned uppermost. . . . " Smile, but not for long, ladies and gentlemen of the patriarchy.

When the endless servitude of woman is broken, wrote the Seer, *then will she*
find things strange, unfathomable, repulsive, delicious, then will she know how
to offer us the song of seaman and mattress instead of the boring laments
on some sad, drifting little woman they vainly try to make us swallow, *she,*
too, will be a poet! It isn't a matter of reversing the roles within the same
stories, of having a King Kong, submitting to the outrages of an amazon in
rut, cry out in fear (however curious it would be to contemplate such a
version), but of discovering *the unknown,* expressing that "other" eroticism
still so badly, so infrequently represented on the screen. On this planet are
a few seers, female ones, who armed with a lens would cause a great stir in
the world of the darkened theater.

That would put the admirable Matilda in *The Monk* or the Rebecca of *La*
Motocyclette in a completely new light. And neither Lewis nor Mandiargues
would be betrayed one bit but, on the contrary, given an extra dimension.

Since you have only your chains to lose and a whole, sensory world to win, erotics of all countries, unite!

From *Positif* (Paris) 61–63 (June-August 1964): 129. Courtesy Nelly Kaplan. The "Seer" is Rimbaud. Marx and Engels, Bataille, Mallarmé, and Nietzsche are also invoked. The title is a play on the phrase "le repos du guerrier," meaning "the warrior's rest," as in Zarathustra's epigram, "Man is made for war, woman for the warrior's rest, and all else is folly."

Female x film = fetish

Gérard Legrand

What is eroticism? It is an ostentatious ceremony in an underground passage. . . .
—Dictionnaire abrégé du surréalisme

In his reply to an inquiry into *Cahiers du cinéma*'s critical methods Robert Benayoun set a cat among the pigeons when he observed that for those people who might otherwise agree on the larger poetic or artistic issues— to say nothing of politics—the merest mention of a film is often enough to cause the outbreak of insoluble controversy. It's as though a person's irreducible singularity suddenly takes the field, this field which to my mind existential doctrine improperly seeks to displace to the conceptual realm, where it engenders excessive confusion.

To this minor problem it is easy to object that *nobody sees the same film.* That much is certain. It is no less true that the same quantity of film unwinds for the same time in the same place before pairs of eyes belonging to brains that are, furthermore, animated by similar or common "ideologies."

Strangely enough, it was a shallow mind that undertook to explicate this banal explanation. In the preface to *La Duchesse de Langeais,* adapted for the screen by its author, Jean Giraudoux emphasized, by contrasting it to the "communion" of theater, the *solitude* of the movie spectator which, he said, is occasionally transformed into a still more complete solitude, "that of the couple." The semidarkness of the film theater may be peopled by other "spectators," but they in turn only perform the role of those mannequins that "furnish" certain old movies. Thus an indifferent paradox points the way to a better understanding of cinema itself.

In addressing itself directly, immediately, to the "subconscious" of each of us the film, *whatever it is,* comes into contact at the threshold of light and dark with that nocturnal face of the mind correctly dubbed "the unconscious system." Since Freud, and despite Jung, we know that this system is entirely modeled on sexual elements. Sexuality, which serves as the invisible quantitative framework of the conscious system, is inversely the flesh, the very stuff, of the structures of the unconscious system. The result is that even where a film without blatant sexual content capable of mobilizing a given spectator for or against it is concerned, such a film acts erotically as a provocation, an act of aggression—or seduction—on each and every one of us. The mechanisms that come into play are the same as those that alight on the erotic object; they are as uncontrollable, tenacious, and sometimes as artful. Even between friends the discussion can very quickly reach the furious intensity we might give it if, for example, we were discussing our most secret preferences for the coital position or for female underclothes, in imposing the sober desire *to be right* in an area where reason only intervenes much later. But exclusive preference as well as superstitious defiance, up to and including disgust for such and such a carnal zone, is an attitude more befitting "cinephilic" discussion than all the phenomena of transference and association introduced by psychoanalysis; and it has a name: *fetishism*.

It was a stroke of genius on the part of Krafft-Ebing (if my memory serves me correct) to propose the word "fetishism," drawn from the history of religion, to designate the ritual passion applied to some part of the body or detail of dress which can go as far as substituting these for all other sexual objects. This passion corresponds to the ancient magical recipe according to which "the part entails the whole." I see no reason not to use this word to describe the motivations that draw us toward such and such a film.

And, notwithstanding the cineastes' claim to restore the "totality" of existence to us, this would explain why many a lover of cinema is so easily and completely satisfied by film fragments. Let us note that all fetishism results in the "cutting out" of the woman and her attributes along a preferred dotted line of oneiric iridescence, barely justifiable in the eyes of someone else. At the same time, the recurrent concept of fetishism sheds light on recent analyses according to which eroticism is inseparable from a certain sense of the "sacred," even though this sacred may be of a sacrilegious kind. We are alluding here to the important contributions of Bataille, Breton, Péret, and even Bellmer (cf. *Anatomie de l'image*), contributions whose contradictory aspects cannot obscure their illuminating convergences.

The "ostentatious ceremony" alluded to in the epigraph to the present text is celebrated by 1 + 1—some might say by $1 + n$—but it is never *collective*. The "global frenzy" of ancient religions is not at all dependent on eroticism, such as one may apprehend it from the *Lexicon* of the 1959 Surrealist Exhibition. . . . Nevertheless, it so happens that the "collective Narcissus" employed as a metaphor by Géza Roheim will never find a larger and truer mirror, even given the bloom of factory film production and the blighted tain of censorship, than *the screen*.

From *Positif* (Paris) 61–63 (June-August 1964): 17–19. Courtesy Gérard Legrand.

Mae Murray

Jacques Rigaut

You can already see how in ten years' time young people will upbraid us for letting ourselves be bowled over by the cinema. The last refuge of sentimentality. Women and travels, what excuses! Drugs don't need justification. An unparalleled miracle, these speechless women. Each one of us will be their victim, once at least.

Coquettish dramas. Her little laugh you'll never control, her latest lies, her next lies, her gowns, her exasperating childishness, her ultimata about a glove or stroll, things you're unaware of, the terror and desire of an inevitable parting, her tenderness when you'd given up hoping for it, her incorrigible gaiety, and the recollection of this long, too agile body, of an extravagant reward, of vice, I'm in love with Mae Murray.

From *Littérature* (Paris) 1 (new series)(March 1922): 18. Jacques Rigaut appears in Man Ray's *Emak Bakia* (1926). Reprinted in Jacques Rigaut, *Écrits* (Paris: Gallimard, 1970). Copyright © 1970 Éditions Gallimard.

"Enchanted wanderer": excerpt from a journey album for Hedy Lamarr

Joseph Cornell

A mong the barren wastes of the talking films there occasionally occur passages to remind one again of the profound and suggestive power of the silent film to evoke an ideal world of beauty, to release unsuspected floods of music from the gaze of a human countenance in its prison of silver light. But aside from evanescent fragments unexpectedly encountered, how often is there created a superb and magnificent imagery such as brought to life the portraits of Falconetti in *Joan of Arc*, Lillian Gish in *Broken Blossoms*, Sibirskaya in *Ménilmontant*, and Carola Nehrer in *Dreigroschenoper?*

And so we are grateful to Hedy Lamarr, the enchanted wanderer, who again speaks the poetic and evocative language of the silent film, if only in whispers at times, beside the empty roar of the soundtrack. Among screwball comedy and the most superficial brand of claptrap drama she yet manages to retain a depth and dignity that enables her to enter this world of expressive silence.

Who has not observed in her magnified visage qualities of a gracious humility and spirituality that with circumstance of costume, scene, or plot conspire to identify her with realms of wonder, more absorbing than the artificial ones, and where we have already been invited by the gaze that she knew as a child.

Her least successful roles will reveal something unique and intriguing—a disarming candor, a naïveté, an innocence, a desire to please touching in its sincerity. In implicit trust she would follow in whatsoever direction the least humble of her audience would desire.

"She will walk only when not bid to, arising from her bed of nothing, her hair

of time falling to the shoulder of space. If she speak, and will only speak if not spoken to, she will have learned her words yesterday and she will forget them tomorrow, if tomorrow come, for it may not." (Parker Tyler)

(Or the contrasted and virile mood of *Comrade X* where she moves through the scenes like the wind with a storm-swept beauty fearful to behold.)

At the end of *Come Live with Me* the picture suddenly becomes luminously beautiful and imaginative with its nocturnal atmosphere and incandescence of fireflies, flashlights, and an aura of tone as rich as the silver screen can yield. Her arms and her shoulders always covered, our gaze is held to her features, where her eyes glow dark against the pale skin and her earrings gleam white against the black hair. Her tenderness finds a counterpart in the summer night. In a world of shadow and subdued light she moves, clothed in a white silk robe trimmed with dark fur, against dim white walls. Through the window fireflies are seen in the distance twinkling in woods and pasture. There is a long shot (as from the ceiling) of her enfolded in white covers; her eyes glisten in the semidarkness like the fireflies. The reclining form of Snow White was not protected more lovingly by her crystal case than the gentle fabric of light that surrounds her. A closer shot shows her against the whiteness of the pillows, while a still closer one shows an expression of ineffable tenderness as, for purposes of plot, she presses and intermittently lights a flashlight against her cheek, as though her features were revealed by slow-motion lightning.

In these scenes it is as though the camera had been presided over by so many apprentices of Caravaggio and Georges de la Tour to create for her this benevolent chiaroscuro . . . the studio props fade out and there remains a drama of light of the *tenebroso* painters . . . the thick night of Caravaggio dissolves into a tenderer, more starlit night of the Nativity . . . she will become enveloped in the warmer shadows of Rembrandt . . . a youth of Giorgione will move through a drama evolved from the musical images of *Also Sprach Zarathustra* of Strauss, from the opening sunburst of sound through the subterranean passages into the lyrical soaring of the theme (apotheosis of compassion) and into the mystical night . . . the thunderous procession of the festival clouds of Debussy passes . . . the crusader of *Comrade X* becomes the *Man in Armor* of Carpaccio . . . in the half-light of a prison dungeon she lies broken in spirit upon her improvised bed of straw, a hand guarding her tear-stained features . . . the bitter heartbreak gives place to a radiance of expression that lights up her gloomy surroundings . . . she has carried a masculine name in one picture, worn masculine garb in another, and with her hair worn shoulder length and gentle features like those portraits of Renaissance youths she has slipped effortlessly into the role of a painter herself . . . *le chasseur d'images* . . . out of the fullness of the heart the eyes speak . . . are alert as the eye of the camera to ensnare the subtleties and legendary loveliness of her world . . .

[The title of this piece is borrowed from a biography of Carl Maria von Weber, who wrote in the horn quartet of the overture to *Der Freischutz* a musical signature of the Enchanted Wanderer.]

From *View* (New York)(December 1941–January 1942): 3. Courtesy Edward Batchellor.

Iron in the wound

Alain Joubert

M any here among us prize cinema as one of the revealers of our anguish and our hopes, and that notwithstanding the endless financial and moral constraints that sunder the free expression of those from whom we might expect so much, the maniacs of the moving image.

Yet if it is often impossible for us to account for the films that attract us, it is because of the distance separating what we'd wish them to be from what they really are. How, in effect, to render an exact account of those particles of our satisfaction, when the latter endlessly slips between our fingers only to reemerge the stronger by virtue of our feelings of regret? To objectify the mysterious powers that drive us would be to try and explain the magical nature of the least *projection,* in other words, to render palpable the reasons that frequently obtain for the addict's cleaving, however furtively, to the darkened movie theater; but here stands revealed the often complete uncertainty of our motivations as to the pleasure we may just have experienced. In the absence, then, of common criteria that might serve as an underlying justification, it is forbidden us to comment on certain films whose value lies essentially in our subjectivity, in the latter's multifacetedness.

Also, when cinema comes to meet us head on there's no question of avoiding contact. All too rare are those films that *totally* excite our enthusiasm for us to ignore the arrival of *Les Abysses,* not to emphasize how this film overwhelms the sensibility of whoever is present during its frenzied unfurling.

To begin with, a harrowing news item, of which this is the gist: "The Papin sisters were brought up in a convent in Le Mans. Later their mother placed them in a 'bourgeois' household in the town. For six years they endured, with complete submissiveness, admonishment, arbitrariness, abuse. Fear, fatigue, humiliation slowly bred hatred, a sweet liquor that secretly consoles since sooner or later it bids violence unite with physical force. And on that day Léa and Christine Papin paid evil back in kind, a payment of hot iron."[1] "They each grab an adversary (*the bosses:* mother and daughter) and tear their eyes from their sockets while they still live, something, it is said, unheard of in the annals of crime. Then they knock both women senseless. And, using whatever comes to hand—hammer, pewter jug, kitchen knife—they belabor the bodies of their victims, smashing in their faces, and, exposing their genitals, they slash the thighs and buttocks of one and daub the other's with the blood. Next they wash the instruments used in these atrocious rites, clean themselves up, and sleep together in the same bed."[2] "Lightning has struck, wood been blasted, the sun finally extinguished. Armed to the teeth, straight out of a Lay of Maldoror's."[3]

To arrive at the sublime excesses of this drama the makers of *Les Abysses* have had to countenance all the secret reasons of a ceremony whose evolution escapes us, the more to overwhelm us given the outbursts we witness.

We soon grasp the apparent motive behind their simmering revolt, but the relationships between the two sisters, and the two sisters and their mistresses, are not as simple as they at first appear. Like a gaze you try and avoid, the gestures of the actresses Colette and Francine Bergé, whose tragic beauty distills an extremely unusual eroticism more suggestive of ambiguity than sensuality, simultaneously express the disquiet that befits the miserable station they occupy and some obscure preparation for an as yet diffuse sacrifice, before arriving at its deeper meaning as the external forms of its appearance gradually become clear.

Likewise the inspiration for a play by Jean Genet, "the maids" and their mystifying, multifarious reflections (which are not necessarily a shortcoming) manifest hostility toward their masters' daughter as a function of the solicitude she pretends to shower upon them so that she might seduce the younger of the two with sophisms inspired by the famous notion, "love one another." We feel ourselves shudder at the horror her infantile verbiage provokes and this inspires our righteous anger. For the first time since *L'Âge d'or* we witness the direct and wholly effective calling into ques-

---

1 Paul Éluard and Benjamin Péret, *Le Surréalisme au service de la révolution* (Paris) 5 (15 May 1933).

2 Jacques Lacan, *Minotaure* (Paris) 3–4 (December 1933).

3 Paul Éluard and Benjamin Péret, op. cit.

tion of the imbecilic criteria that underpin traditional morality and its "progressive" derivatives, a morality which has been inflicted on us for nigh on two thousand years. We feel total solidarity with these two sisters as they deliver their superb riposte to Christendom in the person of this poor young girl, she of the smug smile who asks with a grimace for a second helping of the soup whose recipe she knows well. We recognize the *active* complicity we'd wish to have with their gesture which of a sudden spares us a goodly part of that religious humanism so prized since Pope John XXIII gave it its letters of ignobility.

Nevertheless, there remains the question of broaching the singular core of the intimate relations that exist between the two avenging amazons, each element of their attitude seemingly held in place by secret links only incestuous homosexuality can explain. These cries, outbursts of laughter and tears, these caresses and blows come directly from Christine and Léa's *double* and express the lightning materialization of their unsated instincts. The accumulation of *intense experience* [*des temps forts*] exalts the ultrasensitivity of their bodies, their minds, and permits them to understand the real meaning of objects and of people. We witness something of an initiatory preparation whose unique ceremony is imagined according to the needs of the moment following a method that draws upon *pure psychic automatism.*

By virtue of this, the sisters' final gesture before the explosion of murder is of a rare intensity. The appearance of these robots who *play,* fearfully, the role people have sought to imprison them in till then, the role of "maid-servant" which ladens their personae with the grotesque weight of humiliation, makes them fitfully assume the derisory nature of their condition, owing to reflections perceived in the eyes of the others. Having got this far, they are free and prove it. Their crime, so just because so inevitable, is born of the forces of anger, their discovery of "the mystery of life,"[4] and of those cruel lacerations occasioned by unremitting choice. Its consequences touch our hearts because we know the outcome that awaits its authors. All our pity, all our emotion is focused on the terrible obliteration that will follow, as the execrable symbols of *order* and *submission* die like dogs.

---

4 The phrase used by Christine Papin to the judge who asked her what she'd *sought* in mutilating her victims.

As for the father, a hateful Prudhommesque creature and a perfect foil for the action we've just lived through, he finds himself publicly pilloried by the ideal agents of a society called into question, by reason of his feebleness and his blindness. If they occasionally cause us to smile as we gnash our teeth, his utterances and theirs are of the type we hear every day of our lives and we have to contend constantly with the incredible amount of hypocrisy they imply. We exact a little revenge too in verifying that the wolves—or should we say the swine?—dine well off each other.

We must, then, thank Nico Papatakis and Jean Vauthier for letting us penetrate to the very core of that lucid immoderation which permits beings who thirst for liberty to express, at *last* and with a supreme degree of violence, the totality of *revolt* contained within them.

The first *poetic* sabbath, in the most impassioned sense of the term, that we've ever been summoned to will mark with a whiff of sulfur the history of *our* cinema.

From *La Brèche: action surréaliste* (Paris) 5 (October 1963): 62–65. Courtesy Alain Joubert. The director of *Les Abysses,* Nico Papatakis, produced Jean Genet's film *Un chant d'amour* (1950).

Pornographers & Co.

Robert Lebel

I t is striking that the extremely rapid shift from the total banning of supposedly pornographic films to their almost limitless distribution has only been registered publicly at the level of the entertainment industry. Some were indignant about this, while others claimed to be amused, yet very few people have asked themselves what such sudden liberalization means in relation to other, more tenacious taboos.

It goes without saying that the suddenly permissive attitude of power vis-à-vis these films renders them suspect in advance. What sinister political design is concealed, what revenge is being prepared, behind the calculated risk of this concession to a change in mores that is readily seen to run out of breath at the least semblance of progress? How can it be that a profound breach is suddenly opened in a morality that remains archaic and fundamentally implacable behind the circumstantial flexibility it sometimes affects? It is never through benevolence but from opportunism that a regime, whatever kind it is, consents to grant the people the tried and tested tranquilizers of bread, circuses, and sex.

The "end of guilt" attached to pornography has been triggered, we know, by a general verdict of the United States Supreme Court which declares as unconstitutional, and therefore illegal, any kind of *censorship*. We also know, however, that this is the selfsame word Freud used to designate the braking action the unconscious drives come up against.

When for a time we found ourselves, in France, through contamination more than through genuine emancipation, ruled by a sort of dual legality in which erotic literature was still heavily victimized while film pornography already benefited from widespread tolerance, this unfair treatment was explained by capitalist logic, a logic according to which the legitimacy of any enterprise is evaluated according to the sums of money involved. The film industry got by far the better of marginal publishers on that score, and trading practice aspires to have morality yield, albeit momentarily, to the practical needs of business. Freedom isn't granted, yet it's not forbidden to cash in on it.

This conclusion would be nevertheless incomplete if the other decisive factor behind the change was ignored; that's to say, the irresistible force of repressed desires and fantasy. It should not be overlooked that the law itself is sensitive to this factor and makes a few sacrifices here and there, but each waiving of the rules of the dominant morality has the immediate effect of increasing oppositional pressure and augmenting its strength. The economic expedient paradoxically favors and secretes the revolutionary ferment. And the only true revolution is that of sexuality.

We touch here on one of the irrational mechanisms of a system that deems itself to be rational, and Surrealism has well known how to take advantage of the *détournements* of meaning that the incoherence and ambiguity of power allow to be used against it. This factor alone would suffice to confirm the primordial role of Surrealism in the dismantling of supposed reality.

There is reason, then, to attempt a reconciliation between pornographic movies and the Surrealist circles in which they still sometimes meet with disapproval. Let us state that our aim, here, is not to rehabilitate films with artistic pretensions, which are for the most part overwhelmingly boring, but rather the crudest and most direct of hard-core films. Despite the reactions of disgust they may provoke among the "moral majority," these movies are in league with Surrealism, they fight the same enemy. In this never-ending battle Sade, without the help of Pasolini, teaches us to overcome our repugnance and, if need be, to do our own little bit.

As an essential reference, let us recall André Breton's advice in the *Second Manifesto:* "to aim the long-range weapon of sexual cynicism at the 'moral duties' kind of person." To be sure, in his case this was only an extreme aspiration, counteracted in life by a still more imperious tendency toward poetic sublimation. Today we find ourselves in a situation contrary to his, due mainly to a temporary relaxing of certain constraints, and pornography becomes an incomparably more effective weapon than poetry against the eternal "'moral duties' kind of person."

We will not be surprised to rediscover Duchamp at the origin of the pornographic movie, as he is at the source of so many other demystifications. His Beaubourg retrospective will have at least served to give proof of this antecedence by offering permanent screenings of *Anémic cinéma*, in which Duchamp has divulged and unveiled, in one blinding flash, that which sets apart the lifeless simulacrum of the sex act from its mobile visualization. This occurs almost "abstractly," without the intervention of human actors, through the simple alternation of expansion and contraction, of in/out movement, suggested by the gyration of spirals in "rotorelief."

In the course of its development the narrative cinema would scarcely be aware of this discovery, which long remained hidden, except by way of an accidental allusion during the ardor of a gesticulation or the swaying of a posture. It will only appear in frank terms in such exceedingly rare semiclandestine films as *Un chien andalou* and *L'Âge d'or*, films impregnated by Buñuel and Dalí with a pornography than we can qualify as Surrealist and which would be violently denounced in the name of propriety, good taste, or law and order.

The era will come and go of the "artistic nude" and of museums converted into evil places where troubled adolescents like the Michel Leiris of *L'Âge d'homme* went to seek stimulation. Though the making of pornographic shorts, reserved for *maisons closes* and open minds, remained for half a century the exclusive province of the more dubious dens of vice and their repertoire of lucrative "perversions," the Surrealists never ceased pursuing their own private researches into sexuality. The questions posed during the gatherings of 27 and 31 December 1928, the transcription of which appeared in *La Révolution surréaliste* of 15 March 1929, leave nothing to chance. Setting aside the issues, judged at the time to be secondary, of onanism, fetishism, pederasty, etc., we can reduce the more urgent preoccupations of the Surrealists vis-à-vis their personal sexuality to these three:

1. To what extent is the man aware of the woman's orgasm?

2. To what extent is the woman aware of the man's orgasm?

3. To what extent and how often can a man and a woman making love reach orgasm simultaneously?

It cannot be denied that this collective inquiry into orgasm anticipates by several decades the "surplus-pleasure"[1] in which the braggarts of psychoanalysis, sexology, semiology, and linguistics have so much faith

---

[1] [Lacan's *plus-de-jouir.* —*Trans.*]

today. In 1928 this inquiry led ineluctably to voyeurism, the one thing that seemed capable of providing an answer. This was all very new, no doubt, although for the first-timer, a reader of Sade but someone more at ease with courtly love, the embarrassment might have been nullifying. On the other hand, this embarrassment will accommodate itself better to the unimpeded, irredeemable, and often unwitnessed viewing of an indefinitely repeated film, one which gains its force precisely from the tedious reiteration that refined souls reproach it with, from this repetition to the point of satiety of the Same, from the dispiriting stereotyping of gestures and their arrangements in space.

What occurs is so barely admissible, such a weight of repression subsists in us for disavowing it, that it is constantly necessary to look again, to verify, to convince oneself of not being the victim of a trick. The patient, in his seat, slips without knowing it from voyeurism to a quasiscientific scrutiny, to an almost disinterested quest for knowledge. Never will he have been so close to the essential.

As to the body-object, that of the man or the woman, it is all too ready to exhibit itself in detail and to melt into sighs, with or without pecuniary reward, for us to have scruples about offending it with the gaze or listening in on it with the ears. Those organs that the close-ups, the full-color photography, and the sound track metamorphose into wild beasts, with their squamae, their hirsute pubes, their serous humors, their interstitial lymph glands, their groanings, their splish-splashing, the pulsation of vulvas built like sea urchins, the turgescence of rubescent or black penises, the agitation of all these mutually foreign members which rub against each other, bang together, get tangled up, straddle each other, sometimes unite as if drawn by a sidereal gravitational pull, though for a brief instant and in order to separate in haste—what a dynamic vision of an unnamable groping, of a blind, hesitant, wayward pursuit!

When the compulsorily external ejaculation spurts onto a face, rims the eyes, inundates the lips, rolls down cheeks, chin, throat—what a transgression in terms of socially unproductive, unexploitable, useless, suspended time! This is the fiesta of wasted sperm, from which nothing will be born except a feeling of *vacuity*.

Who's come, who hasn't come, together or alone? The questions the Surrealists debated in 1928 with a certain heterosexual naïveté and ambivalence are more than ever dependent on the still faltering techniques of automatism. Today's pornographic film, however, contributes to loosening the fetters of subjection maintained by the language of sexual encounter and its problematic reciprocity. That which could not be said or explained will be able to be seized directly, if we scrutinize it well or briefly lend it an ear, although any attempt at interpretation is inevitably rendered more opaque with the evidence. Finally, the spectator, overwhelmed by proof and assailed by the doubt of Lacan, is no longer even sure that sexual relations exist as such.

It will be necessary, then, to avoid the disastrous parallel between the libidinous gluttony of the protagonists, pushed to the point of caricature in the case of the women, and his own ability to provide for it. He will have to discern the saturation point beyond which the death instinct and the threat of castration cause impotence in the viewer. As much as the deterrents of the police, this intimate, contagious terror means that the audience of specialized cinemas, like that at initiation ceremonies, is singularly thin on the ground.

It is to a sovereignly Surrealist transmutation that the adept is summoned who will have traversed, without weakening, the often insupportable but salubrious illumination of the hard-core movie. And this so as not to expose oneself to the potential regret of having missed the opportunity of glimpsing the eagerness, *dérive,* and fragility of desire trapped by the specular lure.

From *Surréalisme* (Paris) 2 (1977), 67–71. Courtesy Jean-Jacques Lebel.

Selected films
made by Surrealists

This selective filmography is, it has to be said, something of a shot in the dark. Individual entries have sometimes been pruned (due to space, familiarity of material, degree of pertinence). All films are shorts, i.e., less than forty minutes long, unless asterisked (*). Being part of a marginal—even clandestine—cinema, many of these films are impossible to view.

Henri d'Arche/Georges Hugnet   *La Perle* (1929)
Along with *Un chien andalou*, Hugnet's scenario would seem to have been inspired by Breton and Aragon's theater homage to the film serial, *Le Trésor des jésuites* (1928).

Robert Benayoun

*Paris n'existe pas** (1969)
*Passage Breton** (1970)
*Sérieux comme le plaisir** (1974)

Raymond Borde

Pierre Molinier (commentary by André Breton)(1964)

Jacques Brunius

Voyage aux Cyclades (scenario by Roger Vitrac)(1931)
Autour d'une évasion
(codirected by Silvagni)(1933)
Records 37 (codirected by Jean Tarride; commentary by Robert Desnos)(1937)
Venezuela (1937)
Sources noires (commentary by Desnos) (1938)
Violons d'Ingres (1939)
Somewhere to Live (1950)
Brief City (1951)

To the Rescue (1952)

*The Blakes Slept Here** (1953)

More detail on Brunius's cinematic activities as assistant director, actor, writer is to be found in *L'Avant-Scène du cinéma* (Paris) 67 (February 1967): 47, and in Jean-Pierre Pagliano, *Brunius* (Lausanne: Éditions L'Âge d'Homme, 1987).

| Luis Buñuel | *Un chien andalou* (1929) |
| | *L'Âge d'or** (1930) |

An accessible Buñuel filmography appears in Francisco Aranda, *Luis Bunuel: A Critical Biography* (London: Secker & Warburg, 1975). A more accurate and detailed one is to be found in Yasha David, ed., *¿Buñuel! La mirada del siglo* (Madrid: MNCARS, 1996). The cursory list above shouldn't be read as a polemic against Buñuel's later films; it merely highlights the fact that Buñuel took formal leave of the Surrealist Group at the time of the "Aragon Affair" in 1932.

Joseph Cornell   *Rose Hobart* (1936)

P. Adams Sitney discusses Cornell's undated, but early, collage films—some completed by Larry Jordan, others like *Bookstalls, By Night with Torch and Spear,* and *Vaudeville De-Luxe* seemingly edited by the artist and since restored—in his beautiful essay, "The Cinematic Gaze of Joseph Cornell," in Kynaston McShine, ed., *Joseph Cornell* (New York: The Museum of Modern Art, 1980), 68–89. There is now a whole book devoted to Cornell's own cinephilia: Jody Hauptman, *Joseph Cornell's Stargazing in the Cinema* (New Haven & London: Yale Univ. Press, 1999).

Germaine Dulac/

Antonin Artaud   *The Seashell and the Clergyman* (1927)

Wilhelm Freddie/Jørgen Roos *The Definite Rejection of a Request for a Kiss* (1949)

Eaten Horizons (1950)

Georges Goldfayn/

Jindrich Heisler   *Revue surréaliste* (1951)

Nelly Kaplan   *Gustave Moreau* (some commentary by
                         André Breton)(1961)

Ado Kyrou   *La Déroute* (1958)
                         Le Palais idéal (1959)
                         Port Océane (1960)
                         Parfois le dimanche (codirected by
                         Raoul Sangla)(1960)
                         La Chevelure (1961)
                         Le Temps des assassins (codirected by
                         Jean Vigne)(1961)
                         Combat de coqs (codirected by Louis
                         Seguin)(1961)
                         Les Immortelles (1962)
                         Un honnête homme (1965)
                         *The Monk** (scenario by Buñuel
                         and J.-C. Carrière)(1972)

Roger Livet   *Fleurs meurtries* (1928–1930)
                         Une regrettable affaire (1933)
                         L'Histoire d'Agnès (1949)

René Magritte   *René Magritte cinéaste* (1975)
A compilation of the home movies Magritte made during the last ten years
of his life. The "Nicole and Jean" sequence is very fine.

René Magritte/Paul Nougé   *The Space of a Thought* (1934)
                           "Another Film" (1934)
Both destroyed. Their scenarios appear in translation in *TRANSFORMAcTION*
(Harpford, Devon) 3 (November 1970): 22–23.

Marcel Mariën   *L'Imitation du cinéma** (1959)

Ernst Moerman   *Mr. Fantômas* (1937)

Pierre Molinier   Untitled film (1965)

221

This strictly private exercise in self-glorification, shot on 16mm by the great erotomane painter, was destroyed by him sometime before his suicide in 1976. On Molinier and film—including Jean-Pierre Bouyxou and Raphaël G. Marongiu's portrait of the artist, *Satan bouche un coin* (1967)—see the interview with Bouyxou in *Canal* (Paris) 32 (October 1979): 5.

Paolo Antonio de Paranagua   *Nadja* (1966)

Pierre Prévert   *L'Affaire est dans le sac* (1932)
           Adieu Léonard* (1943)
           Voyage-Surprise* (1946)
           Paris la belle (1928–1959)

An extensive filmography appears in Gérard Guillot, *Les Prévert* (Paris: Seghers, 1967).

Man Ray   *Emak Bakia* (1926)
           L'Étoile de mer (1928)
           Le Mystère du Château de Dés (1929)

To the Man Ray filmography we must now add the eleven shorts, totaling some 55 minutes, revealed since the deposition by the artist of his private archive in the Musée nationale d'art moderne, Paris. This secret oeuvre is treated in full in Jean-Michel Bouhours and Patrick de Haas, *Man Ray, directeur du mauvais movies* (Paris: Éditions du Centre Pompidou, 1997).

Hans Richter   *Dreams That Money Can Buy**
           (episodes by Duchamp, Man Ray,
           Ernst)(1944–1947)

Philippe Soupault/
Walter Ruttmann   Three untitled films (circa 1922)
           (destroyed)

Ludvik Sváb   *L'Autre chien* (1971)
           Backwards to Infinity (1990)

Jan Svankmajer

The Last Trick of Mr. Schwarzwald and Mr. Edgar (1964)
J.S. Bach: Fantasy in G Minor (1965)
Game with Stones (1965)
The Coffin House (1966)
Et Cetera (1966)
Historia Naturae, Suite (1967)
The Garden (1968)
The Flat (1968)
Picnic with Weissmann (1968)
A Quiet Week in a House (1969)
Don Juan (1970)
The Ossuary (1970)
Jabberwocky (1971)
Leonardo's Diary (1972)
The Castle of Otranto (1973–1979)
The Fall of the House of Usher (1980)
Dimensions of Dialogue (1982)
Down to the Cellar (1982)
The Pendulum, the Pit, and Hope (1983)
*Alice** (1987)
Virile Games (1988)
Darkness-Light-Darkness (1989)
The Death of Stalinism in Bohemia (1990)
Food (1992)
*Faust** (1994)
*Conspirators of Pleasure** (1997)

A dossier on Svankmajer's work, prepared by Michael O'Pray in collaboration with Petr Král, appears in *Afterimage* (London) 13 (autumn 1987), an issue devoted to "Animating the Fantastic." There is now a book devoted to this Czech Surrealist: Peter Hames, ed., *Dark Alchemy: The Films of Jan Svankmajer* (Trowbridge: Flick Books, 1995).

Michel Zimbacca	*Square du Temple* (1946)
	Acier et scories Thomas (1949)
	Ni d'Ève, ni d'Adam (1967)
Michel Zimbacca/J.-L. Bédouin	*L'Invention du monde* (commentary by Benjamin Péret)(1952)
	Quetzalcoatl, le serpent emplumé (commentary by Benjamin Péret)(1952)

A parting shot

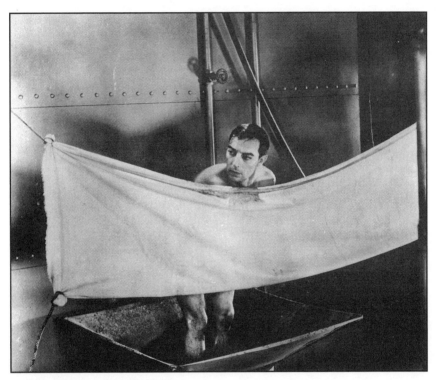

Buster Keaton in *Battling Butler* (1926).

SCREEN. Usually a quadrangular surface, material unimportant, stretched over a frame and intended to be interposed between a cause and its effect. A quintessential example of this device is the screen utilized in cinemas. Thanks to the interposed screen, no representation of the world ever reaches the viewer. In lieu of such protection the spectator finds himself carefully isolated from any kind of reality or unreality that might be noxious, dangerous even, for himself or for his fellows.

Isabelle Waldberg, Robert Lebel, Charles Duits, Marcel Duchamp, eds., *Le Da Costa encyclopédique* (Cussay: n.p., 1947).